Busting Myths about the State and the Libertarian Alternative

Second Edition

Zack Rofer

Mises Institute
518 West Magnolia Ave.
Auburn, Ala. 36832
mises.org

ISBN: 978-1-61016-696-6
ISBN (ebook): 978-1-61016-697-3

Typeset by Mike Dworski

Contents

Preface **1**

I. The Statist's View **5**
People 5
Economics 7

II. Myths about the Nature of the State **11**
Myth #1: The State Is Good and Does Good 11
Myth #2: The State Acts by Consent 18
Myth #3: The State Acts for the "Common Good" 24
Myth #4: The State and Its Personnel Deserve Our Support . 27
Myth #5: Democracy Is Good, Better, Best 35
Myth #6: The State Dispenses Criminal Justice 46

III. The Free Market **57**
What Is the "Free Market"? 57
Economics 101 59
Austrian Economics 65
Myth #7: The Free Market Creates an Inequality Problem . . 67
Myth #8: The Free Market Exploits Workers 78

IV. Myths Justifying the Need for the State **89**
Acquiescence to the State 89
Myth #9: The State Is an Improvement on the Free Market . 94
Myth #10: We Need the State to Provide "Public Goods" . . 106
Myth #11: We Need the State to Deal with Negative Externalities 121
Myth #12: We Need the State to Deal with Anti-Competitive Behavior 138
Myth #13: The "Hobbesian Fear" 141

V. Busting the Myths about Libertarianism **147**
What Is Libertarianism? 147
Myth #14: Libertarians Are Utopian! 154
Myth #15: It's Every Man for Himself! 158
Myth #16: Libertarianism = Chaos! 161
Myth #17: We'd Be Defenseless! 168
Myth #18: There Goes the Environment! 174
Myth #19: Somalia Disproves the Case for Libertarianism! . 179
Myth #20: Libertarians Are Shills for the Powerful! 181
Myth #21: Libertarians Don't Care about the Poor! 183
Myth #22: Libertarians Are Pro-Prostitution and Pro-Narcotics! 190
Myth #23: If It's so Good, Then Why Hasn't It Ever Been Tried? 191
Myth #24: Libertarianism Is a Futile Endeavor! 196

VI. Why Does It Matter? **209**
Minimizing Conflict within Society 209
Opposing War 210
Governing by Principle, Not Arbitrarily 211

VII. Conclusion **215**

Afterword: A Personal Perspective **217**

Reading Guide **219**

Preface

In non-technical terms, the libertarian is simply someone who is against the use of force against peaceful people in civil society. You would think that this would be a universally accepted idea but, as will be discussed in greater depth, to believe in government as we know it is to be at odds with this idea.

The vast majority of people in the world today live under some form of publicly organized government, which hereinafter I'll call the "state."[1] Most people believe that we *should* live under state rule, whether they are classical liberals, communists, conservatives, fascists, liberals, Marxists, neoconservatives, Progressives, Randians, socialists, or any other flavor, all of whom hereinafter I'll call "statists." They simply differ in their views on what powers the state should possess.

Nevertheless, statists of all flavors often react quite strongly to the suggestion by libertarians that a society without a state, operating on a purely free-market, voluntary basis, would be a more just and efficacious society. I believe that this reaction results from three categories of errors by statists: first, they don't fully comprehend the nature of the state; second, they don't fully comprehend the nature of the free market; and third, they subscribe to certain myths about libertarianism and how a stateless society might work. That they make these errors is not surprising, since for the most part their education has been in institutions where no one asks the question "What is the true nature of and justification for the state?", and

[1] All references to the "state" in this book include all arms of the state: the legislature, executive, judiciary, bureaucracy, agencies, etc. While they each have different functions, substantively they are all funded in the same manner, they all have the same inherent characteristics, and they are all responsible for appointing one another and/or working together. The differences between these different arms of the state are trivial compared with the differences between how the state acts and how private citizens act, which is one of the key points of this book.

there is very little discussion about problems with and alternatives to the state.

Given these defects in statists' understanding of this area of political philosophy, what I propose to do in this book is expose some common myths about both the state and libertarianism. Hopefully this will facilitate a more critical view of the state and more openness to the ideas of libertarianism.

Before going further, it's important to note that, in discussing how society should be organized and how individuals should interact with one another, there is a distinction between using "utilitarian" principles and "moral" principles.

Utilitarianism is concerned with discerning what the correct decision should be based on what would "maximize utility" for "society." To pursue this line of thinking, one has to accept that any particular human who is charged with making a specific societal decision is able to (a) appreciate all of the benefits and costs of each alternative course of action to each of the individuals who compose society, (b) quantify each of these benefits and costs in terms of common units of utility, and then (c) dispassionately choose the course of action that will maximize society's utility.

On the other hand, morality is concerned with discerning what the correct decision should be based on a standard of good behavior.[2] A "standard" means something that is universal, i.e., applies to every man. To pursue this line of thinking, one first has to conclude that there *should* be a universal behavioral rule. On this point, if we recognize that all men are metaphysically equal, in the sense of possessing the same fundamental capacity for consciousness, conceiving, rationalizing, and acting, then there is no objective justification to define different rules of acceptable, interpersonal behavior for different men. Every man should be expected to treat others, and be entitled to be treated by others, according to the same code. In addition, this line of thinking also requires one to be able to define an acceptable behavioral rule that, as a purely technical matter, *could* apply to everyone without exception, consistently and continuously (I will develop this further later).

[2]In this book, when I talk about "moral acts" and "morality," I am referring only to an evaluation of *inter*-personal behavior, and not to the evaluation of any actions only involving oneself, which might be better described as "virtues" and "vices."

As will become evident in this book, a number of the common arguments raised by statists are utilitarian, as opposed to moral. While I believe that the fundamental strength of libertarianism is its underlying morality—because it is based on a technically feasible, universal standard of acceptable behavior—and the fundamental weakness of statism is its underlying immorality—because it is inconsistent with the notion of a universal standard of acceptable behavior—even on a utilitarian basis I believe that libertarianism has much more to offer than statism. In any event, I will address the relevant statist arguments from both the moral and utilitarian perspectives (for the latter, chiefly through the medium of economic analysis), even though I believe that the moral argument should suffice.[3]

Finally, there are some upfront, stylistic points that I should make.

First, since in this book I am contrasting those who support the notion of a state with those who don't, I will be using "libertarian" to mean *only* someone who argues for a completely stateless society (as I do), also known as an "anarcho-capitalist," "voluntarist," "libertarian anarchist," or "Rothbardian."[4] There are many people who would not argue for a stateless society but who nevertheless label themselves, or get labeled by others, as "libertarian." I am not referring to them in any way; in this book, they would be "statists."

Second, I appreciate that not all statists think alike; while those on the left, in the middle, and on the right are similarly weak on many issues, they are also differently weak on other issues. Accordingly, when I refer to the assumptions, beliefs, and arguments of statists, I always mean "some" statists, even though I will not always bother using the word "some." One purpose of this book is to lay out the precepts of statist thinking, not the thoughts of every, or any particular, statist.

Third, I have avoided citing too many specific sources in an effort to try

---

[3] I still believe that there is a role for utilitarian analysis, but not the one that is usually cited. If economists believe that a particular outcome would lead to greater benefits (however defined) than the outcome that would result from individuals acting based on their own preferences, then these economists should publicize their analysis and use it to try to persuade individuals to change their decision-making processes. The real problem with utilitarian analysis is that it is used by statists to justify *forcing* individuals to make different decisions, instead of merely trying to persuade them.

[4] The last term refers to Murray Rothbard, who was the libertarian historian, economist, and philosopher who really ignited modern libertarianism in the 20th century.

to create a more conversational tone. Instead, I have included a Reading Guide at the end, which references much of the source material that provided me with the foundations to write this book. That said, all errors of course are mine alone.

Fourth, I would encourage you to read the footnotes, which generally contain additional substantive material or examples, as opposed to just dry source references. Sometimes that's where I have my most fun![5]

It has brought me tremendous pleasure to research and write this book, and I can only hope that you as the reader derive at least a fraction of that pleasure from reading it. If you have any questions or comments that you would like to send me about this book or any topics raised (or not raised) herein, please feel free to email me at TheNAPster3226@gmail.com.

Zack Rofer (August 2018)

[5]Just checking that you were paying attention.

I. The Statist's View

People

The statist perceives the state as a group of individuals who selflessly toil for the "common good," and who have a mandate, through the electoral process, to pass legislation as these individuals see fit to force changes in behavior of those outside the state. The statist lauds "public service," and believes that those at the state are deserving of special privileges and respect given their selflessness and the awesome power they wield. Indeed, many of the most powerful figures at the state, particularly the national leader, generate cult-like followings, where statists identify passionately with them, hang on their every word, look to them for national direction and salvation, and believe that it is not only their task to right every wrong but also that they have the ability and wisdom to do so. Even if there are a few "rotten apples" now and then at the state, this is not seen as an indictment of the notion of the state, just of those individuals. When the state makes mistakes, the statist is very forgiving, almost resigned to the fact that this is to be expected. These mistakes don't cause the statist to question the idea of the state, but simply confirms to the statist that society needs to elect better representatives at the next election.

Contrast this with the statist's views of those in the private sector. These people are seen as individuals who selfishly seek profits by taking unfair advantage of consumers, and who must be brought back into line and closely regulated by the state. Working in the private sector doesn't garner anywhere near the respect that working for the state does, and the statist is constantly critical of any excesses enjoyed by those in the private sector, such as the accumulation of significant wealth. Any "rotten apples" in the private sector only confirm to the statist the wretchedness of the private sector and the need for regulation by the state. In fact, no matter how closely regulated by the state a business may be, if there is a problem that surfaces, the statist assumes that it is solely to do with the nature of the private sector itself, and that the only answer is more state regulation. When businesses make mistakes, statists are unforgiving; as consumers, they may immediately take their patronage elsewhere, often bankrupting such businesses.

The contrast between how the statist views those at the state and those in the private sector is somewhat odd. I can only fathom three reasons for this.

Perhaps statists believe in extra-terrestrials, in the sense that the beings at the state belong to a different species from the mere humans who constitute the private sector. These extra-terrestrial beings do not have any of the foibles of private-sector humans, and thus are perfectly suited to work at the state and naturally gravitate in that direction (I'll call this the "ET Theory").

However, that explanation wouldn't suffice regarding those beings who *move* from the private sector to the state. Thus perhaps statists believe in a special type of machine known as the "Moral-ator." When a person moves from the private sector to the state, perhaps he passes through the Moral-ator, which strips him of his private-sector foibles and converts him into a selfless public servant (I'll call this the "Moral-ator Theory").[1]

Finally, perhaps there *are* some humans who are completely selfless individuals. Perhaps the voters, who apparently are incompetent to manage their own lives without detailed oversight from the beings at the state, nevertheless in a single act of brilliance each election are able to find these special individuals from the broader population and elect them, and *only* them, into office (I'll call this the "Voter Episodic Brilliance Theory" or "VEB Theory" for short).[2]

I will hereinafter call all three of these theories together, the "Tooth Fairy Theories."

[1] It's not clear how the statist thinks about those who move in the reverse direction, from the state to the private sector. Perhaps the Moral-ator works in reverse too, attaching private-sector foibles to former state personnel.

[2] Statists tend to identify passionately with one political party. Given how readily statists overlook or minimize the foibles of candidates from their own party, and how quickly they excoriate candidates from the "other" party for their every foible, no matter how small, statists could only subscribe to the VEB Theory when *their* party's candidates are elected. Which only makes this theory less credible.

Economics

Not surprisingly, the statist subscribes to the Keynesian school of economics. This is not only because this is all that is taught to most students who take economics courses, but also because it gives a very prominent role to the state.

Keynesianism assumes that the economy is a machine, the various economic actors (firms and consumers) are simply cogs in that machine, and the individuals at the state sit poised at the levers to make sure the machine is humming along at the "right" speed, making adjustments as disturbances in the economy occur.[3] It wouldn't be too far from the truth to summarize Keynesianism's key assumptions as follows: consumers are automatons, entrepreneurs are manic depressives, and those at the state are wise, stable, selfless souls who can ably steer the ship through stormy waters.

Fundamentally, Keynesianism is based on the belief that consumer spending creates wealth. Thus the Keynesian solution to depressed economic times is to encourage more consumption spending, and the statist believes that those at the state have the omniscience and natural right to determine when and how money should be spent in the economy.

This is demonstrably wrong on so many counts that an entire book could be written on this topic alone. I will make two quick observations here.

First, this concept reverses reality. People don't become wealthy because they consume, rather, they consume once they become wealthy.

Second, the creation of societal wealth comes from two factors, both of which must be present: (a) the division of labor into specialties, where people do what they are comparatively best at; and (b) savings being channeled into investments in productivity-enhancing new technologies, processes, and capital equipment.

We need to consume to live, but we need to specialize, save, and invest to increase prosperity.

Yet Keynesianism discourages savings in favor of consumption. This is because Keynesians don't recognize that the capital funds and freed-up

---

[3] Although Keynesianism cannot really explain what causes economic downturns; they are just assumed to be a function of human nature.

real resources to make investments can only come from individuals deferring consumption by saving some of their income. Savings become investment through the capital markets directing the saved funds to businesses, and simultaneously release real scarce resources (natural resources, labor, and capital equipment) from having to serve consumption ends so as to be available to serve investment ends. While Keynesians will criticize the wealthy because they don't consume as large a proportion of their income as the less well-off, it is this deferral of consumption by the wealthy that makes capital funds available for investments to make the least productive workers more productive, and thus enhances their ability to earn higher real wages.

Keynesians also believe that if more money is pumped into the economy—money newly created by or with the backing of the central bank—then this will create economic activity and thus prosperity. However, to survive and flourish, humans cannot consume money; they can only consume real goods. To create those real goods, what matters is the amount of real resources available and how they are used. The amount or velocity of money in circulation cannot increase the amount of real resources; rather, money is just a means to enable exchange of such resources.[4] Indeed, if increasing the amount of money in circulation were the means to attain prosperity, why would there be any poor countries in the world? Their central banks could just print up endless amounts of money!

Further, Keynesians believe that economics as a science comprises two distinct sub-disciplines: micro-economics and macro-economics. Whereas the former deals with the laws of economics, which describe how individuals act in a world with scarce resources, the latter attempts to describe, model, and predict how "the economy" behaves. In other words, Keynesians regard "the economy" as a creature distinct from the individuals who compose it. The reality, of course, is that "the economy" is nothing more than the aggregation of all individuals transacting with one another, which we can appreciate through the use of a thought experiment. Imagine taking each person out of "the economy," one at a time; when you have extracted that last person, would there still be a thing called "the economy" remaining?

[4]Note, however, that state-directed or state-supported manipulation of the money supply, and hence the interest rate, can divert real resources from where they could most effectively be used.

One key consequence of considering macro-economics a separate subdiscipline is that statists believe that the laws of economics which govern individual behavior are not necessarily applicable to economy-level policies.

So, for instance, while statists accept that it is beneficial for individual consumers to pay lower prices for goods (i.e., that price deflation is a positive trend), when the state wants to finance its programs through the injection of new money into the economy, thereby causing price inflation—which is essentially a hidden tax—we are told that economy-wide price deflation is something to fear and that, as a country, we must subscribe to "inflation targets."

Or, while statists accept that it is prudent for each individual to save a portion of his income, i.e., defer some consumption, statists believe that the aggregation of all individual savings can be a major problem for "the economy," because it leads to so-called "under-consumption" which, as noted above, statists believe causes economic downturns, the remedy for which is state action to discourage savings and encourage consumption.

As one more example, while statists accept that an individual can maximize his prosperity by not being self-sufficient—meaning that it is highly beneficial for an individual to freely trade with others, producing what he is best at and exchanging this for goods that others are best at producing—this benefit is questionable when the individuals on the other side of such exchanges are residents of a separate state. Statists believe that it could make economic sense for the state to restrict citizens' ability to trade with foreigners, because statists take an "our economy vs. their economy" approach (never mind that national borders are artificially drawn up by the individuals at the state in the first place).[5]

* * * * *

The statist's views on personnel and economics articulated above are consistent themes that permeate the way the statist thinks about the wonders of the state and the depredations of the free market. In the remainder of this book, I will show why these views are specious and hence why we should never settle for the state.

[5] There are many other similar observations to make about statist economics, but that is beyond the scope of this book. I will briefly contrast statist economics with free-market ("Austrian") economics later.

II. Myths about the Nature of the State

Myth #1: The State Is Good and Does Good

Statists like to portray the state as a vehicle through which they can channel their compassion, noble intentions, and moral compasses. They believe that the state brings civility to society. However, as this book will illustrate, the reality is that this vehicle is not as noble or moral as statists like to believe, and it would not be an exaggeration to say that there is no more uncivil institution than the state.

The State Is Coercion

Every action that the state takes is coercive; legislation is passed to compel changes in behavior. Tax legislation is passed to confiscate the income of peacefully acting individuals in excess of what they would otherwise voluntarily give to the state. Regulatory legislation is passed to force peacefully acting individuals to take or refrain from taking actions with their bodies or private property contrary to how they would otherwise act. Failure to comply with legislation, and with the armed agents of the state who seek to enforce such legislation, results in being locked up in a brutal cage (known as "prison") for a number of years as decided by the state. It may also result in the state confiscating some or all of your private property. If you physically resist the state's agents on the grounds of self-defense, these well-armed agents may physically injure you or, in the worst case, kill you.

It is impossible to deny that legislation is coercive: if it is not coercive, how does one explain the violent penalties for non-compliance; if it only represents what everyone would do anyway, why is it passed at all?

The reality is that the state comprises a group of individuals who create and enforce coercive rules about how other, peacefully acting individuals must act with their bodies and private property. No other individuals in society claim legitimacy, or would be recognized by statists as having legitimacy, in doing these things.

This is indeed an awesome power to have over the lives of others. However, it entirely contradicts the notion—and therefore implies that statists do not believe—that all men are metaphysically equal, and therefore should live by the same behavioral code when they interact. To statists, some men are entitled to forcibly dictate to others what they may do with their bodies and private property. Statists are unable to cogently articulate where this entitlement comes from, because there is no good answer. No man is born with any natural entitlement to rule another; he could only gain such power through the other's explicit consent, and subject to the terms thereof.

Thus, absent such consent (which I will deal with below), statists necessarily believe that there are two codes of acceptable behavior for human beings: one code applies to regular citizens; the other code applies only to those individuals at the state. The latter code permits individuals at the state to engage in actions that, if performed by regular citizens, would be regarded as wholly illegitimate, if not moral atrocities. This means that statism recognizes no universal standard of acceptable behavior for man, and thus statism cannot be based on any notion of morality.

To illustrate this point, imagine a street with 10 residents. One resident, X, kicks open Y's door and demands that Y hand over 30 percent of his income, or else he will lock Y in a cage in his basement for five years. Every person would agree that X has no right to do this. What Y earns from his labor or funds is his to keep, transfer, gift, etc., but it is none of X's business. Y may voluntarily decide to give X 30 percent of his income, but he might also decide not to do so. No one on that street has the right to take this coercive action against anyone else. Now, what if six of the 10 residents get together and tell X that he is allowed to do this? Does that change the legitimacy of X's action? If no individual had this power to begin with, how could he delegate it to X, even as part of a group?

Yet this is precisely what statists accept when they claim that a majority of voters could empower an individual at the state to levy a 30 percent income tax.[1] Statists might respond that the money confiscated from Y would be used to help Z, who is needy (by someone's arbitrary definition), and that this is therefore a just cause. However, what the statists are really saying is that the other people on the street have the right to decide whether to give Z a priority right to Y's income!

If these others feel so strongly about helping Z, they are free to do so voluntarily on their own from their own resources.[2] Alternatively, they might try to convince Y of the merits of helping Z. However, to simply arrogate to themselves (through X) the power to forcibly take Y's income has no moral legitimacy.[3]

Or take a second example. A wants to work for B. B offers to pay A a wage of $6.00 per hour, and A accepts this offer. Yet C comes along and says that A is not allowed to work for B unless B pays A $7.00 per hour, and that if, contrary to C's edict, A does work for B at $6.00 per hour, then C will lock up B in a cage in his basement for a year. By what principle does C have the right to interfere in the private arrangement between A and B? By what principle could C prohibit A from working where he chooses, and prohibit B from spending his funds as he chooses? Does this situation change if D, E, and F all tell C that he is allowed to do this? If none of

[1]Since majoritarian democracy is widely regarded by statists as the highest evolution of the state, I will use this concept for these and other examples of how the state works.

[2]Interestingly, most statists who want to help others with their own money would still prefer to hand this money over to the state (in the form of taxes) to disburse to the intended recipients (as transfer payments), instead of finding worthy recipients (or charities) and giving it directly. Why a statist would choose to funnel his money through the state—which has bloated administrative overhead, and comprises individuals with incentives to use the money for their own purposes rather than the intended recipients' purposes—is a question rarely asked, much less answered.

[3]Statists look aghast at Nazi Germany's legislation passed in the 1930s to make "legal" the plunder of its Jewish population's property. Yet why is this different from any tax legislation? The German government was originally democratically elected, and these rules were passed by its legislature. The legislation permitted the state to confiscate the private property of its citizens, which is what the income tax does. Perhaps the statist would argue that it was unfair that this legislation only applied to a segment of the population, yet this is little different from progressive rates of taxation and tax exemptions, which impact different segments of the population differently. Perhaps the statist would be more inclined to support such plunder legislation if it had applied to everyone, which is what statists in fact do support!

D, E, or F had this power to begin with, how could they individually or collectively delegate such power to C?

Yet this is precisely what statists accept when they claim that a majority of voters could empower an individual at the state to legislate a minimum wage rate. Statists might respond that they just want to help A earn more money, and that this is therefore a just cause. Leaving aside whether the policy would actually achieve that objective (B may just rescind his offer to A, or never make it in the first place, if he is compelled to pay more than he wants to pay), what statists are really saying is that D, E, and F have the right to tell A that he cannot work for B, and to tell B that he cannot employ A, unless A earns what they have decided he should earn.

If D, E, and F feel so strongly about helping A, they are free to do several things: offer to employ A at $7.00 per hour themselves; offer to supplement A's income by $1.00 per hour out of their own pockets; or try to convince B of the merits of paying A more. However, to simply arrogate to themselves (through C) the power to forcibly prohibit the private arrangement between A and B has no moral legitimacy.[4]

The bottom line is that there are two ways in which a person could interact with his fellow man: peacefully (through voluntary action) or violently (through coercion). The state is the primary channel for violent interaction between humans.

Is Statism (Like) Mass Slavery?

That sounds shocking, I know, but I will explain.

What is the definition of "slavery"? I would submit that "slavery" means a system whereby A claims the right to initiate or threaten force to require B to do with B's body and the produce of B's body as A directs.

While many Americans—whose only knowledge of slavery consists of what they learned in school about what happened in the American South

[4]It has no consistency either. If statists believe that no one should work for an amount below what the individuals at the state deem a "living wage," then how could they support charity work and volunteers? Heaven forbid, volunteers are working for nothing! Ah, the statist retorts, but they are willingly choosing to use their time to help others. So now the minimum wage principle devolves into statists not being happy about how people are choosing to use their time: apparently those who choose to use their time to earn below the minimum wage are making an unapproved choice. Huh?

before 1865—may instinctively define "slavery" as a black person doing back-breaking work in the fields for a white person, under oppressive conditions, without monetary reward, in reality this is not an accurate definition. Today there are plenty of individuals of varied races who do back-breaking work under the hot sun for employers also of varied races, or for charitable causes, but no one would consider these individuals to be slaves because they can freely quit. In addition, in the U.S. before 1865, (a) there were slaves who performed non-agricultural work (as artisans, in commercial industry, providing domestic services, etc.), many of whom believed that they were well treated by their masters, (b) some slaves were permitted to earn money outside the master's estate, provided that they paid over to the master whatever he commanded, and (c) there were free blacks who enslaved other blacks. More broadly with respect to this last point, throughout world history there have been examples of whites enslaving whites, non-whites enslaving whites, and non-whites enslaving non-whites.[5] Finally, today, regrettably, there are "sex slaves," who are forced to have sex, rather than work in the fields or around the house.

Accordingly, the defining aspect of "slavery" is not the nature of the work, not the races involved, not the amount of actual violence employed on a day-to-day basis, and not the pay, but the fact that a person is compelled by the threat of force to do as someone else directs.

And, if this is true, then consider the ways in which statism is similar to slavery.

First, the most obvious examples are military conscription, jury service, and prison labor. In these cases, individuals at the state force citizens to physically serve as directed until discharged—to go into battle, appear at a

[5]For example, in Ancient Rome and during the Viking Age in Scandinavia, whites enslaved other whites; this was also the case in the 20th-century labor camps run by a number of governments, including those of the Allies immediately after World War II, Germany, the Soviet Union, and Sweden. In Muslim Spain from the 8th to the 15th centuries, whites were enslaved by Muslims, and, in the Barbary slave trade in the 15th to 18th centuries, whites were enslaved by North Africans. Black Africans enslaved other black Africans for hundreds of years before the Atlantic slave trade began, and many of the black African slaves brought to the U.S. had first been captured and enslaved by other black Africans, who then sold these slaves to white Europeans. During the 20th century, a number of Asian governments operated labor camps for portions of their own populations, including Cambodia, China, and Vietnam.

court, or perform manual labor, respectively—under the ultimate threat of imprisonment,[6] or death, if one resists.

Second, a less obvious example is taxation. Individuals at the state force citizens to pay over to the state that percentage of the fruits of their labor, or of their other private property, as directed, under the ultimate threat of imprisonment, or death, if one resists.

Third, the most nuanced example is state regulation of non-violent activity (or victimless "crimes"). Individuals at the state force citizens to do or refrain from doing specific things with their bodies and private property—even though the citizens are not physically harming anyone else—under the ultimate threat of imprisonment, or death, if one resists.

While statists may be aghast at my suggestion that statism is like mass slavery, I would challenge any statist to cogently explain why the relationship between the individuals at the state and each dissenting citizen is any different from the relationship between a master and his dissenting slave.

To anticipate a possible statist objection, I would argue that it's not relevant from the perspective of there being shackles on one's freedom that the individuals at the state are many, but the master is only one. In fact, it may even be worse; one could perhaps escape the clutches of a single master, but how does one escape the clutches of the entire state apparatus?

Statists might argue that the master claims ownership of the slave, but the state does not claim ownership of the citizen. However, that raises two issues.

First, what is "ownership"? I would submit that "ownership" of an object means the exclusive right to control that object. If the individuals at the state, at their whim (i.e., by passing legislation or through executive action, backed up by force), are exclusively able to control what someone does with their body or private property (including income), then that *is* "ownership."

Second, it matters not that one master explicitly claims ownership and another does not; if the latter actually acts in the same manner as the former, then he is implicitly claiming ownership. The act of "claiming" is irrelevant; what counts is the act of using or threatening force to assert control.

---

[6] In the case of resisting prison labor, the punishment would be a longer sentence than would otherwise be the case.

Statists might also argue that slavery is all-pervasive, in the sense that, from the minute the slave rises in the morning to the minute he goes to bed in the evening, every single action is subject to his master's whims. However, I would argue that, given the all-pervasive regulatory and national-security state in which we live today, there is very little, if anything, that a citizen is free to do without permission from or the indulgence of the individuals at the state. Every product and physical activity is state-regulated, all income and assets are liable to be seized by the state, and there are no effective limits on what the individuals at the state may do to disallow a citizen's actions.

Citizens may perceive that they have more freedom in society than the slave does on his master's property, perhaps because a nation, state, province, or town is an enormous property, or perhaps because the edicts and enforcement come from so many different parts of the state apparatus, e.g., in the U.S. there is a "coercion matrix," with the federal, state, county, and local governments on one axis, and the legislature, judiciary, executive, and administrative agencies on the other. In any event, the aforementioned perception is false, because it fails to consider the *aggregate* of all coercion wielded within the property the state claims to control by *all* elements in the matrix, which coercion, as noted above, *is* all-pervasive. Not only that, but, at any time, the individuals at the state may decide to further reduce the citizen's freedom in any way they choose (which has in fact been happening in the U.S. for many years, as all elements in the matrix have continually expanded their range of activity).

So, is statism like mass slavery? It sure seems like it.[7]

* * * * *

It is undeniable that, at its core, the state is simply a group of individuals who force others to do things that serve the ends of those at the state (or their supporters). Indeed, this is the most odious aspect of the state; to use the lexicon of German philosopher Immanuel Kant, the moral issue with the state is that it involves using man as a means for the ends of others, instead of regarding each man as an end in himself.

---

[7] If you want a pithier and more articulate version of this idea, read libertarian philosopher Robert Nozick's piece, "The Tale of a Slave" in his book, *Anarchy, State, and Utopia*.

Myth #2: The State Acts by Consent

The statist will often respond that the state is not in fact coercive because everyone consents to its activities. What the statist could only mean, however, is that *he* consents to the state's activities; he cannot speak for anyone else. The mere fact that I am writing this book indicates that at least one person does not consent to the state's activities (and there are many more like me).[8]

If the response is "Well, the majority of people consent," then what the statist is suggesting is that we live by mob rule. This obviously doesn't address the moral problems raised above but simply restates them in a different way.[9]

Some statists will try to argue that, notwithstanding my making explicit that I do not consent to the state, by my actions I am implicitly consenting, which of course makes one wonder what "consent" really means. It's worth exploring some of the common arguments of statists in this regard.

The Constitution

One argument used in the U.S. is that the Constitution, which established the federal government, binds everyone because it's the supreme law of the land.[10] Sometimes this is embellished by saying that it was passed by supermajorities in each of the ratifying states, so that it's *really* binding. This argument has a number of flaws.

First, no one alive today was part of the original consent. In no other part of our lives do we admit to being legally bound by what our predecessors have done, and nor would we assume we could bind our descendants. No court would uphold this as a valid point of contract law.[11]

---

[8] Lest there be any confusion, for the remainder of this book I will use "coercive" to mean using or threatening force against those who don't agree with the state's existence or actions. Obviously the state is not seen as coercive by those who accept the state's legitimacy in any particular instance under discussion.

[9] As the saying goes, under this way of thinking it would be reasonable for two wolves and a sheep to vote on what's for lunch.

[10] The argument would be similar within a U.S. state with respect to that state's constitution.

[11] As libertarian attorney Stephan Kinsella has put it, it's as if statists are saying that only the first generation had the freedom to make a choice, but no subsequent generation had or will have this freedom.

Second, if anyone today *is* deemed to have consented to the Constitution, they would only have agreed to be bound by what was written in the document, and today's federal government operates well beyond those words. Statists like to say that the Constitution is a "living document" that adjusts over time, but in what other contract is that a valid argument anyone would accept?

For instance, imagine if the Underwriting Department of the bank that holds your fixed rate mortgage contacted you to advise that the mortgage contract is a "living document" and, since times have changed and the bank needs to boost its revenues, your monthly payment is going to increase. Would any person accept this as a valid action? The statist's next argument, that the Constitution's "expansion" is valid because it has been effected through U.S. Supreme Court decision, doesn't hold water either, since the Supreme Court is merely another organ of the state. It would be like your objecting to the mortgage bank's proposed action, and then taking the dispute to the bank's Customer Service Center for resolution. Good luck with that.[12]

Voting

Another argument that statists make is that we consent because we get the opportunity to vote for our representatives in each election. This argument has a number of components that deserve scrutiny.

First, voting is a false choice: you are choosing between being coerced by politician A or politician B. There is no choice not to be coerced.

Second, whether you vote *for* politician A or *against* politician A, or you don't vote at all, if politician A is elected, then he gets to coerce you. In what way is that a valid choice? In every other area of our lives we make real decisions between competing products, and we might choose not to purchase anything in any particular instance, but no vendor could force you to buy his product.

Third, what does it mean to be "represented by" a politician? He does not know you, you do not know him, neither person signs a document agreeing to the specific terms of representation, he cannot be held to ac-

[12]This is not an entirely fair analogy, since it is conceivable that Customer Service representatives might be paid to retain customers, and thus they might try to be helpful when you call. On the other hand, Supreme Court justices are appointed for life, regardless of how helpful or destructive their decisions might be to the cause of liberty.

count or fired by you if he breaches those terms and, by virtue of representing thousands of very different people in your district, he is bound to act in conflict with the desires of many of the people he represents with everything he does.[13] In all other areas of our lives where we hire a representative, e.g. a lawyer, both parties first contact each other and discuss the arrangement and know the specific terms and duties of that arrangement, you can fire your representative at any time if he breaches these terms, and he cannot act against your interests in favor of another client without getting both parties' explicit consent.

Fourth, to exactly which terms does a voter consent when he casts his vote? The platform that the politician campaigned on two weeks ago, last week, or this week, the new ideas the politician pursues after the election, the ideas he later discards, etc.? The fact is, neither the voter nor the politician could articulate the terms to which the voter is consenting.

Living Here

Yet another argument statists make is that, if you live here, then you must implicitly consent to the system. Let's explore this one a little further.

First, since this argument is one of implicit consent, surely raising your hand and explicitly saying "I want to secede from the state" should trump the implicit consent? It also implies that the consent is irrevocable, i.e., apparently you could never withdraw consent. Do we accept these propositions for any other major decision in our lives?

Second, when is this consent actually given: at birth? In no other situation are newborns deemed to have sufficient capacity to give such consent. If not at birth, what is the actual indicator later in one's life that one has consented to the state? For all other major decisions in our lives—such as buying a house or a car—we evidence our consent by signing a contract

[13] In the U.S. (although this is likely true elsewhere too), as populations have grown substantially, the increase in the number of elected representatives has not kept pace, thereby increasing the number of people "represented" by each elected official well beyond what might have been considered reasonable originally. For instance, the Constitution specifies a minimum House of Representatives district size of 30,000; today, the average is over 730,000 (put another way, were the House of Representatives to operate at that original ratio, there would need to be over 10,000 members). This severely further diminishes any notion of "representation" of any individual voter's interests by his elected member of Congress.

which lays out the very specific terms of that agreement. Yet for the *most important* decision—whether we would allow unspecified other men to take from us whatever they choose, and to tell us what we can and cannot do with our bodies and property—we are deemed to have given consent simply by not moving away?

This logic could be easily turned on the statist. When the statist complains about murder in his society, we could ask why the statist doesn't move to a place without murder and, by the statist's own logic, if the statist stays, then he must be consenting to murder!

Third, to what are you consenting by living here: everything the state does now or might do in the future? Who gives that blanket consent anywhere else in their lives?

Fourth, claiming legitimacy as a ruler in a territory is not the same thing as actually having legitimacy. If I put up signs in the neighborhood saying that I am in charge, and that anyone who stays is deemed to consent, who would agree that staying indicates agreement to my authority? I could not point to my own declaration of legitimacy as the source of my legitimacy; that would be circular reasoning.

Fifth, to negate this supposed consent, where could you move to within a territory if every square inch is claimed by the state to be under its control? If beyond your home state, how could you move when other states control passage across their artificial national borders, and the only places not controlled by states are (parts of) the oceans and possibly Antarctica? The exit costs are simply too high to make staying a genuine indication of implicit consent.[14]

A derivative of this statist line of reasoning is that, if you *could* reasonably move to another state, statists argue "Well, choosing to stay here indicates you have chosen this state over another state." However, this is a

[14]To renounce U.S. citizenship is not easy, fast, or cheap. One must fill out a number of forms, participate in several interviews with the state, pay a fee of over $2,000, obtain a certificate of renunciation, and pay an "expatriation tax" on one's entire wealth. The relevant legislation also requires publication of one's name in the Federal Register, meant to "shame" those who expatriate, and expatriates can be barred from re-entering the U.S. if the state determines that they expatriated to avoid U.S. tax legislation (generally the main reason for most!). Moreover, the Internal Revenue Service (IRS) has the power to direct the U.S. State Department to revoke or not renew a citizen's U.S. passport if the IRS claims that the citizen owes more than $50,000 in back taxes (note, the IRS does not have to prove this, just allege it).

false choice. Imagine if someone credibly threatened you with incarceration but gave you the choice of cage A or cage B; if you choose cage A, that only indicates a preference for cage A over cage B, but it doesn't indicate consent to incarceration itself.

Sixth, why should *you* have to move? Why shouldn't the coercive state move out (either physically, or metaphorically by leaving you alone)?[15] Of the two parties—you and the state—it is the state that is forcibly asserting authority. Why should *it* get to stay? Those around you who explicitly want to live under the state's rule could continue to do so, but why should their actions bind you?

If you're born into a neighborhood in which the Mafia requires payments from you to "protect" you, and where the understanding is that, if you don't make these payments, the Mafia will lock or beat you up, if you continue to live there, are you deemed to be consenting to this protection racket?[16] Maybe you just want to live in the place with which you are most familiar.

If a child gets threatened in the lunch cafeteria by the school bully every day, does the child's continued use of the cafeteria evidence his consent? Maybe he just wants to eat his lunch in peace, and is hoping the bully will cease, or be forced to cease, his bullying.

The statist's argument that, if you don't leave, then you are deemed to consent to the state's actions, is subject to the same refutation of the mugger demanding "Your money or your life": just as you have the right *both* to your money *and* your life, so too you have the right *both* to enjoy your private property *and* not be coerced by the individuals at the state.

Using State Services

"Ah," the statist says, "but if you use the local roads, fire department, and garbage services, then you must be deemed to consent." There are several problems with this argument.

First, this argument misses the point that you have no choice in the matter. Since the state has arrogated to itself the responsibility of providing roads, fire departments, garbage disposal, etc., and prohibits competing

[15]One way to effect this governance separation would be through secession, which I discuss in more detail later.

[16]The astute reader will note that the state is no different from the Mafia in this respect.

suppliers, you don't have the option to purchase these services from other suppliers (or not to purchase them at all).

Second, the argument also overlooks the fact these services are supplied using money forcibly confiscated from taxpayers in the first place. How could one party do something wrongful, and then claim that action as the foundation for evidencing implicit consent from the wronged party?

If the Mafia were to build local roads from protection money extorted from local businesses, and then claim that everyone using the roads is thereby deemed to consent to the Mafia's ongoing operations, even (some) statists would reject that argument. Why is it different because the state does this?[17]

Third, in every other area of our lives where we consensually enter into an agreement under which we retain someone to provide us with services, if the services are not provided at all, or are substandard, then we can, at a minimum, terminate the arrangement, if not also sue for money damages. Yet we cannot fire the state as a service-provider, we cannot sue the state for damages (as will be explained later), and if we attempt to stop paying the state for these services (i.e., refuse to pay our taxes), we are liable to be forcibly thrown into a cage.

Fourth, if a thief steals your television, it is not wrong to try to take it back. In other words, if the state confiscates your income via taxes, it is not wrong to try to take back some of this stolen loot by using the state-provided services that were funded with your confiscated income. The alternative is to be looted and get *no* benefit from what was forcibly taken from you!

Fifth, even if one were to concede that, if you use a state-provided benefit, this implies you have "consented," at most this could only imply consent to the provision of the specific benefit in question. Why should it also imply consent to the whole state infrastructure and every single act performed by the state?

* * * * *

When faced with the above arguments, statists often fall back to the question "Well, how would anything get done if we didn't have a state?" That is

[17] It would be a circular response for a statist to retort "Because the Mafia is criminal but the state is legitimate." We are here asking *why* the state is legitimate when it does exactly what the Mafia does.

a (somewhat) reasonable question to ask, but it is not a valid argument for the state's legitimacy or anyone's implicit consent to the state. Rather, that question is a utilitarian one, and there are significant bodies of intellectual writing and historical evidence that suggest potential answers (which will be discussed later). What the statist is implicitly saying, however, is that if he couldn't imagine how things would get done in a voluntary society, then the default response must be to use coercion.

But asking about the state's legitimacy is a *moral* question, not a utilitarian question. Just because the statist cannot conceive of how things might get done without a state doesn't lend moral legitimacy to the state. As libertarian attorney Stephan Kinsella has noted, imagine being in the Soviet Union before it collapsed, and debating the morality of communism: if someone were to ask "Well, who would produce the toothpaste if the state didn't, and how many varieties would there be?" and the answer given was "We don't yet know," would that be the end of the argument, thereby providing the moral foundation for communism?

Myth #3: The State Acts for the "Common Good"

Statists believe that individuals at the state act for the "common good of society."[18] This phrase is thrown about loosely without a lot of thought.

Who Can Define the "Common Good"?

In the U.S. there are over 315 million people. A "society" is not a discrete creature whose objectives can be defined; it is nothing more than many individuals living in proximity to one another. Each person has a unique personality and unique skills, life objectives, perceptions, and needs. What he wants out of life is known only to him, and his wants may change continuously. No one other than this person could really understand his perspective.

If this is all true, then the obvious questions to ask are: what *is* the "common good of society" and *who* could possibly discern this? Even if we used

[18]Other renditions include for the "general welfare" or the "public good."

the most powerful supercomputer in the world, it would be logically impossible for this device to sketch out what is the "common good," and to keep this current with the changing perspectives of millions of people. Does anyone really believe that there is an algorithm that could find a set of objectives which satisfies everyone's unique desires at once, and which could update itself continuously as those desires change? And yet we don't even rely on such a machine; according to statists, the individuals in government are omnisciently able to define the "common good."

In fact, what statists are really saying is that they are willing to let the few munificent beings at the state define the "common good," and then force a change in behavior among the rest of us to fall into line with that definition. However, what about those of us who don't agree with this definition, or with this process of creating the definition?[19]

And one needs to believe in one of the Tooth Fairy Theories to believe that the "common good" would be defined by those at the state as what is good for the population at large, instead of what is good for those at the state.

Do Elections Help?

One statist response might be that voters are not simply letting politicians define the "common good" by themselves, since, through the electoral process, the politicians who are elected reflect their constituents' views. However, which politician's campaign platform maps precisely with every unique constituent's personal definition of the "common good" (this is even harder to answer when one considers those who voted against this politician and those who did not vote at all), and which politician, once elected, acts faithfully to his campaign platform?

Further, each politician is only one member of this group of "common good" definers, and it's not even clear that this group of beings could agree among themselves. The state comprises individuals from different parts of the political spectrum, from different geographical areas, in different branches of government, all disagreeing with one another all the time.

[19]Note that it is possible for a group of people to contractually agree to a common objective, such as in a homeowner's association. But that is a voluntary arrangement in which each member explicitly consents to the definition of the objective, in contrast to the state, which forces a definition upon everyone, whether they agree to it or not.

Even if we fantasize that this group of beings at the state *could* agree on a definition of the "common good," they never actually set out what their conclusions are at the finish of each election so we could decide if we agree, and then subsequently track if they are acting in accordance with that definition.

In addition, the composition of this group changes with each election. Does this mean that each newly elected group coincidentally arrives at the exact same definition of the "common good" as the previous group or, if not, does this mean that the definition changes with each election? If the latter, does this map well with each voter's changing perspectives, meaning that each voter coincidentally changes what he wants out of life only on each election date, and not in the interim?[20]

"Majority Good," Not "Common Good"

If, at the finish of each election, the elected group of politicians did articulate its definition of the "common good," what happens if one citizen disagrees with this definition? Doesn't a single person disagreeing with the state's definition of the "common good" mean that, by definition, it is *not* the "common good," since it is not satisfying *everyone's* objectives at once?

To the statist, however, this is not a problem, for the statist is willing to accept "majority rule" as the philosophy behind defining the "common good." However, this is a logical contradiction: what is being defined is not the "common good" but the "majority good" (and, as noted above, really not even that).[21]

Yet if all men are metaphysically equal, thereby defining how they

---

[20]To the statist who responds that it is impractical to have continuously changing definitions of the "common good," and that once an election cycle is the best we could hope for, I would respond that this is precisely an argument for the stateless society. In that society, each individual could continuously change and acquire his preferences at his own pace, regardless of what others want, without coercing others into his regime nor being coerced by others into theirs. Just because the statist cannot imagine a better system doesn't mean such a system cannot exist.

[21]In addition, as explained by the public choice theory branch of economics, it's not even clear that the majority view prevails in political deliberations. The sequence in which proposals are put up for debate and vote, and the framing of those proposals, impact the actual outcome, which does not necessarily match the alleged preferences of the majority. The individuals who control the proposal process have a huge degree of influence.

should conduct themselves vis-à-vis others, then it must be morally wrong for two men to force a third to accept that what is good for them is good for him too, whether he likes it or not.

Myth #4: The State and Its Personnel Deserve Our Support

Double Standard

Before tackling this myth, it's worth noting that not only do statists hold state personnel in high esteem, they are very tolerant of their errors. Private-sector personnel, on the other hand, are held to a much higher standard.

For instance, national defense is widely acknowledged by statists as one of the core functions of the state. The U.S. federal government confiscates hundreds of billions of taxpayers' dollars per year to spend on national defense, and maintains military bases, ships, and spy networks both in the U.S. and around the globe. Yet when the U.S. homeland was attacked in September 2001—when the state *failed* in its core function, despite all of its massive expenditures and manpower—the state and its key leaders soared in popularity, as people rallied behind the federal government in general, and the president in particular. So too when the Japanese navy attacked the U.S. naval base at Pearl Harbor in 1941.

Imagine, however, if you had hired a private security firm to protect your home and family, and then a criminal invaded the house, killing members of your family. Do you think that if you were asked about this security firm the next day, you would express incredible pride at having contracted with this firm, and pledge to support it going forward, no matter what the cost? I would posit that, after working through your grieving period, the first thing you would do is find another security firm, since this one clearly failed at its core mission.

More generally, the state is legendary for highly documented and deplorable inefficiency, service standards and corruption, yet statists refuse to hold those at the state to the same exacting standards to which they hold those in the private sector. In the private sector, if people buy a product with the slightest defect, then at a minimum they demand a discount, an exchange, or a refund, but they may also decide not to buy from that vendor ever again. Yet with government, even when there are gross defects in service, people just shrug and say "What else could you expect?" and vainly hope that at the next election in a few years time they can vote in someone better.[22]

Statists argue that the state should regulate every industry, yet whenever a problem arises in a highly regulated industry—such as financial services, healthcare/health insurance, or education—this is seen as a failure of the industry, not of the state; in fact, statists then argue, simplistically, that the problem was that there was insufficient regulation. It never seems to occur to statists to ask whether the problem is inherent in the notion of the state itself as a regulator, and whether there are better alternatives.

If statists believe that the state is the answer to what they perceive as "failure of the market," then why do they not believe that the market is the answer to the failure of the state?

For a different take on the notion of a double standard, consider that many statists are comfortable with the fact that states tend to prohibit private citizens from owning and carrying firearms, yet the state's personnel are allowed and, in some cases, required, to carry firearms. This doesn't strike many statists as a double standard but, by any definition of that phrase, it surely must be. If all men are metaphysically equal, with the same right to provide for their own defense, then how could this double standard be morally justified?[23]

Now let's consider some reasons why the state and its personnel do not deserve our support.

Public Service?!

As one steps back and considers what it is that state personnel actually do—force other people to do things they don't want to do—one wonders why state personnel are accorded so much respect, and why "public service" is so venerated.

[22] As libertarian economist and philosopher Walter Block has noted, there are over 30,000 deaths each year on state-managed roads. Imagine if there were this many deaths on private properties, such as in malls, parking lots, or department stores. There would be public outrage, a loss of confidence in the managers of these properties, and calls to do something about it. Yet there is virtual silence from the public about the state's appalling road management.

[23] Perhaps by one of the Tooth Fairy Theories?

The phrase "public service" is itself a misnomer. The politician is not "serving" the public; he is ordering the public around, including ordering them (via taxes) to pay his salary and purchase his products under the threat of involuntary incarceration. Contrast this with those in the private sector, who actually do serve the public by offering up products for purchase and only getting paid if customers see sufficient value in what is offered up to voluntarily part with their money.

It is somewhat surreal that one person would hold in any esteem another person who chooses to forcibly take property from others and tell them what they can and cannot do with their bodies and property, threatening them with punishment if they don't comply. Such a person in any other context (e.g., the Mafia) would receive our severe opprobrium. Yet statists actually laud state personnel on the basis that they are doing wonderful things for others in society.[24]

To pick one example, namely, welfare, why is it laudable and compassionate for A (the state worker) to force B to send his money to C? If A wants to help C, he could give of his own resources, or he could try to convince others of the merit of voluntarily giving of theirs. Either of those activities would be worthy of great respect. But threatening B with incarceration if he doesn't send money to C is worthy only of scorn. This "ends justify the means" approach is not only immoral—in the sense that it admits that some men are entitled to coerce others—it is also very easily abused. Who is to say that A would properly define whether C is in genuine need according to some objective standard, as opposed to a standard that benefits A's own interests?

The State Is an Imposed Monopoly

Statists will constantly warn about the dangers of monopolies, as they correctly understand that a monopoly leads to higher prices, lower quality and less innovation, because the absence of a competitive threat means the monopolist does not have the incentive to do better.

Yet statists don't stop to consider that, while all of this is demonstrably true, the only actual monopoly that exists is the state, which they support.

[24] Not to mention (but I will) the fact that since those at the state can prohibit peaceful individuals from doing relatively mundane things with their person and property, such as opening a business, renovating a house, etc., state personnel can and do extort favors from private individuals in return for not enforcing these prohibitions.

The state effectively prohibits any competition for the services it provides, such as regulation, policing, defense, courts, etc.[25]

In contrast, there could be no monopoly in the free market because (a) new entrants would always be free to enter if they perceived that the incumbent's pricing, quality, or offerings weren't properly satisfying consumers, and (b) consumers could simply stop buying from the incumbent, thereby denying it the cash flow it needed to survive.

However, the state can prohibit competition from new entrants through coercive regulatory legislation, and through coercive tax legislation can force taxpayers to pay for its services (or those of its designated supplier) even if taxpayers don't want to consume these services.

Thus the only sustainable monopolies that have ever existed have been either the state itself, or businesses which receive an exclusive license (and perhaps also subsidies) from the state to operate in a particular territory. Only with the state's coercive powers to prevent competition and fund an incumbent could there really be a monopoly.

As monopoly theory suggests, over time the pricing for state services (taxation) has always increased, and quality of service has deteriorated (or, at best, remained substandard). The most that generally happens when a state is revealed to be underperforming in provision of a service is that the problem is diagnosed as underfunding, and thus pricing (taxation) is increased, as a perverse remedy for the problem![26] Little serious intellectual inquiry is made into the question of whether monopoly provision of the service is the actual problem. Unlike in the private sector, when the state underperforms, a consumer cannot take his money elsewhere.

One wonders why a statist who is able to understand the problems with monopolies would support the large and only possible monopoly that is the state.

---

[25] Strictly speaking, there *are* private-sector security firms and arbitration tribunals operating in parallel with the state's police and courts, respectively. However, taxpayers have to pay for the state's provision of these services even if they choose to use private-sector alternatives. Thus the total cost to a taxpayer of using these alternatives is significantly higher, making for an uneven playing field (and only the well-off can afford to use the generally better private-sector alternatives). The state also coercively limits the activities of private-sector security firms.

[26] Imagine how much success an underperforming private vendor would have if he tried to increase his pricing!

Lack of Proper Incentives and Knowledge

The above discussion explains one of the shortcomings of the state in terms of its institutional monopoly status. However, since institutions cannot act, but only people can act, the real inquiry should be into the incentives and knowledge of the individuals who constitute the state, and whether these factors should cause us to be supportive of these personnel. There are several points to make in this regard.

First, in the private sector, a vendor has to convince *each* individual customer, *each* time he wants to sell his product to that customer, that he is providing sufficient value for the price to be charged. However, for a politician to get elected, he does *not* have to convince every constituent of the value he would provide each time he interacts with that constituent. All the politician has to do is convince a majority of those who turn up to vote, and he only has to do that once every election cycle. Thus, by definition, he is either non-responsive or, at best, only minimally responsive to the needs of many of his constituents.

Second, consider that the principal benefit the individual at the state is able to offer those who support him is the opportunity to rent the state's coercive powers. In other words, he could offer to a special-interest group that he will fight to pass, reject, preserve, strengthen, weaken, enforce, and/or refuse to enforce legislation that would (a) enhance this group's position or weaken or prohibit competitors (through regulations), or (b) forcibly transfer resources from others to this group (through taxation and subsidies).

As a result, state personnel are lobbied intensively by special-interest groups, and the highest bidders tend to win the right to rent the state's coercive powers.[27] What do the bidders typically offer? Campaign contributions, "get out the vote" assistance, special favors for friends and family, or the promise of a private-sector career after leaving the state, to name just a few examples.

Third, once in office, and unlike in the private sector, state personnel do not have to convince their "customers" to pay them for their services. Through taxes and other legislation, state personnel can force their "cus-

[27] Of course those statists who subscribe to one of the Tooth Fairy Theories would object to this characterization, but that rejection practically indicts itself.

tomers" to pay their salaries regardless of how they perform. Thus there is no incentive to continually offer something of value.

In contrast to the strong alignment in the private sector that exists between the interests of vendors and customers—whereby vendors have personal financial upside from satisfying customers' actual preferences, and risk personal financial loss for failure to deliver—state personnel have neither the upside opportunity nor the risk of loss. Thus, unless one subscribes to one of the Tooth Fairy Theories, state personnel's incentives are entirely misaligned with the notion of delivering value to the broader population.

Fourth, for private-sector entrepreneurs to discover what customers really want takes trial and error in producing different products, making quick adjustments to competition, and obtaining continuous market feedback through customers voluntarily electing to buy or abstain from buying on a daily basis. On the other hand, at the state, only one product is offered at a time, it takes years to make adjustments, there is no competition, and there is no continuous market feedback as "customers" have no choice but to buy from this monopolist. Thus those at the state, *even if* they had the best of intentions, are effectively running blind when it comes to satisfying individuals' preferences.[28]

* * * * *

The question we need to ask when faced with human imperfection—whether lack of knowledge, incompetence, or corruption—is whether it is better to have this imperfection decentralized or centralized?

If someone in the private sector is unknowledgeable, incompetent, or corrupt, then only those few who interact directly with that person would suffer loss, and the market would, relatively quickly, ostracize that person (people would stop dealing with him), so overall losses would be minimized. However, if someone is unknowledgeable, incompetent, or cor-

---

[28] Statists may respond that state personnel sometimes do get regular feedback from polls. However, polls group individuals into artificial categories rather than treating them as individuals, so they don't reveal individual preferences. Also, polls suffer from sample size and bias issues. Most importantly, however, individual preferences are only revealed through purchase decisions, not answering surveys; the former has a real financial cost, whereas the latter is costless to the respondent.

rupt in the state sector, then millions could suffer, because the imperfection is centralized and coercively enforced against many. Further, citizens cannot simply and quickly cease relying on this supplier, because the state prohibits competition in the services it provides. Thus such imperfection not only impacts millions, but also tends to endure for much longer than in the private sector.

The State Receives Immunity

As if to rub salt into the wound, the state asserts that both it and its agents should have immunity from suit for causing damage to those in the private sector, unless the state waives such immunity. There are different types of formal immunity standards (e.g., "sovereign immunity," "state immunity," "qualified immunity," etc.), as well as informal immunity (where the state "circles the wagons" around one of its personnel when information comes out about his misdeeds). However, the essence of all of these concepts is that, whereas everyone else in society is held to one standard of liability for causing damage to others, the state and its agents live by a different (and lower) standard. And this different standard is forcibly imposed on society by the state.

It is logically indefensible to claim that some men are entitled to live by a different standard. Further, why should we respect or support any man who forcibly asserts that he lives by a different standard?

In addition, this immunity creates a moral hazard: why should we expect the state's agents to exercise the same degree of care as we expect of others if these agents cannot be held similarly liable? If you know that you can get away with more, then your standards will drop.

This is most dramatically (but not solely) illustrated by the many situations where police personnel use excessive force, causing unnecessary death and injury to private citizens and destruction of their property, and yet private citizens rarely have effective recourse against those personnel.[29]

[29] Another contributing factor to the police using excessive force in the U.S. is the fact that the police are increasingly recruiting or being trained by former soldiers who previously prosecuted the state's brutal "War on Terror," and are also using surplus military equipment from that conflict. Treating civilians like enemy combatants and the streets like battlefields, with the aid of military equipment and tactics, can only lead to bringing the brutality of war to our towns and villages.

Similarly, consider the horrific death, injury, and destruction caused by state personnel initiating war activities around the globe.[30]

But there are other, more subtle, examples of destructive state actions without liability: the state's delay in approving new medical drugs, or denial of such approval, causing suffering and death to those who might have benefited from access to the drugs; the state's refusal to grant an occupational license, or delay in granting such a license, to an individual who wishes to pursue his chosen occupation, causing him to suffer economically; and the state's setting of a minimum wage above the level that employers would be willing to pay for certain lowly productive workers, thereby leading to employers firing or declining to hire such workers, thus prohibiting these workers from earning an income. No private citizen's lawsuit against the state for these types of actions would ever succeed.

Even where immunity might not provide complete legal protection for state personnel, there is practical protection afforded by the forum in which these issues are resolved: the only courts to which the state would submit in a dispute with a citizen are the state's own courts! In other words, the state arrogates to itself the monopoly on deciding if it or its personnel should be liable to private citizens. In what other area of life would we accept that the party with which we are in a dispute can decide if it is liable?

To appreciate the implications of this issue, consider that, in the U.S., courts have held that the police's "duty to protect" is only owed "to the public at large," and *not* to any particular citizen. In these cases, the police were being sued by victims for negligently failing to provide reasonable protection against specific violent crimes, and the state's courts found the police not liable on the aforementioned basis.

Thus, not only do the police benefit from immunity when acting with excessive force, they also benefit from immunity when negligently not acting at all! And we are supposed to support the confiscation of our incomes to pay for the state's protection from violent crime?

[30]Note that these war activities mostly cause death, injury, and destruction to foreigners, for which state personnel are rarely held liable. Yet there is no cogent, logical principle which argues that death, injury, or destruction is excusable if the victim of a state's violence is not currently under that state's territorial control; that victim is still another human being.

Finally, even if liability *were* imposed for destructive action by an individual at the state, who would pay for any damages awarded? Likely not the state agent concerned, but, rather, the state. However, from where would the state get the funds to compensate the aggrieved private citizen? From taxing private citizens, potentially including the aggrieved private citizen himself!

Myth #5: Democracy Is Good, Better, Best

While statists assume that democratic states represent progress relative to the monarchies that existed previously, libertarian philosopher Hans-Hermann Hoppe has advanced the credible thesis that, in terms of how and why rulers make decisions, democracy may actually be a step backward.[31]

Key Characteristics of a Monarchy

According to Hoppe, under the pre-parliamentary, pre-constitutional, hereditary monarchies that characterized Europe through the end of the 18th century, the monarch regarded his kingdom as a long-term capital asset owned by the royal family, the value of which should be preserved for future generations. As such, when it came to governance, the monarch's approach could best be described as "privately owned government." I will discuss the main implications of this below.

A monarch tended to avoid doing things that would profit him in the short term but cause long-term value destruction. Thus the quantity of resources expropriated from the population through taxation would be sufficiently limited to enable his kingdom to remain reasonably productive (and submissive). Similarly, when adjudicating disputes between his

[31] This thesis is laid out methodically in Hoppe's book, *Democracy—The God That Failed*. Note that Hoppe is not suggesting that a monarchical state is acceptable, only that it exhibits characteristics that make it preferable to a democratic state. Hoppe's thesis has been challenged in at least one academic article: see Jacek Sierpinski's work, "A Critique of Hans-Hermann Hoppe's Thesis on Lesser Harmfulness of Monarchy than Democracy," *Res Publica Revista de Historia de las Ideas Politicas*, Vol. 19 Num. 2 (2016): 521–559.

subjects in the royal courts, the monarch would recognize and protect the private-property rights of his subjects, since that was most likely to lead to a more productive society. In addition, only those who, in the monarch's view, could add value to his kingdom would be permitted to enter and settle there, valuable individuals who were already there would be prohibited from leaving, and value-destroying individuals would be expelled.

Wars were "merely" property disputes between individual monarchs. Since the monarch had to personally fund his wars, he would tend to prefer to expand his territory through the more peaceful and less costly means of contractual purchases and/or inter-dynastic marriage. However, if war were deemed "necessary," then it would be conducted privately and on a limited basis, between a monarch and his hired army and the enemy monarch and his hired army—private citizens were understood not to be involved—with neither monarch wanting to destroy the capital value of his kingdom, nor of the property he might end up winning.

Other than soldiers, those who worked for the monarch were rarely paid by the monarch—they had to be able to support themselves—which meant that the number of people who could work in "government" was quite small.

Since the monarch's estate was liable for all debts he incurred, the monarch typically was restrained in his borrowings, and debts were incurred mostly just to finance war. These debts tended to be paid down in peacetime.

While the monarch might have claimed a monopoly on dispute resolution for his subjects, it was generally understood that the royal courts would adjudicate disputes based on pre-existing, customary law that had developed organically over time. As such, the monarch did not seek to "make law" himself. This meant that the law was well accepted and easily understood by the population, and was relatively predictable.

Importantly, everyone in society understood that only a very small number of people could participate in and benefit from the monarchy, namely, blood relatives and those whom they married. Thus there were very clear class distinctions, with the ruled accepting that, although they had numerical superiority, absent a revolution they would never be in power. From the monarch's perspective, he had to be careful about how harshly he ruled, as too harshly might lead to an uprising, which would put at risk the long-term value of his capital asset (if not his life). Thus monarchs tended to be restrained in terms of tax rates, monetary inflation, and regulatory burden, and (as noted above) generally respected traditional law.

Finally, the selection of a monarch was purely a function of the accident of his birth; he needed to display no particular qualifications to attain and hold this position. Thus, as with the potential of any human, while there was some chance that a monarch could be an evil person, there was also some chance that he could be harmless, or even a good person.

Differentiating Characteristics of a Democracy[32]

According to Hoppe, the advent of democracy changes several aspects of societal governance.

First, politicians do not regard society as "theirs," and thus do not take a long-term, capital-asset-preservation view. Rather, they act as temporary caretakers, doing whatever they can in the short term to get elected, or to increase the powers they can rent out for personal gain, regardless of the long-term impact on society. A good analogy for the difference between a monarch and a democratic politician is the landlord/tenant distinction: who is apt to take better care of the property? Politicians simply do not bear the real costs of their actions.

Second, in a democracy, citizens believe, falsely, that they are ruling themselves (the supposed democratic principle of "self-government"), that everyone benefits from the state (the supposed democratic principle of the state acting "for the common good"), and that they each have the opportunity to get elected, or influence the elected, to get a piece of the action. Accordingly, relative to a monarchy, there is a blurring of class

[32]In using the term "democracy" here, I am using it loosely to describe any political system without hereditary rule in which the broad population elects government officials in periodic elections, where such officials are drawn from the general populace and serve for limited terms. Technically, however, "democracy" refers to a specific political system in which, among other things, there is unlimited majority rule and direct self-governance. Contrast this, for instance, with the U.S., which is not technically a democracy but, rather, a constitutional federative republic, because (a) there are elected representatives, and (b) in order to protect the minority, the majority is theoretically limited by a fundamental written law (the Constitution) and the system's structure (different horizontal and vertical branches of government). However, for all purposes going forward I will treat the U.S. as a democracy, since the key point is to distinguish it from monarchies.

distinctions and benefits, which leads to a much greater acceptance by citizens of ever-increasing expropriation and control by the state.

Third, rulers in a democracy can only attain their positions through elections, and, to win an election, a politician must make reproachable promises to a sufficiently large portion of the voting population that he will plunder and/or forcibly restrict the actions of some other portion of the population, for his supporters' benefit. Thus, unlike with a monarchy, it is more or less guaranteed that, in a democracy, those who are attracted to and successfully attain political office will be the worst individuals in society, namely, the most ruthlessly efficient, morally uninhibited demagogues. And, as political competition intensifies, the candidates vying for office must out-compete each other in their immorality.

Accordingly, Hoppe uses his theory to explain that, since the advent of the democratic state—which he labels "publicly owned government"—we have seen much more short-term, reckless thinking by the rulers in society, who willingly and destructively rent out their coercive powers to special-interest groups, in return for immediate personal gain. This has manifested itself in: high taxation, monetary inflation, and public debt; excessive, unpredictable "law-making" through highly complex legislation and judicial activism, most of which overrides traditional private-property rights; an enormous expansion in the number of permanent government employees, paid for by taxpayers; immigration policies more focused on gaining voters than on increasing societal productivity; and ghastly foreign policy, including more horrific wars than previously, well beyond the personal, limited disputes that were a feature of monarchies,[33] and conscription initially becoming the rule rather than the exception, which makes war cheaper and soldiers more plentiful than were the case under monarchies (although, in recent years, some democratic states have suspended conscription in favor of paid, volunteer armed forces, but such states have met these higher costs through increased taxation and/or public debt).

To be more succinct, we have witnessed both the disappearance of any real limits on the growth and exercise of the state's power, and increasingly bad and dangerous individuals being elected as rulers. As such, the state

[33] Whereas war between monarchs was not ideologically motivated, but, rather, a limited dispute over specific property, democratic states make war on broad, nationalistic lines, and seek cultural, linguistic, and/or religious domination of the vanquished population. In addition, democratic states make "total war," as will be discussed later.

is now larger than it has ever been, and the rulers perceive fewer and fewer limits on their powers, amid the (perceived) acquiescence of the citizenry.[34]

State Violence, Democracy-Style

Whether or not one accepts all aspects of Hoppe's thesis, what is incontestable is the development of the large-scale, reckless physical violence initiated by modern, democratically elected governments, both domestically and externally.

Contrary to popular thought, democracy is no bulwark against abuse at the hands of one's own state; it is not just dictatorships that have waged war on their own subjects.[35] Democracy is merely a process for selecting rulers; it does not say anything about how much personal liberty such rulers would permit. And, as noted above, Hoppe's thesis is that, over time, democracies will produce increasingly worse rulers.

Consider, for instance, President Lincoln's waging of war against the people of the Confederate states in the mid-19th century; the democratically elected German government[36] turning on German Jews in the 1930s;

[34] These trends in democracies are empirical, and, as with all historical events, it is difficult to use these observations alone to definitively conclude that this shows causation, as opposed to mere correlation. Thus one needs a plausible theory to explain the different types of decision-making and officeholders in democracies compared with monarchies, which is what Hoppe has attempted to do in his work.

[35] Although it should not be overlooked that dictatorships are states too, and in fact dictators sometimes come to power through elections or, once in office, hold elections as a means to justify remaining in power. While one may be skeptical about elections in dictatorships—due to claims of voter fraud, intimidation, and suppression, and limitations on opposing candidates—those issues are regularly cited as issues in democracies too! In any event, when we include dictatorships, the number of citizens or other subjects killed by their own state totals over one hundred million in just the 20th century alone (this excludes the millions of people killed in wars, which are also initiated by states of all types).

[36] While Germany was a totalitarian state by the time the German government invaded Poland in 1939 at the beginning of World War II, Adolf Hitler and his Nazi Party colleagues were duly elected into office in 1933 as in any other democracy. While the Nazi Party did not initially hold a majority of seats in the Reichstag (parliament), Hitler was appointed by President Hindenburg as Chancellor to head a ruling coalition. Subsequently, Hitler was given emergency powers by Hindenburg according to the Weimar Constitution, and the Nazi Party then won a majority in a general election (in which the Socialist and Communist Parties were banned and their voters

the British Empire's atrocities committed in the early to mid-20th century against its colonial subjects in Africa (Kenya and South Africa), Asia (India, and what was then Malaya), and the Middle East (Iraq and Yemen); and the modern U.S. government's violent actions directed against its own citizens and their private property in the so-called "War on Drugs" (following on from a similar form of persecution in the early 20th century during Prohibition).[37]

There are also plenty of historical instances of democracies initiating war or other aggressive action against nations which have not attacked them.

As just a few examples, consider: the aggressive actions initiated by the governments of Great Britain and the U.S. leading up to and during the War of 1812; the government of Great Britain going to war against Germany in 1914 after the German government had attacked Belgium; the military intervention in the Russian civil war in 1918 by the governments of France, Great Britain, and the U.S.; the governments of France and Great Britain going to war against Germany in 1939 after the German government had attacked Poland; the U.S. government going to war against Germany in World Wars I and II (Germany had not attacked the U.S.); and the U.S. government initiating offensive action in many other states during the 20th and 21st centuries, including (but not limited to) Afghanistan, Bosnia, Cuba, Grenada, Iraq, Korea, Kosovo, Libya, Somalia, Syria, and Vietnam.[38] In fact, the list of aggressive activities initiated by the government of the U.S., the world's largest democracy, is significantly longer when you consider not only the overt military actions carried out by the U.S. government in instances where the U.S. had not been attacked, but also the U.S. government's aggressive, covert actions in many areas of the world for most of the 20th and 21st centuries. The U.S. government

---

intimidated). Hitler's Enabling Law, which gave him vast power, was passed through a vote by the Reichstag, although members of the Reichstag who would presumably have voted against this legislation were not allowed into the Reichstag building at the time of the vote. This is when Hitler began his totalitarian takeover of Germany, and the vestiges of democracy began to disappear.

[37] The "War on Drugs," like Prohibition, should really be called the "War on People Who Believe That They Own Their Own Bodies."

[38] Note that, in many of these conflicts, the U.S. government was joined by the governments of other democracies (such as Australia, Canada, France, and Great Britain).

has carried out these actions through its intelligence agencies and other proxies interfering in the domestic activities of other states (including other democracies), including installing or propping up dictators to do the U.S. government's bidding (e.g., in Chile, Cuba, Egypt, Guatemala, Iran, and Saudi Arabia, as well as in many other states), training and arming local military forces to take aggressive action against their own populations, financing, training, and arming local revolutionaries to rise up against their local governments, and, most recently, through the use of unmanned attack drones.[39]

In addition, the *way* in which war is conducted has also changed for the worse in parallel with the rise of the democratic state. Perhaps because democratic states have ingested the (fallacious) concept of "self-rule," when it comes to conflict and war, democratic states conflate citizens with their respective governments (this is especially incongruous when it comes to conflicts with dictatorships, given that the civilian populations in dictatorships have even less "say" over their rulers than in democracies).[40] Accordingly, when democratic states go to war, instead of combat being confined to the rulers and their military forces, as it was under monarchies, all citizens and all property are regarded as fair game, in what has become known as "total war."[41]

For instance, President Lincoln's generals conducted a brutal form of "total war" against the non-combatant residents of some of the Confederate U.S. states (before turning to the native American Indians), which was a tactic repeated some years later under Presidents McKinley and Roosevelt against the Filipinos in the Philippine-American War. During World War I, the British government's blockade of food deliveries to

[39]For a chilling and thought-provoking discussion of drone aggression waged by the U.S. government in recent times, see Laurie Calhoun's book, *We Kill Because We Can*.

[40]Note that there is also some "self-conflation." That is, the rulers in a democracy promote, and many statists accept, the false notion that a threat to the government's image, power, or continuity is a threat to civil society or individual citizens.

[41]Note that it's not only in violent war that civilians are targeted by democratic states; when such states levy "economic war" against another state, such as through trade sanctions, the explicit purpose is to economically hurt the other state's civilian population as a means of pressuring its government. (Of course the democratic state also hurts its own civilian population by levying such sanctions, since these sanctions prohibit its own civilians from freely trading with the civilians of the other state.)

Germany led to mass starvation among the civilian German population. During World War II, the Allied militaries' bombing of German cities, and the U.S. military's bombing of Japanese cities, made no distinction between those who had declared and were fighting the war and the private citizens. When the U.S. military dropped two atomic bombs on Japan in 1945, killing, maiming, and poisoning close to two hundred thousand civilians, it did not distinguish between the citizens of Japan and their rulers and military. During the Korean War, the U.S. military bombed and napalmed cities, towns, and villages in the north over a period of three years, by some estimates killing 20 percent of the local population; after running low on urban targets, U.S. bombers then destroyed hydroelectric and irrigation dams, flooding farmland and destroying crops. During the Gulf War in 1991, the U.S. military intentionally bombed Iraq's water treatment plants, thereby depriving the Iraqi civilian population of clean drinking water. In addition to these intentional actions, the U.S. military and its allies, many of them democracies, have inflicted substantial "collateral damage"—the modern euphemism for the incidental (but foreseeable) killing or maiming of private citizens and destruction of their property—in many of their aggressive actions in Asia and the Middle East over the past half-century. And so the 20th and 21st centuries go.

To digress slightly, but importantly, it is too easy to overlook the essence of offensive war actions. These actions involve state personnel sending armed forces or unmanned attack drones overseas to kill or maim other men and sometimes also their families (intentionally or negligently), and to destroy their property, very often *in the home territory of these other men*. The aggressor's armed forces are specifically instructed to initiate these acts of brutality and destruction against men they have never met, and who have not initiated violence against these armed forces when they were at home (or against the civilian populations these armed forces are alleged to be protecting). And when these other men fight back to defend their families and property from the foreign aggressors, or seek to exact retribution either in their home territory or by traveling to the territory of the aggressing state, the aggressing state labels these other men "enemy combatants," "violent animals," or "terrorists" who need to be subdued by force or eliminated!

Yet many statists not only support these aggressive endeavors, they also revere the civilian leaders and members of the military who actively participate in these atrocities. Imagine if these same armed forces carried out these actions against domestic citizens; would statists support that?[42] If not, then what is the moral principle that validates engaging in these atrocities against other humans so long as they are outside the state's artificially drawn borders? It seems as if once the individuals at the state declare "We are at war with [name your enemy]," then the statist's definition of "moral atrocity" is substantially relaxed, and the brutality of war is legitimized. Alchemy![43]

The statist will often retort that, prior to the advent of the modern state, there was widespread violence between individuals, families, clans, and tribes. There's plenty of historical evidence to the contrary, namely, that these societal units quickly developed peaceful means of dispute resolution, as they recognized how costly violence is. However, even if the claim were true, such violence was on a very different scale from today's wars. Non-state violence was (and is) limited because it is personal; those engaging in the violence bore the full cost of their actions, and thus there were natural constraints. Contrast this with the massive scale of violence now waged globally by nation-states, including democracies, resulting from the fact that those ordering this violence don't bear the direct costs of their decisions.

If this is our choice, then give me pre-nation-state clan violence any time!

The private citizen cannot escape the war-mongering decisions of his rulers, yet he pays a heavy price for these decisions: death, injury, and mental anguish when conscripted to fight the state's wars, or when those attacked by the state engage in or threaten retribution against the state's citizens (sometimes labeled "blowback"); loss of liberties at home, as the state clamps down on personal freedoms to prevent blowback; deterioration in culture, as society becomes increasingly centered on military and security

[42]For an example in a democracy suggesting that this issue might not trouble statists, consider that, in the U.S., between 1861 and 1865, President Lincoln's generals waged war on the citizens of the Confederate states, which actions many statists still support to this day. Of course one could also argue that, since this war followed the Confederate states' secession from the U.S., this war was actually waged against a foreign nation's citizens. In which case the statist could rest easy, morally speaking!

[43]For a very insightful articulation of the delusions that accompany modern warfare, see Laurie Calhoun's book, *War and Delusion*.

matters; and economic impoverishment, through direct loss of property from blowback, increased confiscation of income to pay for war, reorientation of societal production away from satisfying consumers' wants in favor of tools of death and destruction, and consumption of society's capital base. Whether the private citizen has voted for or against a ruler, or has not voted at all, he incurs the costs of the state's violence.[44]

The conflation of the state's subjects with the state itself is actually an important tool used by state personnel in the context of defending war activities. State personnel (and their supporters) always couch their statements in the first person plural: "We" are at war; "We" have been attacked overseas; "We" need to take action; "We" need to look after "our boys."

Yet there is no "we"; there is only "they." The average peaceful citizen does not engage in violent action overseas, or station himself there to try to interfere with another society. It is obnoxious for state personnel to claim "we" are doing these things. *They* are doing these things, without any direction or consent from the peaceful citizen. *They* start these wars, *they* forcibly take our income to finance them, and then they have the temerity to say "We're all in this together." And it is only *they* who benefit from war: the politicians who gain prestige and power from conquering and occupying new lands; the state agencies which maintain or grow their budgets when there is war (or the threat thereof); the banks which finance war; the vendors of military and other equipment (and their supply chains) which profit from supplying the military; and the favored businesses which gain from new or cheaper access to conquered resources, or enhanced protection of their existing or future foreign investments.[45]

Statists wrap all of this violence in the national flag and collective patriotism, because in this way they can try to convince the average citizen that these violent activities overseas are honorable and necessary—to protect "our national pride," "our freedoms," and "the principles we stand

[44] For an excellent discussion of what war does to a population, see the book edited by John Denson, *The Costs of War*.

[45] Note that not only do the rulers (and their cronies) benefit from war while not bearing its costs, but the most senior members of the state also receive significant personal protection against any blowback—paid for by the confiscated income of private citizens—in the form of massive amounts of armed protection wherever they go (while denying private citizens the right to be armed for their own protection), as well as underground bunkers to which to flee if there is an actual or threatened attack.

for," whatever those phrases mean—so that there will be less objection to pursuing and funding war and "supporting the military."

Statists have been remarkably successful in constructing this delusion. The average citizen is highly deferential to and sympathetic toward military personnel: applauding them in public, providing special ways to honor them (particularly at sporting events), weeping at their reunions with their families, going out of his way to find them civilian jobs, and dutifully accepting the state's claim that he must pay for their physical and mental recovery (in addition to their historical compensation). But these military personnel *voluntarily* chose to go into the morally suspect killing and destruction business![46]

Moreover, 99.9 percent of the time these military personnel are not actually defending the average citizen from any imminent threat to that citizen's life or property. Before the state's armed forces kill or maim each individual regarded as "the enemy," or destroy his property—and most often this target is thousands of miles away from the citizen allegedly being protected—the state doesn't bother to adduce and present evidence of an actual or a threatened wrongful act by that person, nor subject that evidence to any reasonable standard of proof or scrutiny by an independent arbiter. Statists just assume that this person's guilt is proven by the fact that he was targeted by the state, and that the state's violent actions were an appropriate punishment.[47] And the state's honored military personnel eagerly go along with this travesty.

[46]One might have more sympathy for those in the armed forces who are conscripted by the state to fight its wars. Even then, the real honor should be reserved for those who flee conscription to avoid carrying out the state's violence.

[47]Probably the most startling example of this in recent times is the fact that, as disclosed in 2012, during his presidency President Obama regularly presided over a "kill list," whereby he ordered the murder by drone strike of designated individuals overseas, including Americans, none of whom had been tried and found guilty of any violent crime. While many of these strikes also murdered individuals *not* on the list, according to one report in *The New York Times*, the president had a formula for minimizing the official count of mistaken casualties that "in effect counts all military-age males in a strike zone as combatants ... unless there is explicit intelligence posthumously proving them innocent." This is quite a perverse reversal of the usual burden of proof required in capital crimes. Yet this shocking activity quickly ceased being a central discussion point in the U.S.; it appeared that the vast majority of the population didn't know about, didn't care about or, in the case of foreign policy hawks, actively supported, this horrific exercise of state power.

What type of society have we become where we regard proactive killing and destruction as one of the most venerated forms of human endeavor?

To illustrate this delusion further, consider private security guards who are hired to protect people and their property. They don't go in search of other humans to kill or property to destroy, but only react to real situations that endanger their clients or their clients' property. They don't get paid by coercively extracting money from their clients, but have to offer sufficient value for their clients to voluntarily hire them. Do we see a national outpouring of emotion and collective financial support for these private-sector individuals, who are *actually* protecting life and property against imminent threats?

Apparently, honor and support are reserved only for those state personnel who proactively kill foreigners and destroy their property, and who get paid through confiscation of taxpayers' income.

* * * * *

Winston Churchill is reputed to have once noted "It has been said that democracy is the worst form of government except all the others that have been tried." For the above reasons, I would challenge Churchill's conclusion.

Myth #6: The State Dispenses Criminal Justice

The Injustice of It All

The whole area of criminal law is a very odd feature of statist society. Under a just system, the law would recognize that only someone who suffers harm—in the sense of damage to his person or legitimately acquired property (which I'll define later)—would have the right to take action against the aggressor.[48] Yet the statist criminal legal system fails this logic on a number of accounts.

[48] Such person could assign or abandon this right, but that would be his voluntary decision.

First, the system allows the state to take action against an aggressor even though the state is not the victim. In fact, the state could never be a victim of aggression against person or legitimately acquired property, because (a) "the state" is not a person, and (b) any property the state controls has, by definition, been acquired illegitimately, in that the state has used coercive means to acquire it (i.e., by using either tax or regulatory legislation).

Second, under the statist system, state personnel, and not the victim, decide on whether and how to pursue the aggressor, and what penalties he should suffer.

Third, many "crimes" are defined by legislation simply as behavior which the individuals at the state do not approve of, even though such behavior does not cause any actual damage to any individual or his legitimately acquired property. In other words, the state's criminal legal system as a just means to redress personal loss is mostly a fiction.

The History

How did we get here? Statists like to fantasize that there is some deep philosophical or efficiency reason that has driven the state to become the alleged guardian of everyone's interests and to act against criminals "for the common good." However, that's not what actually happened.

Hundreds of years ago there were no "crimes," but only claims brought by victims against aggressors for personal wrongs. These claims were detected, investigated, and resolved locally, and mostly peacefully, according to community customs in locally convened tribunals.

However, at some point when monarchs wanted to raise revenue to help finance their lifestyles and their wars, and to more closely control society and reward different interests who could help in that regard (such as local powerbrokers), they realized that there could be tremendous benefits from running a "justice" system. Accordingly, a wrong committed by A against B or B's property became defined as a "disturbance of the king's peace," and at first such actions were guided, and then later compelled, to be brought before the king's courts. Subsequently, "the Crown" took over detection and prosecution of these actions. In these cases, "the Crown" was able to do several things for the king's benefit: charge fees; fine A and seize his property if he were found guilty; and fine B and seize his property for false accusation if A were acquitted.

As monarchs extended their activities to include forcibly taxing their subjects, it became a crime not to pay one's taxes, and thus the first victimless "crime" was born. In other words, it became a "crime" for one man to try to prevent another man from forcibly seizing part of his income, thereby negating the timeless principle of being entitled to defend one's property from theft. Other victimless "crimes" were also created, which were based on the principle of failing to obey the king's orders in other areas. This led to the creation of vast bureaucracies to try to detect and then prosecute such heinous acts by subjects.

Once monarchs gave way to the modern nation-state, the state simply assumed the same role.[49]

The Growth and Dangers of Victimless "Crimes"

Worse, however, is that the modern state has now created thousands of regulations the violation of which amount to "crimes," and the vast majority of these infractions have no actual victims in the traditional sense, namely, an individual suffering damage to his person or legitimately acquired property. There is an obvious unfairness here in that no citizen could realistically be aware of all or even most of these regulations, and therefore it is very easy for citizens to commit legislated "crimes" without even knowing it. Before the advent of these victimless "crimes"—when a "wrong" was merely defined as causing damage to someone's person or property—citizens could easily understand what was expected of them.

And to enforce these thousands of regulations, the state has established vast, armed bureaucracies.[50]

[49]In today's state "justice" system, to bolster the aura around the supposed infallibility of, and the supreme "justice" imposed by, the state's court system, note how intimidating the setup is, almost as if there are some divine aspects to it. The judge wears a fearsome black robe, is seated higher than everyone else, may be supported by armed guards, and must be addressed using honorific terms (otherwise contempt charges might be brought against the miscreant). This is of a piece with other ridiculously childish aspects of the state, such as the aura created around, and forced respect given to, the presidency, the legislature, and the military. Respect and honor should be earned, not imposed, but the pomp and ceremony is important for the state's illusion of superiority.

[50]For instance, according to a U.S. Department of Justice report from June 2012, just at the federal government alone in 2008 there were 40 federal agencies with over

Each year many thousands of lives are ruined, many permanently, when the state arrests and tries individuals, fines them, seizes their property, and/or incarcerates them based on these regulatory but victimless "crimes." Examples include violations of tax regulations, insider trading and other securities regulations, health & safety regulations, campaign finance regulations, traffic regulations, environmental regulations, prostitution regulations, occupational licensing regulations, narcotics regulations, firearm possession regulations, and immigration regulations.[51]

Marginalizing the Victim's Interests

There are some other disturbing features of modern criminal "justice" systems. Even where a real wrong occurs, in the sense that there is a victim who has suffered personal injury or property damage, the victim's interests are marginalized by the state's system. This happens in several ways.

First, in many modern states, citizens have been disarmed by the state's gun-control regulations, and are vigorously prosecuted should they violate these possession regulations. The theory is that the state's police will protect citizens, so citizens don't need to possess firearms to protect themselves. Yet in the vast majority of violent crimes, only the victim is present when the crime is committed, not the state's police, and thus the victim has been deprived of the most effective method of self-defense.[52]

120,000 officers authorized to carry firearms and make arrests. Unusual examples include the Department of Agriculture, the Department of Education, the Environmental Protection Agency, the Federal Reserve, the Fish and Wildlife Service, the General Services Administration, the Department of Housing and Urban Development, the IRS, the Bureau of Land Management, the Library of Congress, the National Institute of Health, the National Oceanic and Atmospheric Administration, the Park Service, and the Veterans Health Administration.

[51] According to the latest data from the U.S. Bureau of Justice Statistics, approximately one-third of the federal and state prison population in the U.S. (that is, approximately 520,000 prisoners) had been incarcerated for these types of non-violent, victimless "crimes." Note that these numbers exclude another 700,000+ prisoners held in local jails and over 4.7 million individuals on probation and parole, for which "category of offense" data is not available, although undoubtedly a large number of these individuals were also incarcerated for non-violent, victimless "crimes."

[52] To bolster its argument, the state typically claims that reducing private gun ownership would itself reduce violent crime, but that claim is demonstrably false: see John Lott's book, *More Guns, Less Crime*. The aggressor rarely pays attention to gun-control reg-

Gun-control regulations are also immoral. By what right could A forcibly prohibit B from possessing a firearm? B is entitled (as is A) to spend his income as he sees fit, and to possess the means to defend himself from attack. Obviously B is not entitled to use his firearm to initiate aggression against others (nor is A), just as he's not entitled to use any other object, or his body, to commit aggression. The only justifiable exception is that A could tell B that he cannot bring a firearm onto A's private property (if B doesn't like this rule, then his choice is not to enter A's property). However, the state's gun-control regulations often apply everywhere (and the state cannot legitimately own any property and thus cannot legitimately set possession rules), and these regulations prohibit possession, not violent use. With respect to the latter, there are already laws against murder, robbery, rape, etc., so gun-control regulations are redundant (as well as immoral).

Second, the police report to and therefore serve the political class, and thus the police's priorities mostly reflect the political class's priorities. Once the political class sets a priority, that centralized order is what counts, instead of taking into account each individual citizen's desired preferences. Since policing is a scarce resource, every hour spent by the police on task X means an hour less available for task Y.

So, for instance, if the political class wants to raise more revenues, then the police would prioritize enforcement of tax regulations, moving traffic and parking regulations, etc. If the political class wants to moralize and crack down on personal but non-violent vices, then the police would prioritize enforcement of regulations against prostitution, narcotics, etc. If the political class is feeling the pressure from the environmental lobby, then the police would prioritize enforcement of environmental regulations. If the political class is feeling pressure from the anti-gun lobby, then the police would prioritize disarming citizens who possess unregulated firearms (but have committed no violence with them). The time, personnel, and money spent on prosecuting these victimless "crimes" come at the expense of resources that could be devoted to prosecuting crimes *with* victims.

Alternatively, when it comes to actual violent crimes, if the political class

---

ulations, or uses other means to conduct his violence, such as vehicles, knives, clubs, superior strength, explosives, etc. So the only effect of gun-control regulations is to disarm the law-abiding victims.

is feeling pressure from a particular racial, ethnic, or religious group, then the police may reduce their presence in that group's neighborhoods and may reduce arrests of that group's members, even if those neighborhoods and members are responsible for significant violent crime.

These priorities might be quite at odds with what individual citizens want from their police, and what they would choose to purchase if they could individually purchase private security services. However, because the state produces a "one-size-fits-all," politically directed security system, citizens have little individual choice.

Third, the criminal prosecutorial system is designed around the state, not the victim. The prosecutor has no alignment with or responsibility to the victim.

In a private law case, the victim voluntarily chooses his attorney, the attorney contractually must act in accordance with the victim's instructions, and the attorney has the motivation to do the best he can for the victim. This motivation arises because (a) the attorney's compensation may be linked to how well he does for the victim, and (b) how well the attorney performs will impact his reputation, and thus his ability to attract future clients, who will also voluntarily choose their attorney.

On the other hand, under the state's system, the victim is required to accept whichever prosecutor the state assigns, the prosecutor has no contractual relationship with the victim, and the prosecutor is not motivated financially to act in the victim's interests. Instead, the prosecutor is motivated by whatever statistics the state decides it wants to use to measure performance. For instance, if "wins" is important, then the prosecutor may drop the hard cases and only pursue the easy ones; if "case closure" is important, then the prosecutor may drop the long cases and only pursue those that could be resolved quickly; if battling a particular type of "crime" is high on the state's agenda, then the prosecutor would prioritize those cases and ignore others.

The victim also has no ability to direct the prosecutor's actions. If the prosecutor drops the case, against the victim's wishes, then the victim cannot "retain" another prosecutor, as the prosecutor only serves the state, not the victim. If the prosecutor enters into a plea bargain[53] with the aggressor (because he wants the aggressor to help him in a different case, or

[53] A "plea bargain" is an agreement by a defendant with a prosecutor to plead guilty to

the case is going to take too long, etc.), then the victim cannot prevent that. If the prosecutor seeks a punishment that is not in accordance with the victim's wishes, then the victim has no ability to veto that. If the prosecutor does a poor job, then the victim has no claim against him for breach of contract, since the victim is not his client.[54]

In short, the connection between the victim and the aggressor is completely severed, and the state is actually treated as the victim vis-à-vis the aggressor.[55]

Fourth, the victim could end up paying multiple times, without his consent. He suffers the loss from the aggressor's crime, and then, if he is a taxpayer, via taxes he is also forced to pay for the cost of prosecuting the aggressor and, if the aggressor is convicted, for the cost of incarcerating him in a state prison!

Intimidation by the State

Another questionable aspect of the state's criminal legal system is that the state uses its victimless-"crime" legislation as a "stick," to force citizens (and others) to act in accordance with the whims of those at the state.

For instance, in the U.S., in circumstances where those in the federal government are not able to implement their preferred policies directly, they can use their control of the banking system—since it is a (victimless) "crime" to operate a bank without a state-provided license—to indirectly get to the same result. Thus the federal government has been known to insinuate to banks that, if they want to keep their license, then they should not provide financial services to businesses which engage in activities (also victimless) of which those at the federal government do not approve, such as selling narcotics or firearms, engaging in payday lending, and operating escort services or Internet gambling. The inability for these businesses to

certain charges without a trial, in return for other charges being dropped and/or the prosecutor recommending to the judge a potentially lighter sentence.

[54]If the victim tried to sue the prosecutor for negligence, then the prosecutor would likely benefit from the immunity principle discussed earlier, and of course the victim would have to sue the state prosecutor in the state's own courts!

[55]Moreover, in some areas the state may actually prohibit a parallel, private civil action by the victim against the aggressor. Even where both actions might be run in parallel, findings in the criminal case could impact the outcome of the civil case, but the victim has no real input into or control over the criminal case.

use the banking system is a huge impediment, and is akin to preventing them from operating. A similar level of intimidation has also occurred at the state-government level with respect to insurance companies, whereby state insurance regulators who do not approve of firearm ownership have "suggested" that insurance companies cease providing coverage to firearm-owners associations, which provide liability coverage for their members.

Or, if the U.S. government wants to levy economic sanctions against another state for failure to do what the U.S. government has commanded it to do, then the U.S. government has been known to advise all banks worldwide that they should not do business with this other state, or with individuals or businesses in that state, or else these banks will be denied permission to operate in the U.S. Since the U.S. is such an important financial services market, this warning is generally heeded closely by most banks globally.

Similarly, the state makes it a (victimless) "crime" for certain companies to merge without the state's approval. The state has been known to refuse to consent to mergers unless one or both companies do something else the state wants them to do.

The state also makes it a (victimless) "crime" for a citizen to donate more than a specified amount of his own money to other citizens running for political office. These campaign finance regulations are a wonderful weapon for incumbents to use against challengers. The incumbents can use their office and the state's other resources to get their message out, but, for challengers, their main avenue is to purchase media time, which requires funds. When the state limits the amount of money challengers can raise and spend, it favors those already holding office.

To make a somewhat obvious point (by now), all of these victimless-"crime" regulations are immoral, in that they amount to one man forcibly telling another what he may and may not do with his body or private property when he is not initiating aggression against anyone. Thus those at the state are using the threat of enforcing immoral regulations to achieve their desired ends. This is a criminal "justice" system?

There is one other aspect of state intimidation in the criminal "justice" system that is worth noting, namely, prosecutorial intimidation of defendants. At least in the U.S., prosecutors employ three strategies that are manifestly unfair to defendants.

First, when the federal government's prosecutors question a potential defendant who appears voluntarily and is not under oath, the questioners can, without any sanction, lie to the person being interviewed, to trick him into giving up valuable information, but if this person lies to the prosecutors, then he risks being indicted for that victimless "crime" alone.[56]

Second, for a single alleged wrong, prosecutors often charge defendants with many different "crimes" at once, without necessarily expecting all (or any) of the charges to be successfully proved in front of a jury. Since a prosecutor is funded by the state, he has little personal downside in increasing the complexity of a potential trial, but by creating a more complex web of charges to defend against, which also increases the defense's costs, this can be a powerful way for the prosecutor to intimidate a defendant into accepting a plea bargain.

Third, prosecutors are allowed to offer a plea bargain, immunity, or other benefits to a co-defendant in return for that co-defendant testifying against the defendant, which can be a powerful inducement for the co-defendant to give false testimony. Yet a defendant is prohibited from offering any benefit to a witness (other than an expert witness) to testify on his behalf.

Where is the justice in this treatment of defendants?

Prioritizing Crimes against the State

The final point to make about the perversity of the state criminal legal system is to note how the state takes much more seriously "crimes against the state" than wrongs committed against its citizens.

For instance, the murder of a key figure at the state is even given a special term—"assassination"—and it's hard to describe how many resources the state devotes to preventing assassinations, and the lengths to which it will go to find perpetrators. Compare this with the resources the state devotes to preventing and solving murders of ordinary citizens. Those at the state unilaterally elevate the importance of their own lives over the lives of those who both fund the state and are supposed to be protected by it.

[56]The U.S. Supreme Court has ruled that federal prosecutors and Federal Bureau of Investigation agents can use trickery, deceptions, and outright lies (including such things as disguises, verbal traps, and fraud) to help them extract information from a witness or person they are investigating.

Accordingly, through taxes, the ordinary citizen is forcibly required to fund the special protection of individuals at the state, and is not permitted to retain this income for his own protection, or for the protection of individuals of his choosing. Moreover, although the state taxes the ordinary citizen with the promise of protecting him from violence, the state makes this a secondary priority for the use of this citizen's income, behind protection of individuals at the state.[57]

Related to the above point, assaulting a police officer is treated very differently from assaulting an average citizen. For instance, in the U.S., most state legislation elevates the crime from "assault" to "aggravated assault" if the victim is a police officer. Fines and sentences are often greater for this type of assault as compared with assaulting a regular citizen. Further, some of the normal defenses to an allegation of assault are often not available if the assault was directed at a police officer.[58]

Yet, if all men are metaphysically equal, then how could one defend the concept that the penalty for initiating aggression against A should be different from the exact same action directed at B?

Or consider how the state considers the failure to pay taxes, compared with how the state views the failure to pay a private debt that is due.[59] Non-payment of taxes is a "crime," whereas failure to pay a private debt is generally not. Further, the state has a veritable army of tax inspectors and armed tax enforcers to go after tax avoiders.[60]

In addition, to try to prevent non-payment of taxes, the state also establishes many ancillary reporting and disclosure regulations, violations of which are also "crimes." These include requiring use of a tracking iden-

---

[57] And note that the state uses the ordinary citizen's income to fund possession of large amounts of firearms and ammunition to protect individuals at the state, while at the same time, through gun-control regulations, substantially limiting the ordinary citizen's ability to use the same firearms and ammunition to protect himself.

[58] This concept is even more egregious when paired with the immunity concept described earlier: the police get the benefit of immunity when they do something wrong, and when they are wronged, their aggressors suffer greater penalties.

[59] Obviously I'm not suggesting that taxes are a "debt due" to the state, since taxes are forcibly mandated, as opposed to arising from a voluntary payment contract.

[60] In the U.S., quite apart from the IRS's enforcement arm, there are other examples of armed tax collectors, such as the New York state government's "strike force" to combat the heinous crime of trying to avoid payment of state taxes on cigarettes.

tification number by taxpayers, requiring self-reporting of taxable income and of assets held overseas, and forcing banks to monitor and report on customers' cash movements and sources. Sometimes the state even enlists foreigners to become its tax collectors, by requiring foreign banks to report on the overseas holdings of citizens, and by bringing economic pressure to bear on "tax havens."[61]

All of this is a far cry from how the state protects private creditors from non-payment by debtors.

Finally, consider how vigorously the state pursues those who disclose state information, compared with how the state protects disclosure of private information. Again, the former is a "crime" (with its own word: "espionage"), whereas this is not generally true of the latter. The U.S. federal government has often used the threat of indictment under the Espionage Act to try to silence "whistleblowers" who want to publicly disclose information on what they regard as problematic state activities. Also, note how worldwide, state-organized dragnets are established to try to snare those who have the audacity to disclose things the state would rather keep secret, e.g., the U.S. government's pursuit of Julian Assange and Edward Snowden.

Private citizens just cannot expect the same resources to be devoted to protecting their information.[62]

[61] "Tax havens" are simply states that have the temerity to charge lower tax rates than states like the U.S. might prefer. They represent tax-rate competition for higher taxing states, as they attract taxpayers (individuals and firms) who relocate to reduce the theft engaged in by their current state. And if there is one thing a state dislikes, it is competition.

[62] There is some irony to this entire point anyway. In the U.S., the largest danger to the ordinary citizen's privacy is actually the federal government, which spends billions of citizens' confiscated tax dollars each year intercepting citizens' telephone calls and emails, and monitoring their web browsing and physical movement.

III. The Free Market

What Is the "Free Market"?

Why Is This Relevant?

One might ask why I regard the free market, which appears to be merely an economic concept, to be relevant to a discussion of the state, which at first blush could be conceived of as a purely a political concept.

To survive and flourish, humans have wants that must be satisfied, e.g., food, shelter, clothing, healthcare, education, leisure, etc. The only way to satisfy these wants is to take naturally occurring resources, mix them with labor, capital equipment, and managerial skill, and produce the appropriate goods. However, there are never enough resources to satisfy all human wants simultaneously. Thus man's central dilemma is how to allocate scarce, productive resources to maximize the satisfaction of wants; this is an economic question. To perform this productive function in a world with more than one person, humans must deliberately organize themselves and interact with one another in society, and human organization as a society is ultimately a political question. Thus politics and economics are integral to each other.

While there are many different spectrums that could be used to analyze human organization, the one that is most critical to understand in the context of the free market is the liberty spectrum: at one end, the principle is one of voluntary human interaction, where liberty is the prevailing norm; at the other end, human interaction is coerced, where liberty yields to force.

Since the state is a coercive entity, it belongs at one end of the spectrum. The absence of a state, where human interaction is voluntary, is at the other of the spectrum. It is when economic decisions are made within this latter setting that I use the term "the free market."[1]

We Don't Have a "Free Market"

What statists fail to comprehend is that when libertarians talk about the "free market" they mean the *complete* absence of the state (at least in terms of impacting any economic decisions). Accordingly, in any society in which a state exists, there cannot be a "free market."

Hence while statists like to point to perceived problems in any contemporary economy as evidence of the shortcomings of the "free market," the libertarian response is that, since there is a state, there is no "free market." Such problems tend to be caused by one of the following three factors: human error, scarcity of resources, or state intervention.

No political system could eliminate human error or the scarcity of resources. They are natural features of our world, although (as will be discussed later) the presence of a state can exacerbate these two factors. On the other hand, state intervention is entirely of man's own making, and is usually the cause of most of modern society's enduring problems.

When a perceived problem in the economy arises, statists always argue that the state needs to intervene because "The free market has failed." Leaving aside the fact that, by definition, if there is a state to intervene, then there is not a "free market," the statist claim raises the question, "failed" in what sense? The free market is nothing more than the aggregate of the daily interactions of millions of entrepreneurs and customers each transacting voluntarily in accordance with their preferences. The free market cannot "fail" or "succeed," it can only operate. However, down at the individual transaction level, since each transaction in the free market is voluntarily entered into by two parties, by definition both parties must expect to be satisfied with the outcome, and thus *each transaction must be "a success," ex ante.*[2]

The reality is that what statists mean when they say "The free market

[1] In libertarian terms, this is called "anarcho-capitalism." The reference to "anarchy" denotes the absence of a coercive state, not the absence of order; the two are very different things, as will be discussed later.

[2] For instance, if A pays $500 to B for his television, then prior to the trade A must value the television more than his $500, and B must value the $500 more than his television,

has failed" is that the millions of voluntarily transacting entrepreneurs and customers have failed to transact in the way these statists want them to transact. However, what gives statists the right to prioritize their view on how entrepreneurs and customers "should" transact, and to advocate for coercive state intervention to enforce these priorities?

Economics 101

To better understand the difference between the free market and a statist economy, we must first understand economic activity.

Entrepreneurial Activity

As noted above, the purpose of an economy is to allocate productive resources—natural resources, labor, and capital goods—to maximize the satisfaction of human wants. No one can produce all of his own needs, and thus humans must trade; a person produces what he can, and trades this product with others who are producing what he wants but cannot produce for himself. However, productive resources are scarce relative to human wants. Thus choices have to be made in organizing these scarce resources, to try to satisfy those wants that are ranked most highly by each person. The key question is, how can we know which wants are ranked most highly so that we could then try to organize resources accordingly?

Those who organize these scarce resources are society's entrepreneurs. Their function is to try to anticipate human wants, bid for and organize the necessary scarce resources to create goods to satisfy those wants, and then price these goods appropriately and deliver them to consumers.[3]

Those entrepreneurs who are able to successfully bid for and organize resources at a lower cost than what customers are voluntarily willing to

---

otherwise, why would they transact? Only voluntary transactions can be "win-win," since they satisfy the double coincidence of wants.

[3]This is a bit of a simplification of the structure of production. There are entrepreneurs who produce intermediate goods to satisfy the demands of other entrepreneurs who are closer to the end consumer. However, ultimately it is the demands of the end consumer that drive the whole production chain. To recognize the more complex production structure, when I am talking more generally about the production chain I will switch from using "consumer" to "customer."

pay for the end product would make a profit. Other entrepreneurs who are unsuccessful at this task would incur a loss.[4]

The key point, however, is that entrepreneurs cannot force their products on consumers; in the free market the consumer is king, and he votes with his dollars every minute of every day. Those entrepreneurs who make profits would be able to purchase further resources, and those who incur losses would have to yield resources, both of which are beneficial for society, as it means resources are flowing to those entrepreneurs who are best at satisfying actual wants.[5] Since society is more prosperous the more human wants are satisfied, profits are not something we should disdain but, rather, something we should embrace. The lure of making profits is what draws entrepreneurs to take risk with their capital and time to try to find a way to satisfy customers, and losses are a way to discipline entrepreneurs who make mistakes in this process.

An entrepreneur's task is very difficult. The knowledge of what his customers want—in terms of price, quality, location, etc.—is not available in any central database, and there are millions of customers in the economy, each with his own specific wants. Entrepreneurs therefore take their cues from signals given by their customers: if a customer is voluntarily willing to pay for a good at the price proposed by the entrepreneur, then the entrepreneur knows he is satisfying a want; if a customer is not willing to transact, then the entrepreneur knows he is not satisfying a want. The entrepreneur tries to anticipate customer demand, but keeps experimenting every day amid continuous changes in demand, competition, and the availability, quality, and pricing of resources.

The Impact of the State

Now consider the nature of the state. The state comprises a small group of people who have enormous power in the economy through their ability

[4]It's also important to note that production activity takes time, which is also scarce, and thus time can be considered to be another factor of production. To an entrepreneur, a dollar in profits tomorrow is less valuable than a dollar in profits today, and hence entrepreneurs not only have to weigh up the explicit costs of other factors, but also the time needed to generate a profit (which is primarily a function of the production and marketing processes chosen).

[5]Note that there is also a "conservation" benefit to this flow, since the entrepreneurs who are operating at the lowest cost while satisfying demand are using the fewest resources, thereby conserving more of these resources for other uses.

to coercively tax and regulate, and provide subsidies to, other people. Taxation is the forcible taking of money from those who possess it, and who would otherwise have spent these funds in accordance with their individual wants. A subsidy is the transfer of the money seized through taxation to those individuals in the economy whom those at the state believe should have this money instead. Regulations coerce individuals to do or refrain from doing things with their bodies and personal property as those at the state decide, instead of as decided by these individuals themselves. Accordingly, through legislation, those at the state can forcibly redirect resources, funds and efforts in the economy as they see fit.

However, those at the state cannot possibly gather the relevant knowledge that entrepreneurs can gather in terms of individuals' wants, competition, and the availability, quality, and pricing of resources. This is because state personnel are not in the "flow" of signals given to entrepreneurs every minute of every day by customers, competitors, and resource owners.

Moreover, as noted earlier, unlike entrepreneurs, those at the state do not risk their own capital when they act, and thus they do not have the appropriate profit incentives to get things right, nor the same discipline—personal financial loss—to try to avoid making mistakes.

In fact, those at the state have very different incentives than satisfying individual consumers' wants. Given the awesome coercive powers they exercise, state personnel are intensively lobbied by special-interest groups (e.g., businesses, unions, industries, environmental groups, etc.) to exercise these powers in favor of these groups. In return, these groups offer state personnel such things as electoral support, "freebies," and future private-sector positions (this is called "crony capitalism").[6]

These special-interest groups seek subsidies, tariffs or quotas, restrictive regulations, and/or protection from competition, which are all to the detriment of consumers. Subsidies forcibly divert resources to less efficient entrepreneurs, and tariffs, quotas, restrictive regulations, and protection from competition both stifle innovation, and drive up the prices of goods by restricting their availability. Consumers cannot compete in the lobbying game because they are never as organized as special-interest groups.

[6]It's not necessary to attribute any bad intentions to state personnel to support this conclusion. All humans react to irresistible incentives within their chosen careers. What's important when comparing the free market to statism is to recognize all relevant incentives at play, and consider the impact of these different incentives on decision-making.

This is because consumers are a larger and more diverse group, with fewer dollars at stake per individual, than is the case for special-interest groups.[7]

Another important contrast to make between the state and the free market is how they reconcile different interests. In the free market, if one consumer prefers Coke and another prefers Pepsi, then both consumers' wishes could be accommodated: Coke would produce and sell to the first consumer, and Pepsi would produce and sell to the second consumer. However, with the state, only one of these two consumers' wishes could be accommodated at a time, because the state forces a "one-size-fits-all" policy on the population. If one consumer prefers policy X that is campaigned for by party A, and another prefers policy Y that is campaigned for by party B, then whichever party wins in the election would dictate which consumer will be satisfied and which consumer will lose out. To use a Coke/Pepsi analogy, under statism we would all vote on Coke or Pepsi, and if Coke gets the most votes, then Pepsi would be outlawed, and everyone who wanted to drink soda would have to be satisfied with Coke.

For all of these reasons, the state can be described as a relatively small group of people using coercion to reconfigure the economy contrary to how it would be configured if people and resources could flow naturally to maximally satisfy individuals' wants. Hence, by definition, prosperity is reduced by state intervention.

Of course this is all very dynamic. The tendency of each individual in the economy—consumer and entrepreneur—is to adjust to each state intervention in the direction of their actual preferences. Thus, following an intervention, consumers and entrepreneurs would try to get resources flowing the way they would naturally flow, but now subject to the constraints of the new state intervention and/or any adverse consequences. This is because individuals' inherent preferences cannot be changed by those at the state; the state can only impact the ability and priority of entre-

[7]This is known as "concentrated benefits and diffuse costs." For example, successfully lobbying for a particular regulation might yield a particular firm $100 million in incremental revenues from consumers, and thus there is a real benefit to the firm in engaging in aggressive lobbying. If these benefits are extracted from five million relevant consumers, then that's only $20 per consumer. Thus no consumer would have any reason to spend time and money to look into this particular matter, nor to try to counteract it.

preneurs to satisfy preferences (this is like water always trying to find the cracks in a rock).[8]

Once those at the state realize how the private sector has adjusted to try to satisfy actual preferences that are not in accordance with the state's preferences, they feel compelled to implement more interventions to try again to redirect resources in the way they want. Similarly, once those at the state observe the adverse consequences resulting from their prior interventions (although they rarely confess to appreciating the link), they feel compelled to implement more interventions to try to address those consequences. Then the private sector adjusts again, and/or more adverse consequences arise, and then the state intervenes again.

This is how problems arise in the modern economy. Statists don't like the choices consumers and entrepreneurs are making, so they exclaim "The free market has failed!" and then the state intervenes. This causes new, artificial problems, and then statists exclaim again "The free market has failed!" and argue for more intervention.

It would not be an exaggeration to claim that all enduring (as opposed to temporary) economic problems in modern society are demonstrably traceable back to state intervention. Relative to the free market, in a market with state intervention there are fewer goods available, and those that are available are more expensive;[9] there are fewer jobs available; there are fewer workers available; the purchasing power of money and the benefit from traditional cash savings are lower; capital accumulation is lower, leading to less innovation and lower sustainable economic growth; and we have dramatic, economy-wide business cycles (the more the state intervenes, the more frequent these cycles and the greater their duration and intensity).[10]

The state is also responsible for broader social problems in two senses:

---

[8] In the extreme case where the state actually outlaws a product that consumers want, all that happens is that a "black market" develops, and transactions move "underground" at higher prices and with less oversight than would otherwise have been the case, e.g., narcotics today, and alcohol during Prohibition. In fact, "black market" is really just the statist's pejorative phrase for a free market that has been outlawed.

[9] In addition to the cost, the quality of goods is also adversely impacted by state intervention. For instance, with respect to passenger vehicles, the safety, emissions, and fuel efficiency edicts issued by the state have dramatically reduced the variety of available styles, visibility, and performance.

[10] That these economic problems are directly attributable to the state can only be fully ap-

the state creates intra-societal conflict, because different interests aggressively compete to rent the state's coercive powers to use against others; and there is more inter-societal conflict, because of state-initiated or state-provoked war.

Statists only look at the symptoms of a perceived economic problem and conclude that the free market has failed. They don't dig deeper to understand the root causes, or consider the logical fallacy behind their conclusion. By its nature, the free market—as defined above—could *only* naturally act to try to maximize the satisfaction of human wants. On the other hand, as discussed above, the state can *never* be as efficient towards this end as the free market.

To be clear, free-market advocates do *not* claim that the free market would be a perfect solution. It could not be perfect because the combination of human imperfection and scarce resources means we could never satisfy all human wants simultaneously. Rather, free-market advocates claim that if the objective is to *maximize* the satisfaction of human wants, then the free market would be more effective than state intervention. The free market, through the continuous experimentation of millions of entrepreneurs, would represent not one but countless possible solutions to the problem of allocating scarce resources to satisfy human wants. On the other hand, the state represents only one possible solution. Thus we should not think of the comparison as the free market vs. the state but, rather, as the comparison of many experimenters vs. one.

To think of this another way, if an entrepreneur in the free market fails to adequately provide a solution to consumers' wants, then other entrepreneurs tend to enter the market and try to arbitrage away the imperfection (meaning improve upon this entrepreneur's shortcomings). However, when the state fails to adequately provide a solution to consumers' wants, since the state is a coercive monopoly there is no one who could legally try to arbitrage away the state's imperfection.

Finally, in addition to these utilitarian observations, it bears repeating that, due to the absence of coercion, the free market is also the *only moral solution*.

---

preciated with a good understanding of free-market economics, known as "Austrian economics," which will be discussed briefly below.

Austrian Economics

Technically speaking, economics as a science is supposed to be "value-free," meaning that it doesn't seek to prescribe what economic policies a society should or should not adopt; rather, it simply outlines what the consequences would be of adopting specific policies. On the other hand, political philosophy *is* prescriptive, and thus does seek to suggest a set of principles on which society should be based. So, for example, economics would explain that an increase in the minimum wage would, all else being equal, cause relative unemployment for workers whose productivity is lower than the new wage level, and a higher wage for certain other workers, and leave things at that. It would be up to political philosophy to argue whether, given this outcome, an increase in the minimum wage should or should not be adopted.

Libertarians favor a school of economics dating from the late 19th century known as "Austrian economics" (since the early founders were all from Austria). Austrian economic analysis explains that intervention by the central planners at the state can only hamper the ability of entrepreneurs to maximally satisfy consumers' preferences.[11]

Austrian economics differs substantially from Keynesian economics which, as noted earlier, is the statist's preferred school of economic thought.[12] Keynesian economists are famous for simplistically classifying into uniform categories millions of uniquely different individuals, and concepts comprising countless different components, such as "consumers," "labor," "the economy," "the environment," "the financial sector," "the money supply," or "exports," and then theorizing about how these allegedly uniform groups or things act, or interact with one another, and how the state could forcibly improve such actions or interactions. To lend *faux*-scientific credibility to their analyses, Keynesians try to reduce

[11] Conceptually, someone could subscribe to Austrian economics but still be a statist, as that person could agree with the conclusion from Austrian economic analysis, but believe that there are higher priorities than maximizing the satisfaction of consumer preferences.

[12] Some statists claim to be monetarists (the so-called "Chicago school" of economics), but monetarism is so close to Keynesianism compared with Austrian economics that monetarists may as well be Keynesians, for all practical purposes.

human activity to a series of mathematical formula which, through their intricate econometric models, are used to predict with utopian accuracy how an economy or these groups would respond to state action; when reality doesn't conform to these models, Keynesians question reality, not their models. If the economy is not in equilibrium, then the Keynesian regards this as a problem. To Keynesians, the state has *the* central role in the economy, and the purpose of economics is to prescribe what the state should do to get the economy "back" into equilibrium.

Unlike Keynesian economics, Austrian economics doesn't use aggregate mathematical models to quantitatively or temporally predict economy-wide outcomes. This is because these outcomes *cannot* be modeled, since the economy is simply the aggregate of millions of unique consumers and entrepreneurs interacting continuously, based on their ever-changing subjective preferences and assessments of the future. Accordingly, Austrian economics is focused on using the logic of purposeful human action, and the concept of subjective costs and benefits, to examine cause and effect at the level of the individual consumer and entrepreneur. Instead of looking at all firms as uniform actors, and the economy as a single entity, Austrian economics takes into account differential impacts at different stages of the consumption and production cycles. In fact, while the state is central to Keynesian economics, the entrepreneur is central to Austrian economics, where "entrepreneur" is defined as a profit-seeker who commits and risks his capital in deciding when, what, and how much to produce, under the condition of uncertainty.

Austrian economists focus on the market *process* as opposed to the market equilibrium, and are not troubled by the fact that the economy is in a perpetual state of disequilibrium because everything is constantly changing; this is the inevitable outcome of purposeful human action amid uncertainty, which is the environment under which the entrepreneur must operate. Keynesianism has no theory of or role for the entrepreneur, because Keynesianism focuses on the long run, where the economy is supposed to be in an idyllic equilibrium, and entrepreneurs could not exist in equilibrium.

The purpose of Austrian economics is not to explain how to guide the economy to a utopian equilibrium, but to describe the less-than-obvious trade-offs involved when humans make economic decisions amid changing circumstances. In this respect, Austrian economics employs the concept—first articulated by 19th century French economist Frédéric Bastiat—to focus not just on what is seen, but on what is unseen, when state interventions occur in the economy.

Austrian economics is also much simpler and more intuitive to understand than Keynesian economics. Austrian economists like to say that Keynesians have "physics envy," since they are fixated on defining everything via a fancy model. In contrast, Austrian economists are well read in history and philosophy, and seek to understand the reality of purposeful human action, not the fantasy world of mathematical models.

There are other substantial differences between Austrian and Keynesian economics, in areas such as money, heterogeneity of capital goods, savings and investment, anti-trust, entrepreneurship, and the business cycle, just to name a few. A full comparison of the two economic schools is beyond the scope of this book; suffice to say, it is difficult to fully appreciate the economic benefits of libertarianism over statism without a good understanding of non-fiction (i.e., Austrian) economics.[13]

Myth #7: The Free Market Creates an Inequality Problem

Statists claim that state intervention is needed to address the "inequality problem" which arises in the free market. This is a misguided claim, both because it is "tilting at windmills," and because it incorrectly attributes causation.[14]

[13] For a detailed comparison of Keynesian and Austrian economics, the *Liberty Classroom* online educational series produced by libertarian historian Tom Woods includes a course entitled "What's Wrong With Textbook Economics," taught by Professor Jeff Herbener. In that course, Herbener takes one of the standard Keynesian textbooks, *Economics* (written by Paul Samuelson and William Nordhaus), and provides a chapter-by-chapter Austrian critique. Alternatively, for an excellent introduction to Austrian economics, I can strongly recommend Robert Murphy's book, *Choice*.

[14] The inequality discussion often swings back and forward loosely between "income" and "wealth" inequality. However, the two concepts are quite different. "Income" is one's earnings in a particular period; "wealth" is the amount of assets one owns, net of one's debts. One could have low income in a period but still own a lot of assets (as

Equality Is Impossible

To claim that inequality is a problem caused by the free market implies that it is natural for all men to have equal income or wealth, and that this natural state is disturbed by peaceful, voluntary exchange among men.

However, no two men have the same physical or intellectual attributes, nurturing, or luck, and there is a wide variety of other differences that could be important in each man's economic evolution (such as personal choices, culture, and geography). Accordingly, and assuming no criminal aggression by or against any man, why should we expect any two men to end up in the same place in terms of career skills, family, education, health, etc.? If these and other factors impact what one earns, then why should we expect any two men to end up with the same income or wealth?[15]

In other words, inequality is actually society's *natural* state. And, leaving aside voluntary gifts by those with more to those with less, there are only two ways to change this natural state.

First, by physically rebalancing men's natural attributes or their developmental environments. Some examples would include: taking one good eye from each person with two good eyes and giving these excess good eyes to the blind; ejecting the more advanced students from school a few

many elderly do); alternatively, one could have high income in a period but own few assets of value. As a related point, many of the wealthiest, highest profile statists often take advantage of the terminological confusion in this area to try to appear "socially conscious" by championing higher income tax rates to fund statist social programs; they know full well that this is not going to materially impact them, because most of their well-being is tied up in wealth (assets), which are not caught by income taxes, as opposed to income (also, they have paid tax advisors to organize their affairs to ensure that much of their income is sheltered from income taxes). One wonders whether these wealthy statists would, instead, champion high "wealth taxes" to fund social programs; after all, the success of these programs is not a function of the specific source of their funding.

[15] Statists frequently make the remarkable claim that inequality can *only* arise because of "discrimination." In other words, they assume that, but for "discrimination," every person would end up in the same economic situation as every other person. Apart from the fact that this wouldn't explain inequality between two people of the same class (e.g., two white, heterosexual, Protestant men of the same age, with no disabilities), no allowance is made by this argument for the myriad of other factors that influence where someone ends up in life. This whole area is very well covered in Thomas Sowell's book, *Wealth, Poverty and Politics*.

years early to let the others catch up; and pulling children out of nurturing households and raising them in less helpful environments.

Second, through forcibly taking income or wealth from one person and giving it to another.

Yet, with respect to either solution, if all men are metaphysically equal, then surely no man possesses the right to initiate force against another man's body or property? Thus, to ensure income or wealth equality requires acting immorally.

In addition, even if one could, at some point in time, equalize all wealth for a moment, this doesn't solve the "Day Two" problem. On the day after equalization, if, to satisfy their individual preferences, people were free to trade what they have for what they want, and to build upon what they have, then inequality would immediately arise once again as each individual makes his unique choices. Accordingly, unless we prohibit free trade and entrepreneurship by individuals, the entire effort to achieve the prior equalization would have to be undertaken again and again until eternity. Think of the futile cost, bureaucracy and immoral intrusion into people's lives that would entail. Well, welcome to the modern state!

Membership of Income and Wealth Groups Is Dynamic

Statists define inequality by using categories. They refer to the "top 1 percent" or the "bottom 10 percent," and track what happens to the income or wealth of those groups over time. However, those are meaningless statistics because they represent groups in which the members are constantly changing.[16]

A person's income and wealth typically change over time. In a normal career, you would start out with low income and few assets; over time, your income might grow as you progress in your career, and you might start acquiring assets; near the end of your career, as you retire, your income might drop significantly but you might have built up a substantial asset

[16] There are other problems with the widely used inequality statistics. For instance, the statistics often fail to take into account significant cash and in-kind benefits provided to individuals by the state. Also, by only focusing on dollars, they don't measure the much higher level of consumables that can be bought with these dollars today compared with in the past.

base. Along the way you might have had some years where you received a big bonus, and thus your income would have spiked upwards, and you also might have spent some time in between jobs, so your income would have spiked downwards. In some years you might come into an inheritance, or your stock portfolio or house might increase substantially in value, so you look wealthier, and in some years your assets might be worth much less, so you look less wealthy.

Thus, at different points of time when inequality is measured, one could be in the high income group one year but the low income group the next, and similarly be in the high wealth group one year but the low wealth group the next. Any particular person who might fall into the "bottom 10 percent" one year, perhaps early on in his career, could be in the "middle 10 percent" in a few years time, and might even spend some time in the "top 10 percent," before falling back down again later when he retires or has some bad luck.

Accordingly, measuring income and wealth for categories of people tells us nothing about what is happening to *actual* people. For that, one must track the ups and downs of those actual people. And it is quite logical that people would move into and out of different income and wealth groups over their lives.[17]

How Much Inequality Is the Problem?

When a statist claims that there is "too much inequality," the right response is, "Well then, how much inequality *would* be appropriate?" The statist cannot answer this question because there is no answer, or at least no objectively verifiable answer.

What the statist really means is that the level of inequality which he perceives to exist is too high for his taste. Presumably, with millions of dif-

[17]This is illustrated in the U.S. by IRS data released in 2014 analyzing the frequency with which actual individual taxpayers appeared in the top 400 income-earner group from 1992–2010. Of the 7,600 tax returns filed over this period (400 highest earners in each year × 19 years), there were 4,024 unique, individual taxpayers, since obviously some taxpayers made it into the top 400 in more than one year. It turns out that 85 percent of these 4,024 individuals made it into the top 400 only once or twice over that 19 year period, and only two percent (95 individuals) made it into this group 10 or more times. Other IRS data illustrates similar mobility of specific individuals over time through the various quintiles of income distribution.

ferent statists, there would be millions of different views on this concept. How are we to reconcile all of these views into a target inequality amount that is acceptable to everyone? If we can't define an objective, then how could we design a process to achieve success?

The statist would likely fall back on the democratic process, i.e., the right amount of inequality is whatever those who hold elected office at any point in time tell us is acceptable. In other words, this is an entirely arbitrary target based on the whims of our rulers.[18]

And of course, as noted above, whatever the target is, the only way to move towards that target is through immoral action, i.e., the application of force by some men to other men.

How Inequality Arises in the Free Market

All of the above points aside, one of the biggest misconceptions statists harbor about an economy is *how* people become wealthy in the free market. This misconception then causes statists to perceive significant wealth as something to condemn, which leads to the misplaced concern about income or wealth inequality.

In the free market, no entrepreneur can force any customer to buy his product. Every transaction is a voluntary exchange: the customer voluntarily gives up some of his money in return for the entrepreneur's product. By definition, the customer must value the product he receives more than the money he gives up, otherwise why would he trade?

Similarly, no entrepreneur can force any person to work for him. Every labor arrangement is a voluntary exchange: the worker voluntarily gives up some of his time and effort in return for wages. By definition, the worker

[18]It's even more arbitrary when one considers that statists' concerns about inequality seem to stop at national borders artificially contrived by the state. As libertarian historian Tom Woods has pointed out, the inequality between the richest and the poorest in the U.S. is trivial compared with the inequality between the U.S. population and the populations in many of the world's poorest countries (e.g., parts of Africa, and Cuba, North Korea, and Venezuela). If statists truly believe in the morality of forcibly reducing inequality among humans, then they should be in favor of a massive, forced transfer of income to these poor populations from everyone in the U.S. (and other wealthy countries), including from those in the lower income quintiles in the U.S. who are doing much better, relatively speaking, than even the "middle class" in these extremely poor countries.

must value the wages he receives more highly than the time he has given up and the effort he has made, otherwise why would he work?

This is also true for owners of natural resources, capital equipment, and financial capital: they only exchange these factors voluntarily with the entrepreneur in return for acceptable payments (rent, interest, dividends, etc.).

I want to digress for an instant and anticipate an objection at this point from statists. Statists might argue that a consumer or a worker could be in very difficult circumstances with no other attractive options, and thus really is "forced" to buy the product or accept the job offer, as the case may be, and accordingly these are not voluntary exchanges. However, this places the fault in the wrong place. What is forcing the consumer's or the worker's hand is *not* the entrepreneur who is offering the product or the job. Rather, it is reality that is responsible for the consumer's or the worker's tough situation: it could be bad luck, bad prior decisions, bad education, etc. The consumer or the worker could always decide *not* to purchase the product or accept the job offer; he would consider his predicament, and decide whether continuing to look for a different product or job is preferable to buying this product or accepting this job offer.

Moreover, *the one party* to which the consumer or the worker should be *thankful* is the entrepreneur who is offering the product or the job. At least this entrepreneur is giving the consumer or the worker a way to improve his situation relative to where things currently stand. Consider all of the other individuals in the economy who are *not* offering any product to the consumer or any job to the worker. Surely they are not as noble as this entrepreneur when it comes to this consumer or this worker? Yet the statist's ire (and call for state action) is often directed at this entrepreneur for "overcharging" the consumer or "underpaying" the worker.[19,20]

---

[19]The statist who claims that the entrepreneur is taking advantage of this consumer or worker by pricing the product "too high" or offering wages that are "too low" (as if there is some objectively ascertainable correct price or wage, which is a whole other fallacy) simply illustrates a poor understanding of how the free market operates. An entrepreneur who prices his goods above competitive goods, or proposes underpaying a worker relative to what competitors are offering, would see his competitors lure away the customer or the worker, as the case may be.

[20]With respect to the worker whom the statist believes is "underpaid," as Austrian economist Don Boudreaux has noted, worker compensation is only half of the living stan-

In any event, to return to the main topic, now consider how an entrepreneur runs his business in the free market. He engages in voluntary trades with the owners of productive factors—workers, owners of natural resources, and capital-goods and capital-funds suppliers—to acquire use of these factors. He then organizes these factors in a process over time to produce goods for which customers would voluntarily pay the entrepreneur if the goods satisfy their wants. If the entrepreneur can purchase and organize the productive factors at a cost lower than the price at which customers are willing to buy his product, then he makes a profit.[21]

Is it wrong for the entrepreneur to seek a profit? As noted earlier, since no human is self-sufficient, every human must produce what he can, and trade it for the product of others who are able to satisfy those of his needs that he cannot satisfy himself. A worker sells his time and effort for wages, and uses those wages to buy what he cannot produce himself; a land owner sells possession of his land for rent, and uses that rent to buy what he cannot produce himself; a capital-goods supplier sells or rents his equipment for proceeds, and uses those proceeds to buy what he cannot produce himself; a capital-funds supplier lends or invests his funds for interest or

---

dards equation, the other half being the cost of living. If statists want to improve the worker's situation, then why don't they campaign for economy-wide low price ceilings on all goods, which would allow the worker to buy more with his income, instead of campaigning for action by the state to raise the worker's wages? That would be a way ostensibly to improve the worker's living standards without targeting the one party—the employer—who is actually providing a benefit to the worker. The reason this is not done is because (a) people instinctively know that price ceilings create shortages of goods, although for some reason these same people don't see that price floors, like the minimum wage, create surpluses of workers, thereby taking some bargaining power away from the least productive workers, and (b) the employer is a more convenient target to attack, and many statists harbor the Marxist belief that all employers "oppress" all workers. This is despite the fact that, in the U.S., about 95 percent of workers are paid more than the minimum wage; wouldn't true oppressors only pay exactly what the state demanded and not a penny more? Boudreaux has also suggested that if statists really believe they can just "will" higher pay for workers through legislation, without any adverse side effects, then why not just ban part-time work? If everyone had to work full time, then they'd all get paid so much more...

[21] Of course this is a gross simplification of the complexity and risk in the entrepreneurial process. An entrepreneur must compete with others for productive factors and the consumers' money, and he must keep up with new technologies and other changes in the overall environment in which he operates. If he stops innovating and satisfying consumers, then he would eventually go out of business.

dividends, respectively, and uses the interest or dividends to buy what he cannot produce himself. Similarly, an entrepreneur employs his expertise for profits, and uses those profits to buy what he cannot produce himself.

How does an entrepreneur in the free market become wealthy? He could only become wealthy if he can consistently satisfy the demands of workers, natural resource owners, capital-goods and capital-funds suppliers, and customers and, while doing so, make a profit. If we ignore the cost structure to make the key point, then the only way an entrepreneur could become wealthy is if he consistently delivers to a large number of customers a product for which they are voluntarily willing to part with their money. In other words, only by satisfying other humans' wants could he become wealthy.

Why is this worthy of any disdain? The entrepreneur is in the business of organizing resources to satisfy human wants, and if he does a great job, then he becomes wealthy. No free-market advocate argues that the entrepreneur is a "do gooder"; he is in business to make a profit, but the fact is that, in a voluntary economy, he could *only* make a profit if he made his customers happy. Conversely, those who cannot make their customers happy lose money and do not end up as wealthy, perhaps even living in relative poverty.

This is how inequality of wealth arises in the free market: those who have done a better job for customers end up with more wealth than those who have done a poorer job.

With one exception discussed below, the history of entrepreneurs attaining great wealth is the history of those who have best satisfied customers' wants on a large scale. They have brought new products at affordable prices to the mass market, raising the living standards of many individuals in the economy.[22]

When one looks at a wealthy entrepreneur, one only sees his wealth—meaning the assets that define his living standard—but that fails to appre-

[22]In this respect, the wealthy perform a valuable testing function for society. When innovations are first developed they are relatively expensive to produce, but the entrepreneur needs some way to test his innovations in the consumer market. Wealthy consumers, since they can afford expensive products, constitute the "test laboratory" for entrepreneurs to try out their innovations. Those innovations that pass this test then become the focus of entrepreneurs' efforts to bring down production costs to create mass market appeal.

ciate that his ability to acquire these assets was bestowed upon him voluntarily by the many customers whose lives or businesses were bettered by purchasing his products. Through the sale of his products on the market, in no sense has the entrepreneur "taken" anything away from those who have less—he has exchanged his products for customers' money—and therefore he does not deserve to be forcibly required by the state to "give it back" through taxation or other means.

The critical point to appreciate is that "wealth" is not something that descends from heaven and simply cries out for distribution among the population. Too often statists just assume that wealth has always been there and will always be there, and that the only point for discussion is how to distribute it. Statists would do better to consider how wealth is actually generated. The default for most of human existence has been absolute poverty and, if no entrepreneur got up in the morning to produce goods in demand, then poverty is where we'd all be headed. In other words, wealth doesn't just exist, it has to be *created* by entrepreneurs in a complex process fraught with risk, and requires that these entrepreneurs have the freedom to organize their activities to produce goods desired by customers, and be able to keep any resulting profits as the reward for taking the risk to create such goods.[23,24]

But because the state infringes on entrepreneurial freedom and incentives, and thus the creation of wealth, it can only suppress human well-being, since it means fewer quality goods at affordable prices to satisfy human wants.

Focus on Absolute, Not Relative, Poverty

In focusing on inequality, statists are wrongly concerned with *relative* poverty; as noted above, there will always be those who are more and those who are less wealthy, given that individuals have different skills,

[23] The statist view here is at least partially a consequence of subscribing to Keynesian economics, which pays no attention to differences in entrepreneurial activity, but simply looks at the economy as a mass of uniform firms all doing the same thing.

[24] It's also worth pointing out that wealth is not fixed in amount; in the free market, there is no limit to the amount of wealth that entrepreneurs could create. If an entrepreneur creates one unit of wealth, that in no way detracts from the amount of wealth that others could create and enjoy.

upbringings, and luck. Moreover, relative poverty data tells us very little about someone's living standards. If A earns $4 million a year and B earns $500,000 a year, then the statist concerned with inequality would complain that A is earning eight times what B is earning (8x!), yet B is not exactly destitute. Now assume that five years later, A earns $10 million a year and B earns $1 million a year; the statist focused on inequality would complain that things are measurably worse because inequality has widened, since now A is earning 10 times what B is earning (which is clearly a sign of the coming Armageddon).

It is better to focus on the living standards of the least well-off, or *absolute* poverty. Living standards are a function of the quantity, quality, and price of products available which satisfy consumers' needs. Absolute poverty has declined—that is, living standards of the least well-off have increased—dramatically thanks to entrepreneurial activity; the poorest individuals in the U.S. live better than European royalty lived a couple of centuries ago, due to the fabulous, plentiful, and affordable innovations produced by entrepreneurs in search of profits.[25]

How Inequality Arises with a State

There is, however, a form of wealthy entrepreneur who *is* deserving of our disdain. He cannot exist in the free market, but he is quite common in the statist economy.

This is the crony capitalist: the entrepreneur who gets assistance from the state in generating his wealth, also known as the "political entrepreneur" (as opposed to the "market entrepreneur," who operates without state assistance). Such assistance could be in the form of monopoly or monopoly-like privileges (through state licensing), subsidies, protective tariffs or import quotas, eminent domain, newly created money, etc.[26]

[25] However, even relative poverty has been reduced by entrepreneurial activity. For want of a better term, "stuff" inequality has declined the most in the countries with the least state intervention (which is another way of saying the most-free entrepreneurial activity). For instance, a couple of hundred years ago in England, the poor traveled barefoot while the rich traveled fully clothed and in horse-drawn carriages; today, the poor travel fully clothed in modest cars and the rich travel fully clothed in fancy cars. In addition, inequality as measured by the widely used Gini coefficient is much less dramatic in the countries with less state intervention than in those with more.

[26] Statists lament the fabulous wealth of those in financial services ("Wall Street"), but

Since every action by the state is coercive, any of these forms of assistance means the state has either coercively taken resources from another person and bestowed them on the political entrepreneur, or has coercively restricted the political entrepreneur's actual or potential competitors from competing as vigorously as they might. As noted earlier, such political entrepreneurs are able to obtain this assistance through aggressive lobbying of the state, and in effect are paying to rent the state's coercive powers.

It is somewhat obvious to note, but statists often overlook, the fact that if there were no state, then there would be no coercive powers to rent and thus no political entrepreneurship. Statists prefer to believe that crony capitalism is a problem caused by businesses, not the state, but of course there are two parties to every instance of crony capitalism. This is an issue which flows naturally from the very *existence* of the state, and a proper survey of economic history would reveal that this is an issue as old as the state itself. As long as the state exists, each business's calculus would be "If I don't reap the benefits of the state's coercive powers, then my competitors will."

Efforts to regulate crony capitalism out of existence have always failed, and will always fail, because they attack the symptom, not the cause.

* * * * *

The implication of the statist myth that the free market creates an inequality problem is that the state is able to provide an appropriate solution. However, all that happens when the state coercively imposes a "solution" in this area is that we shift from inequality of income/wealth to inequality of power. That is, those at the state who would construct this "solution" wield significant power over ordinary citizens, and special-interest groups will lobby state personnel aggressively to rent the state's coercive powers to influence the alleged solution.

---

that is greatly a function of state privilege. The state creates, and enables banks to create, substantial amounts of new money—which will eventually cause consumer prices to rise—and much of this new money flows to the financial sector first due to how the new money is created (through central bank open-market operations and fractional-reserve banking). Those in this sector therefore get to buy products with the new money before it has filtered into the rest of the economy, and thus before price inflation sets in, which is highly beneficial to these early recipients. On the other hand, the average citizen, who is the last to get the new money, has had to buy higher-priced goods in the meantime with his prior income. In this way, state privilege widens inequality.

Accordingly, while the outcome might (temporarily) reflect less inequality of income/wealth, it would definitely reflect an enormous inequality of power. Who is to say that this is a reasonable trade-off?

And since such a solution would rely on one man coercing another, we know it cannot be a moral solution.

Myth #8: The Free Market Exploits Workers

Income Inequality among Workers

There are some points I wish to make regarding workers, inequality, and the free market which parallel those made above regarding entrepreneurs.

We could think of a worker as an entrepreneur, whose product to sell is his labor and whose customer is another entrepreneur (who runs a firm). As noted above, in the free market the worker cannot force his product on his customer. He has to offer sufficient value to his customer for his customer to be willing to voluntarily part with some of his income to purchase the worker's labor.

If the worker could consistently provide enough value to his customer, then he would be paid well and may end up relatively wealthy as a result. The worker can add to the value he can offer his customer through obtaining experience or education in a relevant area, remaining in good health, having a good attitude, etc., and with this increased value may be able to command an increased price for his product in the form of higher compensation (subject, of course, to the impact of competition from other workers competing to sell their labor to the same entrepreneur).

However, a worker who doesn't have the same experience, education, health, attitude, etc. would not be able to earn as much because he wouldn't be providing as much value to his customer, and such a worker may end up living in relative poverty.

This is how inequality of income for workers arises in the free market: those who do a better job as employees end up with more than those who do a poorer job. Those workers who attain very high incomes in this manner are not deserving of any disdain. Like the entrepreneur, their high incomes simply reflect the fact that they have contributed significant value to their customers (in this case, entrepreneurs) who have been willing to voluntarily compensate them for such value.

However, there is also a parallel to the "political entrepreneur" who does deserve our disdain, namely, the "political worker." This is the worker who seeks to use the state's coercive powers to get special privileges vis-à-vis employers, principally through regulations relating to labor unions, minimum wages, working conditions, and anti-discrimination (affirmative action).

Labor unions are not objectionable per se, since there is nothing wrong with employees banding together to try to negotiate better terms from an employer. However, what *is* morally objectionable is when unions obtain special rights and protections from the state.[27] It is one thing for employees to collectively bargain with an employer where all parties are voluntarily engaging in such discussions, are free to accept or reject any proposal and any representatives without any violent consequences, and are free to enforce their legitimate property rights. It is quite another for a labor union to use the state's coercive powers to (a) force an employer to negotiate exclusively with the union (including providing the union with organizing space on the employer's property), and to require all employees to be represented exclusively by such union, whether they want this or not, (b) force an employer to make or accept any particular proposals, or (c) restrict the range of defensive actions an employer may take in response to any threatened or actual violent strike-action implemented by the union against the employer or the employer's property, as well as against any workers who might not want to abide by the strike action.

Regarding working conditions, anti-discrimination, and minimum wage regulations, I will deal with these below.

Worker Exploitation in the Free Market

Statists often argue that workers are liable to be unfairly exploited economically by entrepreneurs in the free market, and thus state intervention is necessary to prevent this. However, this doesn't make any sense. It suggests that the relationship is coercive, as if the employer could force the worker to take a job with low pay and terrible working conditions, the

[27] Note that labor union regulation is often as much about feathering the nest of union leaders vis-à-vis union members as it is about "helping" employees vis-à-vis employers. Through labor union regulations, union leaders often force workers to become union members, pay dues, strike, and support action programs to which the workers might object, all of which increase the power and compensation of the union leaders.

worker would have no option but to submit, and the employer would be immune to outside pressures when setting these terms. It also suggests that statist intervention could improve on the free market. There are several points to make about this.

First, a worker's potential total compensation (comprising cash, benefits, and working conditions) has a lower bound and an upper bound. The lower bound is determined by competition for the worker from other employers. If there is vigorous competition, then the lower bound would be higher, and if there is little competition, then it would be lower. The upper bound is determined by how productive a worker is, i.e., how much value he can provide to the employer. The more skills a worker has, or the more capital equipment or technology available to make the worker more productive, the higher the upper bound. Low-skilled workers and workers in economies with little capital equipment or technology tend to face a low upper bound.

In the free market, both of these bounds would be higher than in a statist economy, and thus workers would tend to do better.

Regarding the lower bound, the free market would be characterized by an absence of artificial restrictions on new firms entering an industry and on small firms competing effectively, i.e., no state-awarded monopoly privileges, no licensing requirements, and no regulatory costs or taxes, thus leaving more financial capital available for businesses to use in productive operations. Hence there would tend to be more firms bidding for a worker's services.

With respect to the upper bound, there would be no artificial restrictions on human and financial capital formation, i.e., no hindrances to competition among education-providers, leading to higher-quality education; no artificial price inflation in education caused by state subsidies; no taxes on individuals' incomes, thereby providing workers with more money to invest in their personal development; and no taxes or regulations on financial capital, allowing firms to utilize more of it. Hence workers would tend to be better educated, and have more capital and technology at their disposal, making them more productive.

Second, the employment arrangement in the free market is voluntary, and thus the worker could always refuse to work under the proposed terms and seek employment elsewhere if he thinks he could do better. And it's wrong to characterize the situation as the worker being the only one in need: the employer obviously needs the worker to perform *some* labor, otherwise he wouldn't make an employment offer. It is just a question of price and conditions.

As noted above, the employer would offer no more than the value he thinks the worker could add relative to the total cost of employing him.[28] In the free market, other employers who are interested in the worker are free to make competing offers, and thus if the worker wants to figure out what he's worth, then he could solicit as many offers as possible. If there are no competing offers, or the worker doesn't like the best terms available to him, then this is not the fault of any employer. It's the fault of reality. Perhaps the worker doesn't have as valuable a skill set as he thinks he has.

The important point to note is that if an employer has a need for a worker, then it makes no sense to intentionally underpay him and risk losing him to another firm. However, "underpay" always means relative to the lower and upper bounds noted above, as subjectively assessed by that employer, and not according to some third-party-determined, utopian, centralized, "objective" value, such as that often imposed by the state or its proxies.

Third, the whole notion of "exploitation" is a misnomer, since it implies some wrong on the part of the employer. Yet there is no principle which supports this conclusion.

No worker can possess a positive "right" to a job, nor to any particular compensation. If an employer makes an offer to a worker, then the employer is making a voluntary decision to divert some of his income to purchase the worker's services and to provide particular working conditions. To claim that a worker has a "right" to a job, or to any particular compensation or working conditions, implies that the worker has a right to the employer's income that is *superior* to the employer's right! What principle could justify this?

---

[28] This is where state intervention has an adverse impact: if the state sets a minimum wage above the worker's productive value, or requires the employer to pay payroll taxes or to provide specific benefits to a worker, thus raising his total cost, then the employer may either determine not to make an offer, or to reduce his offer of cash wages to keep the total cost to where it makes sense to employ the worker. The important point is that the state would be an outside party imposing these costs on an employer, even if the worker and employer would be willing to engage in a differently structured arrangement.

To illustrate this in a different way, consider another type of commercial relationship, namely, the customer/vendor relationship. No statist ever accuses a customer of "exploiting" a vendor if the customer decides to withhold his dollars and not purchase a product from the vendor for any reason whatsoever, or requires a lower price before he would purchase that product. In fact, customers regularly bankrupt vendors whose products they no longer wish to purchase for whatever personal reasons they have. Statists are rightly of the view that the customer is free to do with his income as he pleases.

So how could it be that there is a different principle when the customer is an employer and the vendor is a worker selling his services? The explanation cannot be that the worker is a unique vendor case because he is not a product but, rather, a person offering a service; there are plenty of personal service vendors in business. What if a vendor is operating a business as a house painter or a gardener? For a customer to withhold a purchase of those services, or require a lower price, is to act exactly like the employer who decides not to employ a worker or to offer lower wages than a worker is demanding. Is one case "exploitation" and the other not?

What if the same person is *both* a customer and an employer? For instance, consider the following example: businessman X decides to purchase outsourced janitorial services from A and not B, because A's prices are lower, and when X advertises for a new receptionist, he prefers C to D, because C is willing to accept a lower wage. Would the statist argue that, to avoid the charge of "exploitation," X must spend his income on *both* of the higher priced vendors (B and D)? If not, why not? To ask these questions is to answer them.[29]

The folly of the "exploitation" thinking can also be illustrated by considering the proposed employment relationship from the reverse perspective. If a worker decides to work for an employer, then he is making a voluntary decision to use his body in the employer's production process. It would not be wrong for the worker to withhold his body, nor to demand more

[29] Or consider this situation: E quits his job and opens up his own lawn mowing business. Does it make sense to say that before E quit he could have looked to the state to force his employer to employ him and pay him a certain amount, yet after he quits he cannot look to the state to force his ex-employer to purchase his lawn mowing services at his specified price?

attractive compensation before he supplies his body. Would this mean that the worker is "exploiting" the employer? No! The employer has no right to the worker's efforts that is superior to the worker's right; that would be chattel slavery. If this is true, then why should the worker have any superior right to the employer's income? That would be theft.

Statists are conditioned to assume that the employer is always in the superior bargaining position compared with the worker, and that it is the task of those at the state to use coercion to balance this out. As noted above, even if that were true, the worker's bargaining position would be a function of reality (or of prior state intervention), not a fault of the employer against whom the coercion would be levied (i.e., why punish the employer for committing no wrong?). And using coercion is never moral.[30]

However, even this assumption is not generally true; in fact, anyone who claims it is has probably never run a business, since the biggest ongoing concern of most managers is attracting and retaining productive employees. Moreover, if employers always had the superior bargaining position, then presumably they would only pay employees the legislated minimum wage (why pay more than the state forces you to pay?). Yet the vast majority of employees in the U.S. who are paid on an hourly basis are paid more than the relevant minimum wage, suggesting the importance of non-state factors, e.g., competition for workers.[31]

Fourth, statists also overlook the fact that in the free market, where the customer is free to purchase the employer's product or not, it is the customer who ultimately controls the employer's revenues, and therefore the funds from which the employer could purchase future factors of production, including labor. If customers turn against the employer because they wish to use their dollars elsewhere, and the employer anticipates that this will continue in the future, then the financial pressure on the employer would cause him to recalibrate the mix of factors to purchase, and how

---

[30] In addition, consider highly sought-after executives, athletes, and movie stars. Who generally "calls the shots" in those instances? Why don't statists propose using coercion to deal with the exploitation of those who hire these workers?

[31] Note that Switzerland has *no* minimum wage, and yet we're not used to thinking about Swiss workers living at a subsistence level; in fact, according to some reports, they're among the highest paid workers in the world. Just based on the interaction of the supply of and the demand for labor. Imagine that.

much he could pay for them if he wished to remain in business and generate an acceptable return on capital.[32]

In this respect, for the most part (activists aside), customers are cold hearted. They care not one whiff about the plight of the employer or his workers, and would pull their dollars for the most feckless or even indiscernible reasons. Thus, if the statist wants to levy blame at any party in the free market for downward pressure on workers' compensation, then he ought not forget the customer.

Discrimination in the Free Market

Statists also worry about another form of exploitation in the free market, namely, class discrimination. It is claimed that if the state does not protect certain classes of individuals, then some employers would simply not employ them due to their race, gender, sexual orientation, etc.[33]

Once again this shows a profound misunderstanding of how the free market would work.

In the free market, discrimination has an economic cost to the discriminator. For instance, if an employer refused to employ Jews, then he would be artificially reducing his supply of labor; as basic economics teaches, if there is a reduced supply, then, all else being equal, the price would be higher. Thus this employer would end up paying more for his labor than if he did not discriminate. If he were willing to bear that cost, then that would be his choice—employing someone means using the employer's own income, which surely he must be free to spend as he sees fit—but his competitors who are willing to employ Jews would have a cost advantage in terms of a wider pool of labor.

Similarly, if an employer decided to underpay women relative to men for the same value labor, then his competitors would be able to offer more to

---

[32] The corollary to this is that if the state artificially raises the cost of labor (such as through the minimum wage or required benefits), and the employer anticipates that he would not be able to pass this additional cost onto the customer, then, all else being equal, the employer would have to scale back his purchase of labor.

[33] So far statists haven't defined ugly people, fat people, or short people as protected classes, even though some employers might well have strong and often times justifiable views about not employing these types of people. Perhaps when these groups get sufficiently organized to lobby the state, they too will attain state-protected status.

entice his women employees away, and he would be left with higher-priced male labor and thus lower margins than before.

The other aspect to bear in mind is social ostracization.

If an employer is known to refuse to employ (or serve) a certain group, such as blacks or Asians, then, as word gets around, those customers who object to his views would cease patronizing his business, which would have a real economic cost. Competitors may open up close by and make it very clear that they employ and serve everyone, thereby putting acute pressure on the employer in question.[34]

In other words, in the free market, class discrimination would likely not endure, as a discriminating employer would be at an economic disadvantage relative to those who don't discriminate, and thus he would likely not survive.[35]

This is why so much of the history of class discrimination has been brought about *by* the state itself: those who favor class discrimination cannot reliably depend on the free market to help their cause, and thus they have always resorted to lobbying for legislation to legally discriminate by coercive means.

For instance, in the antebellum north in the U.S., a number of states, such as Illinois, Indiana, and Maryland, passed legislation to prevent or restrict free blacks from moving to these states, owning property, and working in certain trades. Similarly, in the post-Reconstruction south, the "Jim Crow" legislative enactments were passed to mandate segregation of blacks and whites in many areas of society. In all of these cases, those who wanted to discriminate against blacks saw that too many whites were willing to trade with, employ, and generally fraternize with blacks, and thus the only way to enforce discrimination was to use the state's coercive powers. This was also the reason for the enactment in South Africa of its apartheid legislation in the mid-20th century.

---

[34] Statists also miss the fact that, in this way, the free market *exposes* the discriminator for all to see. However, if state legislation requires the discriminator to employ or serve those whom he despises, then his racism, sexism, etc. would remain hidden. Wouldn't the statist prefer to know who the discriminators are?

[35] That is, unless the discriminator could serve the likely small pool of like-minded customers who would be willing to pay more to buy from the discriminator. If so, that would be their collective choice. Who is the state to say that they cannot do this? Their money is theirs to spend as they see fit.

The same theme applied in Nazi Germany in the 1930s: those who wanted to discriminate against Jews couldn't depend upon the free market, and thus they had to pass numerous pieces of anti-Jew legislation.

As a final example, labor unions in the U.S. aggressively lobbied the federal government in the early 20th century to pass minimum-wage legislation. The unions would not accept black workers as members, but black workers were willing to work for lower wages than the white union-workers, and employers were willing to employ black workers at these lower wages. Thus the free market was a threat to white union-workers' jobs. However, by setting the minimum wage above the black workers' productive value, state intervention effectively priced black labor out of the market.

State Discrimination

Through today's affirmative-action legislation, individuals at the state routinely intervene on behalf of protected classes of workers, either requiring employers to hire workers in these classes, or fining employers if they don't treat such workers the way the individuals at the state deem appropriate.[36]

However, what exactly is denied to a worker when they are discriminated against? As noted earlier, from the employer's perspective, offering a job requires the diversion of some of the employer's income to the employee. How could a worker have a "right" to that portion of the employer's income? Also as noted earlier, if the worker could deny his bodily efforts to the employer for any reason whatsoever, then why could the employer not similarly deny the diversion of some of his income to the worker for any reason whatsoever? In other words, if it is deemed actionable if an Asian employer refuses to employ a Hispanic worker because he is Hispanic, then why is it not also actionable if the Hispanic worker refuses

[36]It's worth noting that, through this legislation, there is a substantial compliance and recordkeeping cost imposed on employers, which simply means fewer employer resources available to hire workers. In addition, to the extent that they have a choice, employers are likely more reluctant to even interview, never mind hire, workers in protected classes, for fear of the additional liability they bring if the employer doesn't comply with the whims of those at the state once the employer has made first contact with the worker. This can hardly be to the benefit of those who are allegedly protected by affirmative-action legislation.

to offer his labor services to the Asian employer because the employer is Asian?[37]

And, to extend a broader analogy raised earlier in the customer/vendor situation, why is it not also actionable if an Asian customer refuses to buy from a Hispanic vendor because he is Hispanic?

What state action in this area represents, in essence, is the individuals at the state arrogating to themselves the right to tell an employer how to spend his income and how to treat others; in other words, the individuals at the state (on behalf of the protected classes) claim a priority property right in the employer's personal resources and body. From where do these individuals at the state get this right?

Moreover, the state divides the world into two groups—the protected classes and everyone else—and uses its coercive powers in a discriminatory manner in favor of the protected classes and therefore *against* everyone else. Predictably, this leads to aggressive lobbying by groups not in a protected class, either to be defined into the existing protected classes or to expand the range of protected classes to cover their own situations. In other words, there is now lobbying to rent the state's coercive powers to discriminate.[38]

This is the solution to the perceived free-market "problem" of discrimination?

[37] To be clear, I am not suggesting that these forms of behavior should be socially acceptable, only that they do not represent the taking or denial of anything to which the aggrieved party is properly entitled, and thus do not justify the use of force or the threat of force by the state as a remedy.

[38] For instance, in the U.S., the original "anti-discrimination" legislation covered race, religion, nationality, and gender. Later legislation added age, pregnancy, familial status, disability, veteran status, and genetic information.

IV. Myths Justifying the Need for the State

If the above commentary about the state and the free market is true, then why does the state exist? This is a complex question, the answer to which has several aspects to it.

As has been discussed earlier, no individual—not even the most ardent statist—signs a contract explicitly consenting to the state's existence or actions. Instead, the state exists through the implicit acquiescence of the non-libertarian population. I will discuss below how different forms of this acquiescence arise, and then go on to review some of the key fallacies underlying this acquiescence.[1]

Acquiescence to the State

Host/Parasite Analogy

The individuals at the state live off the productive capacity of the rest of the population. It is the rest of the population that produces the real wealth in society, namely, goods and services which satisfy human wants. When these products are created and traded, they generate the base on which state personnel can forcibly levy taxes to fund their personal incomes and professional activities. This is why, to libertarians, the state is analogous to a parasite living within the body of civil society as the host.

Biologically speaking, a parasite cannot exist without a host, for the host is the source of the parasite's sustenance. Accordingly, unless a parasite is highly mobile, it does not want to completely destroy its host, as then the

[1] There is a very good book by Michael Huemer, *The Problem With Political Authority*, which goes into a lot of interesting psychological detail about why such acquiescence persists when it is illogical to support the immoral institution that is the state.

parasite would perish too. Moreover, the host is always more powerful than the parasite, pound for pound, so in some sense the parasite depends for its existence not only on the host's survival (even flourishing), but also the host's passive acquiescence.

Thus state personnel have to be careful not to milk society so extensively during their time in office that they drain it of some base level of productive capacity. In those states that have historically gone too far, civil society exists in dire poverty, e.g., Cuba, North Korea, the Soviet Union, Venezuela, and Zimbabwe, and this can only end in total system collapse (as happened eventually in the Soviet Union).

More importantly, however, the individuals at the state are numerically always a small fraction of the overall population. If the population as the host were to rise up in a coordinated fashion to rid itself of the state parasite, then state personnel would be powerless to stop this. This has occurred historically through successful revolutions, the most famous of which are the French and American Revolutions of the late 18th century.

Accordingly, to try to prevent such revolutionary action, the modern state uses three different means to ensure the population's acquiescence.

Fear

Individuals at the state can act with great physical brutality against anyone engaging in revolutionary action, or those merely suspected of thinking revolutionary thoughts. This is designed to instill fear in the minds of citizens, to suppress acting on any revolutionary inclinations they might harbor. This is a key feature of most totalitarian states, and its effect can be described as "fear-based acquiescence."

However, in modern democracies, where there is no ongoing, widespread physical brutality, the mere awesome power of the state in concept, along with periodic displays of its power by its military, police, and other executive bodies, could be sufficient to induce a "Stockholm syndrome" among the population. This syndrome is a psychological phenomenon in which hostages express empathy with, and have positive feelings toward, their captors, sometimes to the point of defending and identifying with them. These feelings are generally considered irrational in light of the danger or risk endured by the victims, who essentially mistake any lack of abuse from their captors for kindness.

So, for instance, even though state personnel could at any time decide to forcibly confiscate up to 100 percent of an individual's income, the fact that they "only" choose to confiscate, say, 35 percent, is regarded as a beneficent act that should not be questioned by the population, and should even be applauded for its restraint. Or, if, for many years, the state prohibits a pharmaceutical company from selling to those afflicted with a painful condition a drug which alleviates their pain & suffering—in what would be a purely voluntary exchange between the parties—then once the state removes the prohibition by approving commercial sale of the drug, the approval is cheered by the population as a beneficent act, notwithstanding all the agony suffered in the meantime by those afflicted with the condition.

Participation

State personnel can also divide and conquer. By renting out its coercive powers to special-interest groups, the state can, in effect, invite a percentage of civil society to live as parasites too. This involves the state using subsidies, monopoly licenses, protective tariffs, welfare or other transfer payments, etc. to benefit many different sub-groups in society, who thereby live off those who are not so well organized to demand these benefits or oppose these programs.[2]

This practice ensures that there are many individuals who become dependent on the state for their own well-being, such that they are unlikely to rise up and reject it. "Don't bite the hand that feeds you" is the adage that comes to mind. This is a feature of every state in existence today, and its effect can be described as "participation-based acquiescence."

Education

In addition, the political class can seize control of the minds of the population and pump them full of fallacies about why we need the state. In this way, such subversive ideas as rejecting the parasite never even arise, or don't develop very far. The state does this primarily by controlling education.[3]

---

[2]As explained earlier, this is known as "crony capitalism" or "political entrepreneurship."

[3]Other means include the ridiculously childish pomp and ceremony that citizens are subjected to from a very young age when it comes to state institutions and personnel:

The state sets or influences educational curricula through many means: licensing of teaching professionals, accreditation of educational institutions, funding the development of learning materials, funding the budgets of educational institutions, and subsidizing key intellectuals to produce "thought leadership" that just happens to favor the state.[4]

Further, the state either compels the population to sit and listen to its educational content (as is the case with compulsory K-12 school attendance), or bribes the population to sit and listen (as is the case with heavily subsidized "college-for-everyone" programs).

As a result, the state can rightfully expect very little host resistance. When one looks at the history of state-provided and state-financed education around the world, it is quite clear that the original purpose was to mold each child into a state worshipper, euphemistically called a "good citizen." This is not supposition; when state education was first conceived, its creators were not shy about making this point explicitly.[5]

This indoctrination is a feature of every state in existence today, and its effect can be described as "fallacy-based acquiescence."[6]

The impact of this indoctrination is that the statist could be likened to the proverbial "frog in boiling water." While to the libertarian, each new action of the state is a moral outrage, because the libertarian's benchmark is fixed, namely, the absence of coercion, to the statist, each new action of the state is acceptable or, at worst, tolerable, because the benchmark is dynamic, namely, the status quo immediately before the new action. The statist has been taught to accept the status quo, and thus each incremental

---

honoring the national flag; emotionally singing the national anthem; treating politicians and the military with a reverence they have done nothing to deserve; in the U.S., reciting the Pledge of Allegiance at school, etc.

[4]To reward its intellectual supporters, the state provides intellectuals with research grants, retains intellectuals as consultants, funds educational institutions that employ intellectuals, and offers intellectuals prestigious positions at the state itself.

[5]Note too that in the early 19th century, before state education was imposed in England, the state actually tried to discourage independent thought by taxing paper, newspapers, and pamphlets, to make it too expensive for ordinary citizens to access unapproved information. These were essentially "taxes on knowledge."

[6]By "indoctrination," I mean "The process of teaching a person or group to accept a set of beliefs uncritically." Statist education in history, economics, and politics assumes, without any critical evaluation, the necessity, and sometimes even the moral virtue, of the state.

state action seems quite bearable, whereas the libertarian does not accept the status quo, and thus views the totality of all state actions together as a gargantuan abomination.

This is not to imply that "good citizens" are stupid. To claim that someone believes in a fallacy is not a statement about that person's intelligence, which is biological, but rather about that person's knowledge, which has to be actively sought. One could have a high IQ but not know anything, or anything correct, about a particular subject, and thus have erroneous views with respect to that subject. Thus, while to a libertarian it seems unreasonable for a person to support the state given the depth and breadth of the moral, economic, and historical cases against the state, one must take account of the fact that few statists have devoted any time to learning about libertarianism, and most have spent much of their lives drinking from the fountain of statism.[7]

It should be noted that a key component of generating this fallacy-based acquiescence is creating and furthering the illusion that voting makes one an active participant in, and influencer of, the state. The more that people believe that the broader the suffrage, the more "We're all in it together," the more the state can get away with, because it can always retort that its decisions reflect the "general will" of the population, or that "The people have spoken." In this sense, it is no coincidence that the growth of the state has been greatest in modern times in parallel with the growth of democracy and broader voting rights among populations.

* * * * *

Fear-based acquiescence and participation-based acquiescence are mostly immune to rational debate; one could understand the issues with the state, but still support it for one of those two reasons. However, fallacy-based acquiescence can and ought to be addressed by remedial action. The issue for libertarians, though, is that the underlying fallacies as to why we need the state are rarely challenged, much less addressed, in regular discourse among the population. Accordingly, below I will address some of the larger fallacies about the need for the state.

---

[7]In my case, I had 19 years of formal schooling in statism, and many years of imbibing statism by osmosis. A mere three years of intensive self-education in libertarianism, Austrian economics, and revisionist history completely changed my views.

Before I do so, however, I am willing to concede that there might be statists who are quite cognizant of all of the failings of the state, and who might even doubt the need for a state in its present form, but who nevertheless support today's state simply because they believe that there is no better alternative. I see this as resulting from a lack of imagination, a lack of intellectual curiosity to search for a better solution, and/or an inadequate education.

Myth #9: The State Is an Improvement on the Free Market

Inappropriate Benchmarking

The public has become conditioned to believe that if a market is not "perfectly competitive" (defined below), then it is broken, and this calls for state intervention.

The state, aided by its intellectuals, has convinced the population that "perfect competition" should be the benchmark against which all private-sector entrepreneurial activity is to be graded. However, as defined, "perfect competition" is never attainable, anywhere. It requires all firms in an industry to have the same products, cost structures, information, market shares, etc., so all they do is produce as automatons and sell to uniformly demanding consumers. Just to state this is to explain why this is an unrealistic view of human action. The "perfect competition" model takes no account of the realities of, and continuous changes in, individual consumers' subjective preferences, or of continuous changes in resource availability and pricing, technology, and entrepreneurial insights and errors.

More generally, however, this approach is misguided because it uses a comparison between reality and perfection as the criterion by which to decide whether the state should intervene; this is a common mistake made by statists. There could only be one answer if that is the question asked. The more reasonable question to ask is, which is better, reality *without* state intervention or reality *with* state intervention?[8]

[8] I addressed this earlier under the section dealing with the realities of the free market.

Failure to "Keep Score"

Moreover, if the comparison between reality and perfection is the criterion statists use to decide whether the state should intervene, then this suggests that statists see the state as the agent of perfection. Yet statists never go back and ask whether state intervention has ever led to the nirvana for which they were hoping, i.e., the standard to which they hold the private sector.

As discussed earlier, statists hold the state to a much lower standard than they hold the private sector. Not only is the private sector blamed when it doesn't achieve outcomes statists (unrealistically) believe should be attained, the private sector is also blamed when it reacts to state intervention. In other words, the private sector can only do wrong. On the other hand, statists never hold the state to *any* meaningful benchmark—certainly not the perfection benchmark to which they hold the private sector—so in their eyes state intervention can always be justified.[9]

If, at any point in time, the state hasn't achieved its objectives with a particular program, then the usual answer given is that the state is not large enough, i.e., the solution is that we need *more* regulation and/or taxes. Yet no state program—every one of which starts out with absurdly lofty objectives such as "We're going to eradicate poverty," or "We're going to ensure that everyone has healthcare"—has ever been declared successful such that it could be shut down. With that track record, you would think that statists would at least conclude that the state is awful at estimating problems or awful at solving them, or both.

And, as noted earlier, if the state is the statist's solution to "market failure," then why isn't the market the statist's solution to state failure?

The most the statist will ever admit is that, in some areas, the state needs to be reformed. However, statists never ponder that perhaps the state is inherently incapable of being reformed, given that its personnel are able to exercise unrestrained coercive powers, and have incentives and knowledge

[9]Part of the reason statists believe the state is an agent for good and the private sector an agent for bad is that statists are suspicious of the profit motive, which the state does not pursue but the private sector does. This suspicion simply reflects a woeful understanding of (a) how profits are generated in the free market; (b) how the profit motive ensures resources get most efficiently allocated within society; and (c) the different and suspect incentives of those in the state sector.

misaligned with maximizing the satisfaction of human wants. When the statist says "We need to reform government," what the statist is saying is that we should plead with those exercising power "Please sir, make yourself better. Only exercise your power omnisciently and magnanimously." The state metaphorically must chuckle at this plea.

Yet, in the private sector, no such pleading is necessary. If consumers don't like what a firm is producing, then they put it or its relevant product out of business by abandoning it; witness, for instance, the respective fates of Blockbuster Video, the Ford Edsel, New Coke, and Wang Computing.

However, there is no way to effectively abandon the products supplied by the state, no matter how bad they are.

Incorrect Analysis of Causation

The public has also been trained by the state to look at imperfection in the world and blame the "free market" (which, as previously explained, doesn't even exist, so the fault is misdirected), and then to believe that only the state could make things better. There are two fundamental points to make about this conclusion.

First, as previously discussed, the world is imperfect because of human imperfection and scarcity of resources. Neither issue is the fault of the free market, and nor could the state solve either issue. It is difficult to comprehend why the statist would believe that the imperfect human beings running the state could be a better solution to the imperfect human beings involved in the private sector.[10] And it is equally hard to comprehend how entrepreneurs organizing scarce resources to meet customer preferences, with the risk of going out of business if they get it wrong and the upside of personal profit if they get it right, could be bested by central planners at the state, who neither have the necessary knowledge of customer preferences nor the incentives of entrepreneurs.

Second, and not surprisingly, statists have been taught a version of history which credits the state with most of the positive developments in the human condition, and blames the private sector for all of the negative aspects. Statists then take this mistaken view of history and apply it to all current problems, so the only possible result can be a call for state inter-

[10]Unless one subscribes to one of the Tooth Fairy Theories.

vention. However, this shows a poor appreciation of economic principles and history.

Sweatshops.[11] To give a classic example, statists will bemoan the operation of sweatshops in poor countries, and regard this as a problem of the free market.[12] They reflect on their comfortable personal situation, and demand that we somehow stop sweatshop labor elsewhere in the world because "I wouldn't want to live that way." This ignores a number of key facts.

First, sweatshop labor is a feature only of poor countries and, these days, countries tend to be poor mostly because of heavy state intervention. Most poor countries suffer from central planning of the economy, regulations that make it unattractive for foreign financial capital to be invested locally (e.g., high taxes, exchange controls, complex bureaucracies that firms are required to navigate, etc.), and dismal healthcare, education, and banking sectors due to significant state control.

Second, sweatshop labor is not usually forced labor (if it were, then the statist's concern would be valid). The companies employing these workers are not using armed personnel to round up the workers each morning and march them to the factory floor; these workers are voluntarily choosing to work in the factories. This means that, as bad as the working conditions might be, they must be better than the alternatives these workers face, otherwise, why would the workers turn up each morning? The reality is that these workers and their families live in abject poverty and face a miserable existence. The traditional alternative for these workers is to engage in back-breaking and dangerous agricultural labor on the family farm to eke out a subsistence lifestyle, or, failing that, to turn to prostitution, begging, or violent crime to generate income.

Thus, when statists insist that sweatshop labor be made illegal, or that the employers be boycotted out of business, they are likely pushing these workers into these less than savory alternatives; in this light, factory work is a relative "luxury" for these families. From statists' unique vantage points thousands of miles away, and based on their own existence and values, they

[11]The key material to read in this area is Benjamin Powell's book, *Out of Poverty*.

[12]Similarly, statists regard the sweatshop labor that was an early feature of the Industrial Revolution as an example of the dangers of the free market.

are seeking to impose their views on what is the "better" choice for these workers, without appreciating the actual alternatives that reality (or state intervention) has served up to these families.

Third, as noted earlier, basic economics teaches that the upper bound on what employers would pay workers is based on their productivity level (why would an employer pay a worker $2.00 per hour when the worker can only add $1.00 per hour of value?), and the lower bound is based on competition, as employers must compete for workers and so cannot underpay them relative to their alternatives. The usual reason sweatshop workers are paid so little is that their upper bound is quite low, because they are lowly productive. The reason for this is twofold: they aren't well trained, and there is insufficient capital equipment available locally to make them more productive.

In the free market, as foreign entrepreneurs begin to invest in the local economy, given its cheap labor, they make more capital available (through machines, processes, training, etc.) to make these workers more productive, and thus able to command higher compensation. Provided there is free competition for these workers, employers would compete to hire and retain the more productive workers through some combination of higher wages and better working conditions. This is the only sustainable way for wages and working conditions to gradually improve, even though statists believe that these things could improve simply by the state commanding that this be so.

To that end, statists will often retort that the state could accelerate this process by forcing employers to pay higher wages, and offer better working conditions, more quickly than the rate at which things would naturally evolve.[13] This is labeled a "moral imperative" to improve these workers' lives. However, there are a few problems with this line of thinking.

First, statists ignore the fact that sweatshop wages are often significantly above poverty-level income in these regions, and even compare well with average incomes, making sweatshop employment a step *up* the local career

[13]This is often pursued by statists in a First World country lobbying their government to impose trade restrictions on exports from these Third World countries, unless these countries bring their labor standards up to those demanded by these activists. It is also pursued via private citizen boycotts which, while misguided (for the reasons to be discussed), at least don't involve state-imposed, coercive restrictions on free trade.

ladder. Rather than bemoaning these opportunities for these workers, we should be supporting such jobs if we care about these workers having a real chance to pull themselves up out of poverty.

In fact, history shows that sweatshops are an important positive development for the poorest in emerging economies, as they evolve from subsistence agriculture to the living standards that we enjoy in the First World today. This was true in England during the Industrial Revolution, then subsequently in the U.S., and then more recently in the "East Asian Tigers" of Hong Kong, Singapore, South Korea, and Taiwan.[14] The same could be expected in the sweatshop economies of other parts of Asia, and in Central America, if they are allowed to run their natural course too.

Second, those at the state cannot possibly appreciate the economics of each employer, nor each employer's market. Statists incorrectly assume that, just because a business has an existing profit margin, the entrepreneur would voluntarily absorb higher costs imposed on him by the state. Yet all economic decisions are made at the margin.

The entrepreneur has choices as to what to do with the firm's financial capital, which production processes to use, where to locate, what mix of labor and capital equipment to use, etc., and he would have a view on what is an adequate return for the risk he is taking. If labor costs (cash wages, benefits, and working conditions) are forcibly increased at the margin, then the entrepreneur would adjust to counteract that increase to try to preserve his profits. For instance, if cash wages are forced up by legislation, then the entrepreneur may reduce working conditions or benefits, such as free meals, air conditioning running time, or vacation days; more generally, he may substitute machines for labor, or he may relocate to a cheaper region (in either case, the effect is to reduce the cash income of the workers who desperately need it). An entrepreneur who was contemplating opening up in the region may reconsider his decision in light of the higher costs, thereby adversely impacting those poor workers in this region whom the entrepreneur might have hired.[15]

---

[14] Even more promising is the fact that each of these evolutions was faster than the prior one, due to the increasingly rapid pace of global trade and financial capital flows.

[15] That said, it's worth pointing out that often times if there is one large employer in a region, then that employer may actually *support* the state imposing these higher costs on all employers, since this increases the entry costs for, and thus reduces the number

As noted earlier, the only sustainable ways to improve a worker's plight are to improve the two factors that bound the compensation a firm would pay him: at the lower bound, facilitate increased competition for workers, by reducing the costs for new firms to enter the market and for existing firms to remain in the market (mainly by reducing or eliminating taxes and regulations); at the upper bound, facilitate increased worker productivity, by reducing restrictions on financial and human capital investment (mainly by reducing restrictions on education and funds flows, reducing taxes on income, etc.).

Third, employers look at the *total* cost of employing a worker relative to his productivity, but are agnostic as to how that cost is distributed between (a) cash wages, (b) benefits (vacation, healthcare, etc.), and (c) working conditions (safety, air conditioning, etc.).

Accordingly, in the free market, the mix of cash compensation, benefits, and working conditions that an employer offers to his workers tends to reflect workers' choices, because employers would have to offer the best mix of these factors to keep the best workers satisfied. Often times the poorest workers are first interested in cash, which they can use to buy food, clothing, and shelter for their families, and they are willing to forego benefits and better working conditions to maximize cash. As their productivity increases, and thus so too their ability to command higher compensation, beyond some level of subsistence cash they may start to demand better working conditions instead of more cash. At still higher levels of compensation they may demand more vacation time, or health benefits, instead of more cash or better working conditions.

The key point is that the individuals at the state are in no position to second guess the mix of compensation components that workers desire.

---

of, potential new competitors (another instance of crony capitalism). The incumbent may figure that this dampening of competition is worth the additional labor costs (or he may *already* be offering these higher wages or better benefits or working conditions to his employees, so the new regulations wouldn't really impact him). The incumbent may actually help write the regulations, to ensure that they are tough enough to keep competitors out, but not so tough that the incumbent would have to change what he does. This is also why large employers support minimum-wage legislation; often they are already paying their employees more, so the legislation only impacts would-be competition.

Those statists who try to force improvements in wages, benefits, and/or working conditions on employers in these regions are simply imposing their compensation-component preference rankings, instead of allowing employers to respond to their workers' actual preferences.[16]

Fourth, what's odd about the statist's criticism of the sweatshop factory owner is that the statist is not also taking aim that those who do *not* choose to open factories in this region. Those who choose not to open a factory are doing *nothing* for the poorest in that region; they are not offering them higher wages than they could earn elsewhere, better working conditions than they presently endure, or the opportunity to develop their skills through gainful employment. In contrast, the sweatshop factory owner is the *only* one who is offering to use his financial capital to improve these individuals' lives. If there is a "moral imperative" to improve the plight of these workers, then why don't statists target people who are doing nothing to contribute to this imperative, instead of picking on the one party who *is* doing something positive?

Instead of burdening this entrepreneur with state intervention, we should be applauding and encouraging his actions which, though born out of self-interest, are also providing the poorest with an opportunity to reach the first rung on the ladder towards improved living standards.[17]

---

[16] If the statist is so sure of his arguments that it's economically possible to improve workers' conditions beyond what is being offered by firms actually operating in a market, then why doesn't the statist either start his own business in that market, or offer to buy out the factory in question, and then offer those working conditions (or send his cash to those workers directly)? The response that it is too difficult and complex for the statist to do that, and that the statist isn't really familiar with running a business or with the particular industry or region in question, *is* the key economic argument against the statist's demand that others do what he wishes! It's easy to be an armchair entrepreneur and command others to do what you want with their financial capital. As described, there *is* a private-sector solution to the problem perceived by the statist, but to the statist it's just much more convenient to coercively force the factory owner to do what the statist wants.

[17] If statists really cared about the plight of the poorest in these regions, then they should argue for states to *force* entrepreneurs to open factories. This might sound ridiculous, but it is less ridiculous than the statist's attack on those who *do* open factories. Alternatively, and as noted earlier, if statists want to improve the living standards of the poorest, then why don't they campaign instead for economy-wide low price ceilings on all goods, so the low income of the poorest could buy more? That would be a

Unseen Costs

Statists often observe reality at time t_0 when there was no state intervention, and then at time t_1 after the state has intervened, and conclude that, if the latter reality is better than the former, then the state's intervention was beneficial. However, this conclusion ignores economics, morality, and history.

Economics. Each time the state intervenes there is a cost, but this cost is never compared with the alleged benefits from the intervention. The state forcibly diverts scarce resources from where they would have flowed naturally in order to satisfy customer preferences, to where the individuals at the state define as the priority. While we see the impact of this diversion of resources in the form of the end result, we never see the impact of this diversion in the sense of how the resources might have otherwise been deployed. Thus it is impossible to know if the benefits of that diversion exceeded the costs.

For instance, if the state imposes significant compliance costs on drug developers, requiring them to jump through the process hoops the state has designed before the drug developers can market their products, then we can never know if the scarce resources that were diverted into such compliance activities could have been used to develop other valuable drugs, perhaps saving lives and alleviating suffering.[18]

If we judge state intervention just by the visibly positive outcomes, without considering its hidden but very real costs, then we are making uneconomic decisions, in the sense that we are assuming that there are no trade-offs, which is contrary to the reality of a world where resources are scarce. By this (unrealistic) rationale, state intervention could never be the wrong decision.

---

way ostensibly to improve the lot of the poor without targeting the one party—the sweatshop factory owner—who is actually helping these people.

[18]The uglier truth is that, before these state regulations were written, the incumbent drug companies would have aggressively lobbied the state to ensure the regulations were written to favor them over potential new competitors. So we also could never know if the resources diverted to this lobbying could have been used by the incumbent drug companies to develop other valuable drugs, nor whether those entrepreneurs who cannot enter the market because of the regulations might have developed other valuable drugs.

How do we know that the free market can do better? In the free market, entrepreneurs from different industries and at different firms bid against each other for scarce resources. This tends to drive their prices up, but there is a limit, as an entrepreneur is not going to purchase a resource at a price which he doesn't think would allow him to make a profit on selling his final product to customers. Customers are willing to pay more for products that satisfy their more important needs than those that satisfy their less important needs. Thus, as customers express their relative preferences through the prices that they are willing to pay for different products, this guides entrepreneurs as to how much to bid for scarce resources. By definition, those entrepreneurs satisfying customers' most important needs would be able to bid more for scarce resources than those who are not. In this way, we know that resources would tend to move to where they can bring the most value, which is another way of saying that we know that the cost/benefit trade-off is being appropriately considered.

To illustrate this point, assume that input X is used both by entrepreneurs supplying product A and by those supplying product B. If customers value product A more highly than product B, and thus are willing to pay more for product A than for product B, then in bidding for input X, entrepreneurs who manufacture product A would be able to outbid those who manufacture product B, and more of input X would flow to these entrepreneurs. Through this process, resources would flow to their most important uses as "voted" by customers with their own dollars. Contrast this with state intervention, which would forcibly direct input X to the use deemed most important by individuals at the state, even though they are not the customers. Which process is more apt to appropriately weigh trade-offs and maximize satisfaction of customers' wants?

Often statists will point to a product developed with the state's backing and note the absence of a private-sector alternative, and then claim that this product would not have been developed by the private sector, so that there must have been a significant benefit from the state's intervention. However, this is quite disingenuous on several counts.

First, it's possible that there is no actual, substantial, voluntary customer demand for the product, so the claim might indeed be partially correct, namely, that the private sector would not have developed this product (which would have been a good thing in terms of resource usage!). Some examples might be nuclear weapons, "bridges to nowhere," and monuments deifying former presidents, generals, or others in the state sector.

Second, we can never know if the claim is true but, given the incentives in the private sector, the chances are high that, if there were real demand, then the private sector would have developed a relevant product to address that demand.

Third, when an entrepreneur in the private sector tries to develop a product that competes with an effort backed by the state, the private-sector product is normally crowded out by the state. Since the state can forcibly divert resources to its project, whereas the entrepreneur has to bid for resources, and can only obtain them if others voluntarily yield them, the state has a huge advantage in terms of the resources it could throw at a project. Further, since the state is not concerned with profitability—it cannot go out of business, as it uses taxes to fund its expenses—the state can price its products well below private-sector prices. In addition, the state can of course use its regulatory muscle to further handicap or outright prohibit the private-sector alternative.[19]

Morality. While some individuals in the economy might appreciate that the state produced the outcome that occurred, by definition, the state would have forced other individuals in the economy to pay for an outcome that they might not have wanted (either at all, or in priority to other outcomes for which they might have preferred to use their income that was taxed away).

[19] A good example of crowding out is the development of the Internet. While the packet-switching technology that underlies the Internet was developed by two individuals in the private sector, the concept of a global network was developed concurrently by a U.S. government-backed effort and several alternative private-sector efforts. For various reasons, these private-sector efforts—whose networks were more advanced than that being developed for the U.S. government—fell away in the face of the U.S. government's funding and other actions (and those of some European governments which sought to protect their state-run telephone companies). Thus we ended up with the Internet we have, not because it was the best solution (technologically, it wasn't), but because the private-sector efforts were crowded out, leaving the U.S. government's project as the "last man standing." Money has suffered a similar fate: originally, sound money was developed by the free market, but then the state needed to control the money supply for its own ends, and thus legislated away private money.

As raised earlier, statists have no good response to the moral question, namely, if all men are metaphysically equal, so that no man has the right to rule another without his consent, then by what right can those at the state seize an individual's income to use in ways that this individual does not want?

History. Almost every example that statists rely on to "prove" the benefits of state intervention is, in fact, belied by the trends that preceded the intervention.

For instance, statists will cite examples of where, following the state's imposition of health & safety regulations, workplace accidents declined; what they will fail to observe is that workplace accidents were already declining for a long time before the introduction of the regulations, and usually at a rate faster than after the regulations were implemented. In fact, the history of sweatshops globally shows that legislation dealing with minimum wages, benefits, workplace conditions, etc. mostly *followed* voluntary industry developments caused by the economic dynamics previously discussed, rather than preceding these developments and causing them to occur. Tellingly, where this type of legislation sought to get out in front of economics—meaning it attempted to prematurely force adoption of uneconomic workplace improvements—the various parties (factory owners and employees) simply ignored the legislation, and operated in non-compliance.

Similarly, statists will cite the implementation of a state-provided option for health insurance as a positive factor in increasing the percentage of the population that has health insurance, ignoring the fact that this percentage had been growing more rapidly before the new state scheme was introduced.

More generally, economic history shows that where there has been real demand for something—be it safer working conditions, or health insurance—entrepreneurs have always worked to develop a product to meet that demand in the most efficient manner possible. On the other hand, all that state intervention has ever done is increase the cost of supplying products, leading to lower supply, and impose centralized resource direction on the economy, leading to misdirection relative to satisfying actual preferences.

Myth #10: We Need the State to Provide "Public Goods"[20]

The Theory

Another fallacious belief purportedly justifying the state is the notion of so-called "public goods." The supposed argument is that there are some goods that no private firm would supply at all, or that wouldn't be supplied in sufficient quantities by the private sector, but which are beneficial to society, and so the state must forcibly direct resources towards the production of these goods and even provide these goods itself.

As the theory goes, private firms wouldn't produce these goods for one of two reasons.

First, because of the so-called "free-rider" problem, namely, private firms wouldn't be able to prevent people from benefiting from these goods without paying for them. Commonly cited examples of these goods include lighthouses, national defense, and police.

Second, because these goods are just too difficult for the private sector to handle: they require complex arrangements or huge amounts of financial capital, and profits would be too hard to generate or would be too distant in the future. Examples of these goods include roads, schools, money, courts, railroads, power, and scientific research and development.

Actually, for many of these goods, the statist argument goes further: not only must the state produce these goods, but it must do so as a monopoly, i.e., it must prohibit others from trying to produce competitive goods.

It's hard to know where to start in refuting the many fallacies bound up in these assumptions.

History to the Contrary

Probably the easiest place to start is to review history. Every single good that statists now claim is a "public good," and thus must be produced by the state or else it would not be produced at all, has at one time or another been produced privately, until the state forcibly intervened. In addition, in

[20] I will use the phrase "public good" in quotation marks to indicate that, when one considers it logically and using credible economics, this is not a separate category of economic good.

different parts of the world many of these goods are still produced privately. In other words, the private sector has not found providing these goods to be too complex, too capital intensive, or too distantly profitable.

For instance, lighthouses were originally provided by the private sector before the state took them over. Similarly, originally roads were privately built, and there are still many private roads in gated communities, strip malls, office parks, and private cities. Schooling was originally private until the state intervened, and private schools still exist and are growing globally (even in the poorest slums in the Third World). Originally policing was private, and there are now more private security guards than state police in the U.S.; in addition, when private citizens are free to carry personal firearms, they are more effective at preventing crimes against themselves (or others) than the police are.[21] Law and courts originally developed from the ground up before states took them over, and private mediation and arbitration are growing as forms of dispute resolution. The first successful railroad in the U.S. was privately built, and there are privately run railroads globally. Money was historically developed privately before being taken over by the state for its own ends. Walt Disney World is an entirely privately constructed and privately run "village" with its own security, roads, immigration rules, etc.

Why Insist on a Monopoly?

Even statists accept that monopolies are bad because they lead to higher prices and less innovation compared with when there is competition. If so, why would the statist argue that the state must monopolize the production of a "public good"; what would be the harm in allowing genuine competition? If the statist is correct, namely, that the private sector would not produce such a good, then the statist should not be concerned if the state doesn't outlaw competition.

Note, however, that what I am advocating is *real* competition, where consumers could opt out of paying for the state's "public good," and instead purchase only the competitive, private good. There is no real compe-

[21] As noted earlier, when a violent crime occurs, we can only guarantee that there are two people present: the aggressor and the victim. The police are hardly ever there. Thus armed potential victims are much more successful at preventing such crimes than the police could ever be.

tition if the state forcibly extracts payment for its "public good" from all consumers, in the form of taxes, but then allows competitive, private suppliers to also produce the same type of good. This puts these suppliers at a tremendous disadvantage, since it raises the effective price to consumers of the private good because the consumers have to pay for the state's "public good" via taxes, and then also for the supplier's good.[22]

In addition, as noted earlier, the state is not concerned with profitability, because it can force taxpayers to fund its operations. Thus the explicit prices of state-provided "public goods" are typically set well below the prices of competitive, private goods. This makes the state an even more formidable competitor to private-sector suppliers, tending to depress the demand for competitive, private goods.[23]

All of this generally means that private-sector goods that compete with "public goods" are well out of the reach of the less well-off. Only the wealthier citizens can afford to purchase the relatively scarce, competitive, private goods (which tend to be of much higher quality), while the less well-off are left to consume the state-provided (lower-quality) goods.

The "Free-Rider" Concept

The most fundamental point relating to "public goods," however, is that statists cannot convincingly answer the question "Which goods are 'public goods' and which are not?" Often times the statist's simplistic response is to cite those goods currently produced by the state. However, that is circular reasoning. The question is asking for the principles from which one could deduce which goods should be produced by the state and which should not; just because the state is currently producing a good doesn't provide any principled argument for the necessity or morality of its production by the state.

As noted above, the statist's most common justification for "public

[22]The classic example of this is education. While the state allows private schools to exist, the consumer who wants to send his child to a private school has to pay twice: once through his property taxes for the local government school, and then again for the private school's tuition.

[23]Typically the explicit price for "public goods" is zero, but of course to calculate the true economic price one must factor in the taxes paid to fund such goods.

goods" is the so-called "free-rider" problem. However, there are moral, economic, and practical issues with using this as a workable principle.

In terms of the moral issue, what the statist is saying is this: I want this good, but you benefit from it even if you don't pay for it, so I'm going to force you to pay for it. The moral counter-argument is this: I don't want to pay for this good, and am not asking for this benefit to be freely bestowed upon me, so why should I be forced to pay just because you want the good and can't figure out how to exclude me?

In fact, it is more likely that the statist is *really* saying this: I want this good, but can't afford it myself, so I'm going to enlist the state's help to force others to contribute—using the argument that they benefit—so that I can get what I want. Thus the alleged solution to the "free-rider" problem is to create "forced riders"!

In terms of economics, one of the key insights of Austrian economics is that all benefits are subjective. Thus it is not correct for A to tell B that B is benefiting from a so-called "public good" (and thus must pay for it); only B can make that call.[24]

In practical terms, the "free-rider" principle is capable of expanding the range of "public goods" to absurd levels.

If a company provides a significant number of jobs in a local community, then this could provide certain benefits to that community which flow from lower unemployment, such as lower crime, greater vibrancy, etc., yet the community is not reimbursing that company for these benefits. Shouldn't the "free-riding" community be obliged to pay for these benefits? If a person works on his front garden extensively to make it beautiful, then this could provide benefits to his neighbors in terms of beautifying the street, yet his neighbors are not paying for this. Shouldn't they be obliged to contribute to the upkeep of his garden, lest they "free-ride"? If a person wears deodorant, then this could provide benefits to those commuters who are jammed up against this person on the subway, yet they are not paying for his deodorant. Shouldn't these "free-riders" be required to

[24]So, for instance, in the case of national defense, a pacifist might not obtain *any* benefit from provision of this service. Even a non-pacifist might not obtain any benefit from a particular defense-services bundle if, for example, he believed that the services were in fact *increasing* the likelihood of enemy attack (unless the non-pacifist were a masochist), such as would be the case with the U.S. government's aggressive, global "defense" policies, as discussed earlier.

pay? If a person pays a dog trainer to teach his dog how to behave in public, then those who come across this dog could benefit from that training, but they are "free-riding" on this person's investment; shouldn't they be required to contribute? If a person installs smoke detectors in his house to provide early warnings about fire, then this could provide benefits to those neighbors whose houses are close to his house (if a fire is contained early, then it won't spread to the neighbors' houses), yet they are not paying for these smoke detectors. Shouldn't these "free-riding" neighbors be required to pay?

The point is, so-called "free-riding" is *everywhere*. Yet statists conveniently only choose to use this as a justification for the state's provision of "public goods" if the product is something they really want but (a) could not afford to purchase for themselves, and (b) don't think they could persuade others to voluntarily pay for too.

The Statist Economist's View

More technically, statist economists use fancier terms to try to create a definition of and justification for "public goods." They claim that "public goods" are those which are both "non-rivalrous" and "non-excludable."

Non-Rivalrous. The term "non-rivalrous" means one person's consumption of the good does not interfere with another person's consumption of the good, so the additional cost to the producer of supplying an additional consumer is perceived to be zero. The statist economist points out that since (as he sees it) it doesn't cost the producer to serve an additional consumer, the producer should be required to supply at full capacity without charging, because if he doesn't, then society wouldn't be supplied with "enough" of the good (according to the statist economist's estimation). Since private producers might object to this business model, the implication is that the state must be the producer of this good (assuming the good is also non-excludable).[25]

[25] Of course the idea of the state not charging for any good is illusory. The state charges (at a minimum) through taxation, but the charge is levied on all taxpayers, as opposed to only on those individuals who consume the good.

A classic example often given is the less-than-full cinema. If a movie is going to be shown at 80-percent capacity, then the perceived marginal cost of admitting one more patron is zero. However, this is problematic for two reasons.

First, it is not true that admitting one more patron has no marginal cost. The next patron might be noisy, tall, smelly, or too large to comfortably fit into just his seat, and thus might adversely impact the other patrons' experience. In addition, the next patron requires additional effort by the cinema in terms of clean-up afterwards (this patron might contribute additional trash), and at some point additional ticketing staff and security might be required as the number of patrons grows. Also, each patron increases the "wear & tear" on the carpeting and seats.

More generally, however, one of the key insights of Austrian economics is that all costs are subjective. Thus no one other than the cinema owner can legitimately judge whether there is a cost to admitting one more patron. In fact, the owner's decision *not* to admit an additional patron for free demonstrates that he believes that there is a cost to doing so.

Second, this principle can be applied to other situations which illustrate the principle's absurdity. For instance, if someone's living room is not filled to capacity, then should the house owner be expected to admit a small group of strangers who want to use a comfortable space for a meeting? Would this justify the state taking over and opening up all houses that are not used to capacity?[26]

In fact, the logical extension of this principle would suggest that *all* products should be given away for free, for once a good is manufactured and is sitting idle somewhere, the statist economist would have to conclude that the additional cost to the vendor of a customer wandering in and picking up that good is zero.

Other examples often cited include roads and the Internet. However, each person's use of a road or the physical equipment constituting the Internet's "pipes" impacts others' usage by "clogging up" the resource (in the case of roads, traffic; in the case of the Internet, waiting for a video to buffer or an email to download). Further, each person's usage also in-

[26]This is a relevant example because both the cinema and the house are instances of privately owned property.

creases the "wear & tear" on the relevant resource, thereby increasing the maintenance costs.

Non-Excludable. The term "non-excludable" is the fancy term for a good that is subject to the aforementioned "free-rider" issue. It means that the supplier of a good could not exclude any particular consumer from benefiting, even if the consumer did not pay for the good, and thus, faced with this issue, private producers wouldn't produce the good at all, as there would be no viable business model. Therefore, the state must be the producer (assuming the good is also non-rivalrous).

The classic example often given is the lighthouse. Once the light is shining on the water, all ships out there could benefit from this, so how would the lighthouse owner be able to charge for his service?

The problem with this line of thinking is that it speaks of no logical principle but, rather, simply a lack of ingenuity on the part of the statist economist. Just because the economist cannot conceive of how to make a business out of this service doesn't mean that entrepreneurs could not come up with a solution. In fact, historically, lighthouses *were* privately owned. Ships and their insurers voluntarily paid to ensure this service was provided, because the cost was very cheap compared with the potential cost from the loss of a ship and/or its cargo due to a collision with another ship or rocks.

Consider also what happened with analog radio. While it is not possible to exclude listeners from analog-radio programming, radio-station entrepreneurs figured out a way to create a viable business model, by charging advertisers who wanted access to the radio station's listener base.[27]

The critical point to note about goods that are supposedly "non-excludable" is that, for the private sector to supply such goods, it is *not* necessary that entrepreneurs would be able to charge everyone who benefits. All that matters is that entrepreneurs could produce the goods at a lower cost than the revenues they generate. That's where entrepreneurial ingenuity trumps the limitations of the statist economist's imagination.

The other key point to note, which statist economists overlook, is the fact that the benefit of many of these allegedly "non-excludable" goods

[27]With advances in technology, today radio listeners are excludable, which is how the satellite-radio business model works.

could be tied to living in, visiting, or using a particular territory (either physical territory, or intangible "territory," such as the abovementioned radio programming). This has two principal implications.

First, since people *can* be excluded from any territory, the benefits of such goods are, in fact, excludable.

Second, if the provider of the goods in question also owns the territory, then he could build the cost of providing such goods into the territory-use fee that he charges residents or visitors, on the basis that provision of these goods enhances the quality of living in or visiting his territory.

So, for instance, a developer of a residential community could establish roads, security, parks, etc. and then price the provision of these goods into the sale price of individual plots of land and/or residents' annual maintenance dues. The owner of a road could supply streetlights as a service to those who pay his toll fee, which would incorporate the cost of providing such lighting. In the case of the lighthouse example, since each ship ultimately calls into a port, and it is to the port's benefit to provide its customers with light to make the approach to the port easier, the port owner could easily build the cost of providing the lighthouse into docking fees charged to ships.[28]

Combining the Two Concepts. As noted earlier, the statist economist only classifies as a "public good" something which is *both* non-rivalrous *and* non-excludable.

The classic example of what a statist economist would call a true "public good" is national defense. However, even this can be shown to be a false assumption.

National defense is not "non-rivalrous." "National defense" is a concept, not a product. Real resources are required to create a real defense product, and thus questions arise as to how much defense do we want, and in what form?

Do we just want to protect the coastal states, or the interior too? If we choose the interior too, then we need to spend more money than if we just protected the coastal states, so the marginal cost of producing that extra

[28]Or, if libertarian thinking catches on and portions of oceans are able to be privately owned, then an ocean owner could incorporate the lighthouse fee into the price of a permit to sail in his waters.

defensive capability is not zero. Do we want to protect citizens who are abroad, or just those who are in the homeland? If the former, then we need to spend more money than if we just pursued the latter. Do we want to offer citizens protection in the air, in the sea, or just on the ground? Each of those decisions entails different costs. Looked at another way, if a fixed set of protective resources is deployed to cover a larger area or population, then this would detract from the quality of protection that would otherwise be provided to a smaller area or group of citizens.

Neither is national defense "non-excludable." It only appears so, given the way that individuals at the state, in their infinite wisdom, have decided to provide this good.

National defense is ultimately about protecting lives and property from damage. Each individual and each piece of property could either be included in the protection umbrella or not; private security agencies do this all the time, as do insurers. Property, life, and health insurers could offer their policyholders compensation against destruction, death, and injury from attack. If you bought such a policy, then you would be compensated if you suffered this type of loss, and if you didn't, then you wouldn't. The insurers would then invest in defensive capabilities to protect their policyholders from attack, since done efficiently, this would be cheaper than making large payouts. As technology improves, the exclusion of non-payers could become more precise.

A good illustration of this was provided by the operation of Israel's Iron Dome defensive missile system during the 2014 conflict with the Hamas group based in the Gaza Strip. When Hamas fired a rocket into Israeli air space, Iron Dome would calculate where the rocket would land, and if it would do damage to houses or people. If the calculations showed that the rocket would be landing harmlessly, then Iron Dome would not fire off an intercepting missile; if the calculations showed that Israelis were at risk, then Iron Dome would intercept and destroy the rocket. One could imagine insurers offering this precision protection only to their policyholders.[29]

The "non-excludable" argument is also belied by the fact that adjacent nations have their own defensive capabilities. If it were true that

[29]In a similar vein, one could imagine a private company's "SEAL team" that would rescue only paying customers if they were taken hostage overseas.

national defense is "non-excludable," then neither Canada nor Mexico would bother having defensive capabilities, as they could just "free-ride" on the coattails of the capabilities of the U.S. Similarly, it would make no sense for some states in the European Union to have their own defensive capabilities, since they are all in close proximity to other states, on whose capabilities they could "free-ride."

Finally, to the extent that there is some perceived "free riding," the statist economist overlooks the remedy of ostracization. The citizens of adjacent territories tend to have significant commercial and personal interaction. If the citizens of one territory had invested in defensive protection which might also benefit the citizens of an adjacent territory, but the citizens of the adjacent territory refuse to contribute to the cost of this protection, then if it were sufficiently important to them, the citizens of the paying territory could threaten to reduce trade and other interaction with the citizens of the non-paying territory. In this way, there *would be* some exclusion of benefits; not of the defensive protection, but of other items of equivalent value.[30]

How Much Must Be Supplied?

More broadly, there are two fundamental problems with the concept of the "public good" justification for state action. There is a practical problem and a moral problem.

First, the practical problem. The "public goods" argument implies that there is in fact a set, socially optimal amount of the good that must be produced. The theory runs that if, in the state's estimation, the private sector would produce less than this level, then the state must step in. However, statists never ask, much less answer, how one could derive this "socially optimal production level," and who has the omniscience to do this?

[30] To digress slightly, there is also a self-contradictory element in arguing that national defense must be provided by the state. As noted above, "national defense" is essentially about protecting human bodies and property from external aggression. Yet when the state provides national defense, what does it do? It forcibly confiscates property from individuals to fund its activities, and it may even forcibly conscript individuals to serve in the armed forces. In both of these activities, the state itself, as the purported guardian against aggression, is forcibly aggressing against bodies and property!

In the private sector, the "socially optimal production level" is pursued by individual entrepreneurs trying to anticipate individual consumer preferences based on pricing signals given to them in the market by individual consumers and the owners of factors of production. As noted earlier, those entrepreneurs who anticipate correctly and please voluntarily paying consumers would make profits, and thus would be able to bid for more scarce resources, and those who fail to do this would tend to go out of business, and thus would yield scarce resources. Note that this "socially optimal production level" continuously changes with consumer preferences and resource availability, so entrepreneurs must continuously adjust.

Practically speaking, it is impossible for individuals at the state, or their economists, to make a credible theoretical calculation in advance, or to adjust on the fly, regarding the "socially optimal production level" of any "public good." State personnel cannot know consumers' changing preferences, since they cannot know what is inside each consumer's head, and nor does the state, as a coercive monopoly, get any actionable, market feedback from consumers, since consumers are not making voluntary purchases of state-provided "public goods."

In addition, if state personnel get the production quantity or quality wrong relative to what consumers actually want, then the state does not go out of business, but rather continues to divert scarce resources into producing these goods away from goods that consumers actually want.

Accordingly, in justifying the state's provision of "public goods," the state can only rely on models produced by intellectuals, which models (like their intellectual creators) are entirely divorced from the real world.

Further, even if the state *could* know each individual's preferences, how on earth could it reconcile them into one production decision (this is analogous to the "common good" issue discussed earlier)? Society is not a single consumer, but rather the aggregation of many individuals, and while the private sector can satisfy all individuals concurrently through competing products, the state (at best) can only satisfy a subset of individuals who are in favor of the single production decision made by the state.

Second, the moral problem. Any time the state produces a "public good," it is charging every single taxpayer whether that taxpayer wants that good or not. Taxpayers do not have the opportunity to opt out. By what right can the individuals at the state tell each citizen that he must pay for those goods that state personnel decide they want to produce? This means that state personnel have a claim over the income of individuals which is superior to the claim of those individuals themselves! How could this be justified?

Basic Science. The typical statist claim that basic science is a "public good" illustrates both of the above issues. The statist believes that basic science is a "public good" because it involves significant sums of money, doesn't always have a commercial payoff—either because not everything works out, or the benefits might occur too distantly in the future—and all of society could benefit from scientific advances. Apparently these are reasons why the private sector—entrepreneurs and philanthropists—will not fund "sufficient" basic science, and thus the state must step in to fill the gap by coercively diverting taxpayers' money.

Just on the surface, the given reasons are not compelling: there are plenty of projects that involve significant sums of money which get funded by the private sector (e.g., airplanes, cruise ships, oil rigs, satellites, and skyscrapers); the private sector is comfortable spending money on uncertain outcomes, both in terms of quantity and time (e.g., the development of new blockbuster drugs, and the funding of new technology companies); and society always benefits from advances created by the private sector (which is why people are willing to voluntarily purchase products that incorporate these advances).

However, there are deeper arguments against basic science being a "public good." Below I'll focus on the core principled arguments, and I'll leave aside the empirical evidence, of which there is plenty, that (a) the private sector has historically funded enormous amounts of basic science, and still does, and (b) the majority of advances in technology have come not from basic R&D, but from applied R&D conducted by commercial enterprises under pressure to innovate to beat out competition.[31]

How could the statist know that the private sector wouldn't fund "sufficient" basic R&D? That implies that there is some objective definition of "basic R&D," some objectively identifiable minimum required amount,

[31] This is all very well documented in Terence Kealey's book, *The Economic Laws of Scientific Research*.

and some ability to foresee what the private sector would and wouldn't fund. From where does the statist derive this minimum required dollar amount? Could the statist even specify this amount, much less defend it? Could the statist specify which types of basic R&D require which minimum amounts? No!

If the statist cannot credibly specify how much basic R&D is required, nor in which areas, then how could we know whether the state is even carrying out its stated task sufficiently? Essentially it becomes an arbitrary "gut" calculation: the definition of "sufficient" is the opinion of whoever is in power at any one point in time.

This is not to say that any single person in the private sector knows the answers either, but (a) the private sector is not coercively taking anyone's income when it hazards a guess, (b) the private sector is taking multiple guesses at any point in time, since many people are simultaneously personally funding their different ideas, and (c) those in the private sector pay a personal financial penalty for guessing wrong, and stand to make a personal financial gain if they guess right, and thus the incentives are much more aligned with guessing correctly over time.

The statist's usual retort is to point to some beneficial development that he believes only came about through the state funding the basic research. However, just because the state coercively diverted resources out of the private sector towards state-identified research priorities doesn't mean that this is efficient or moral.[32]

There is nothing special about basic R&D spending. Like any other investment that occurs in the economy, basic R&D spending just represents the allocation of scarce resources towards an objective. Thus the same core principles apply to basic R&D as to any use of resources in the economy. If the state funds this good, then it is engaging in central planning. It is diverting resources that would have been used otherwise by the private sector, which has better incentives than the state to use scarce resources efficiently,

[32]More often than not, the actual history of development of such a good is contrary to what the statist would hope or was taught. Often times the private sector was already funding or developing the good anyway, or the actual breakthrough came from private-sector work. As noted earlier regarding the Internet, for example, typically the state crowds out private-sector efforts, and we are left with a sub-optimal, state-backed effort by default.

and can better take account of dispersed knowledge and preferences in the economy than could the central planners with their "one-size-fits-all," coercive approach.

It also means that the state is forcibly diverting resources away from individuals in the economy who might have preferred to use their resources in a different way. Some people might indeed be glad that the state diverted resources to help develop a particular good, but not everyone might have seen this as their top priority. No one was given a choice.

As noted earlier, statists don't appear to fully appreciate the notion of trade-offs. Given scarce resources, it's not the case that we could spend on basic R&D without a cost; we would have to give up something to devote resources in that direction. So even saying "We should spend more on cancer research" is not a reasonable proposition. We have to ask "Using resources taken from what other activity?" To stay focused on R&D trade-offs in medicine, spending more on cancer research might mean spending less on AIDS research.[33] How do we know that this priority reflects the preferences of each individual whose money was confiscated by the state in this endeavor? The individuals at the state cannot efficiently or morally make these decisions, as they are making "either/or" decisions for everyone at once, without knowing their actual preferences.

State personnel react to political causes, which they can easily perceive and benefit from, but not to consumer preferences, to which they are blind. For instance, whereas combating Ebola in Africa might become a hot political cause, leading to the state diverting resources into this area as politicians respond to special-interest pressure or polls, it could be the case that there is actually very little consumer demand for an Ebola vaccine, and much more demand for a malaria vaccine (malaria kills far more Africans than Ebola). These actual consumer preferences would be thwarted by such state intervention.

In fact, given the incentives for those at the state to respond to the most aggressive lobbying by those seeking to rent the state's coercive powers, it's usually a very safe bet that the process by which basic R&D funding was

[33]Of course the trade-offs are much broader than this. Spending more on cancer research might mean spending less on food, shelter, clothing, education, etc. We couldn't know exactly what we are giving up, only that we are giving up something.

created was highly political. The politicization of this decision could manifest itself in matters such as the choice of field to research, the specific scientists or institutions involved, the geographic location of the research, the privileged beneficiaries of the research, and the definition of the objectives and benchmarks.

Consider the vast amount of societal resources diverted by the state to defense companies in the U.S., some of which is spent on military R&D. Each year billions of dollars are drawn out of the portion of the economy that serves actual consumer preferences, and these dollars are plowed into researching and developing products the main purpose of which is to kill humans or destroy property. These products are then used aggressively around the globe by the U.S. government in activities having nothing to do with defending U.S. citizens against actual threats to the homeland. That hardly satisfies consumer preferences.

Or consider the whole NASA space R&D program. This was ramped up in the 1960s as part of a testosterone-laced competition with the Soviet Union to waste the most money in outer space, which in some way was supposed to express "national pride" (as defined by the state). Neither the Soviet Union (now Russia) nor the U.S. has ever derived any substantial, non-military benefits from their respective space R&D programs, yet we are continually told by the state that it is critical that we forego our actual consumer preferences to forcibly fund this R&D. The defense, aerospace, electronics, and communications industries have lobbied hard to promote taxpayer funding of their R&D, but which consumer preferences does this satisfy?

As a final example, consider how AIDS became a high profile political cause in the 1980s, which meant that dollars were politically diverted into AIDS research, when in fact it might have made more sense to allow these dollars to flow into other deserving areas. Taxpayers were never given the choice.

The last point to make about the basic science area is that, in addition to the state's R&D funding process being driven by politics, it also tends to be driven by scientists who are not risking their own financial capital, and thus who are not concerned with any particular return on the funds invested; remember, these funds represent scarce resources forcibly diverted from other uses in the economy. If scientists want to "dream big" about breaking new frontiers without worrying about returns on capital, then they and their supporters should "dream big" with their own funds, and not with those funds forcibly taken from others. Let these scientists engage with philanthropies or with private-sector firms which don't contract with the state, and thereby raise the money to pursue their dreams from the voluntary sector.

Myth #11: We Need the State to Deal with Negative Externalities

The Theory

There is another justification for the state, which is the inverse of the "public goods" argument. This is referred to as "negative externalities." The argument is that the production of some goods involves costs to society which the entrepreneur does not incur, and thus he does not factor these costs into his production function (these costs are said to be "externalized," in that they are shifted to society, instead of being "internalized" into the good). Accordingly, the consumers of these goods, in paying a price that doesn't account for these costs, are getting a "free-ride" on the backs of those who do suffer these costs but don't get the benefit of the goods. Or, looked at another way, these goods are over-produced.

The state is therefore required to intervene to prohibit or reduce these externalized costs, or shift them back onto the entrepreneur.[34]

Pollution

The classic example given in this area is pollution. For instance, if an entrepreneur's factory emits toxic chemicals into a river and this causes damage to people downstream who use the river's water, but the entrepreneur does

[34] Negative externalities are the inverse of "public goods" because, in the case of the latter, statists believe that insufficient goods would be produced because entrepreneurs could not internalize the social benefits; in the case of negative externalities, statists believe that too much would be produced because entrepreneurs don't have to internalize the social costs.

not have to pay for this damage, then, when he prices his goods for consumers, he would not need to factor in this pollution cost, and thus could offer consumers a lower price than if the entrepreneur *were* to factor in this cost. Those who suffer from the pollution damage therefore would bear some of the production costs, even though they didn't buy the entrepreneur's goods. This is supposedly an argument for the state to step in and regulate the entrepreneur, either to prevent such pollution, or to make the entrepreneur pay for the associated costs.

The main argument against this situation being a justification for the state is that the reason the entrepreneur "gets away" with not paying the costs of his pollution is due to a weak system of private-property rights. This is generally due to state interference with property ownership and the enforcement system. Too much property such as water sources, roads, parks, etc. is regarded as owned by the state instead of by private citizens, which means there is less efficient stewardship—no one takes care of property as well as someone who has their own financial capital invested—and no obvious defendants to sue when things go wrong.

In the above example, if instead the river were privately owned, then the downstream users of the river who buy their water from the river owner would take action against the river owner for supplying them with polluted water, and the river owner would have a strong interest in taking action against the entrepreneur for polluting his water. The action by the river owner against the entrepreneur would be for what is called "nuisance," a well-established cause of action developed in the common law hundreds of years ago, whereas the downstream users who buy their water from the river owner would likely have a claim for breach of contract against the river owner. Faced with these actual or potential liabilities, the entrepreneur and the river owner (either on their own initiative, or as required by their liability insurers) would quickly take effective action to reduce toxic emissions, because this would be a cheaper way of running their businesses compared with being subject to continual liability (I will discuss the libertarian take on this issue in greater detail later).

Instead, statists argue that the state should (a) own the river, (b) direct the entrepreneur how to organize his operations, and (c) be able to fine (and ultimately imprison) the entrepreneur if he doesn't comply with the state's directives.

However, this is a very ineffective and an immoral system for regulating the relevant activities. As in many other parts of the economy, once the state moves in, it crowds out more effective private-sector solutions. This regime forcibly substitutes the inefficient state for those who have a direct interest in the outcome, and weakens the regulation against wrongdoers. I will elaborate on the deficiencies of a state regulatory regime below.

First, recall that the alleged justification for the state to intervene here is because the statist believes that the entrepreneur could externalize his pollution costs to society. However, when the state intervenes to try to internalize the pollution costs to the entrepreneur, the state externalizes the *enforcement* costs to society! Every state-instituted regulatory regime involves significant costs to set up and support large state bureaucracies to write, pass, and enforce regulations against entire industries, as opposed to against just wrongdoers within those industries. All taxpayers foot the bills for these enforcement systems, not just those who might benefit directly. In contrast, in a purely private-sector system based on private lawsuits, the enforcement costs—as well as the liability for pollution damage—would mostly, if not wholly, be internalized just to the wrongdoers.[35]

Second, the state will produce standardized regulations for an industry, which necessarily can't take into account each entrepreneur's unique production methods and situation. This "one-size-fits-all" approach can only mean overkill for some entrepreneurs, and too light regulation for others, when compared with a system of individual private lawsuits (or the mere threat thereof). Such lawsuits would impose a customized regime of damages to be paid by each individual entrepreneur who is guilty of wrongdoing, and thus would create incentives for each individual entrepreneur to fine tune his own situation (mainly to avoid such lawsuits in the first place).

When centralized regulations are overkill, this means an entrepreneur's costs would increase by more than is just, thus artificially reducing his ability to supply goods, leading to higher prices for consumers. When the regulations are too light or are out of date, not only would this not prevent damage from occurring, but the entrepreneur who complies with the

[35] Some private systems may require the wrongdoer to pay all of the legal costs of the victim, while others may settle on different standards.

regulations would have less incentive to actually reduce his harmful activities, since he would have a valid defense to any lawsuit, namely, that he was fully compliant with the state's (inadequate or antiquated) regulations.[36]

Even assuming that those writing the regulations have the best of intentions (which is a dubious assumption, as to which see below), given the reality of human imperfection, there is a huge difference between (a) having regulations imposed centrally from the top down, and (b) allowing regulations to develop from the ground up (via private lawsuits). If those at the state make a mistake issuing regulations, then it impacts millions of people at once; if a private-sector entity makes a mistake, then it only impacts those who interact with that entity. As noted earlier, we should all want the issues with human imperfection (whether incompetence or corruption) decentralized as far as possible, as opposed to becoming more centralized.

Statists tend to scream out for centralized state regulation in particular after the occurrence of a low probability but high profile accident. The mere fact that this event occurred is cited as evidence of the need for regulating the activity which caused the harm, and regulations may then be written to try to prevent this event from ever happening again.

However, what this inevitably leads to is society incurring all of the problems and costs associated with a state regulation just to mitigate a small risk; it takes no account of the benefits that accrue from the activity that accidentally caused the harm, which activity would be curtailed by the new regulation. It is as if the statist believes that it's possible or desirable

[36]For instance, it took New York City until 2008 to comprehensively update its 1968 building code. The periodic revisions over 40 years had led to conflicting and confusing requirements, and did not keep pace with modern construction materials and practices. Yet highly competent architects and builders couldn't stray from these regulations, lest they risk fines and prosecution. As another example, while British Petroleum was attacked for its lack of readiness to handle the 2010 Gulf of Mexico deep-water oil spill, the company had long been required by federal regulators to base its spill preparations on federal rules last updated in 2004, which focused mostly on oil released onto the surface, as opposed to in deep water. As one further set of examples, in a series of U.S. Supreme Court cases on the federal Clean Water Act of 1972, the court held that federal environmental standards must prevail over conflicting state-level environmental standards in setting the benchmark for activities impacting the cleanliness of bodies of water, even though the federal standards were *lower* than the state-level standards!

to eliminate all risks in life, no matter how small, regardless of the cost. Yet every action every person takes is fraught with risk: driving a car, crossing the street, flying on an airplane, etc. Each person has a different tolerance for assuming risk, as each person would implicitly first weigh up the perceived benefits against the perceived risks. How could the state assume that it could create a centralized regulation which satisfies every person's benefit/risk trade-off calculus? Obviously this is an impossible task, so why take it on?

When regulations are written in response to an accident, this is usually due to some single-issue, special-interest group lobbying the state for the new regulation. In essence, then, what actually happens is that this group effectively rents the state's coercive powers to impose the group's benefit/risk assessment on everyone else.

Third, there is deeper point to make about the trade-offs that are ignored with centralized regulations. As noted above, every person has his own sense of how much risk he is prepared to assume; in the case of pollution, this means weighing up the risks to his personal health and/or property from the pollution against the benefits he expects to gain from the production activity leading to the pollution. Production activity, while creating pollution, provides goods which satisfy human wants, as well as employment opportunities. Probably the only thing we know for certain is that very few people, if any, would argue that zero pollution ought to be the standard by which we live. This would cause all production activity to grind to a halt, which would lead to a return to the significant human poverty and misery that was a feature of pre-Industrial Revolution society.

However, the level of pollution above zero that we *should* accept as the trade-off for production activity is where each person's standard starts to diverge.

For instance, the least well-off might prefer more production activity and less pollution regulation (i.e., potentially more pollution), since their highest priorities would be the availability of affordable goods that meet their basic needs, and employment income to purchase these goods. As people become wealthier, it makes sense that they start to prefer less production activity in return for a cleaner environment; in this sense, a cleaner environment is a "luxury good." We have seen this in operation all throughout history, and still see it today, whereby in those countries that are emerging from poverty, such as China and India, the populations are more concerned about production activity than the environment, but in the wealthier countries there is a tendency to prefer the inverse.

However, this is not just a principle that applies across national borders. Within national borders, even one as wealthy as the U.S., there is still a spread of preferences among the population. In other words, while in the U.S. there are those who would prefer less pollution even though it means less production activity, there are still many whose highest priorities are satisfaction of their consumption needs and steady employment, and, accordingly, they would be willing to live with more pollution. This is what statists overlook, or perhaps intentionally ignore. Those who are clamoring for more stringent, centralized environmental regulation are often the same individuals who have attained sufficient wealth such that they could now afford to "purchase" a cleaner environment. They never consider the costs that they are imposing on others who don't share their views. While the cleaner environment is the visible outcome, there are unseen costs of less production activity, including the lower living standards of those who might not have made this choice, resulting from there being fewer or more expensive consumption goods, and fewer employment opportunities.[37]

For instance, statists like to point to the environmental regulations that preceded the improvement in the air quality in Los Angeles. This supposedly positive outcome is regarded as proof that the state "can get the job done" where the market "failed." Leaving aside the issue of whether the market failed and why (since, as noted above, this is generally due to a weak system of property rights established by the state in the first place), the conclusion that the solution was positive for everyone concerned is dubious.

For the sake of illustration, let's assume that there were local restrictions placed on production and driving activities in Los Angeles, and costly, mandatory "clean" vehicle production specifications introduced.[38] Now

[37]To provide an analogy, consider the serious side effects that come from certain therapies used to combat the most severe diseases. Those who are healthy wouldn't want to suffer those side effects because they are in a different position from those who are afflicted with these diseases. The latter group, however, might be very willing to suffer these side effects if they are the price of mitigating the worse effects from the diseases. To complete the analogy, those who would argue for centralized environmental regulation to reduce pollution to the lowest levels are effectively arguing that these drugs should be outlawed because of their awful side effects.

[38]I'm not saying that this is precisely what happened in Los Angeles; I'm just using Los Angeles as an excuse to make a point.

consider the interests of those at the lower end of the economic spectrum who (a) lost their actual jobs when their factory had to shut down, move, or cut back due to higher regulatory costs, (b) were deprived of a potential job by the production that was now too costly to establish or expand, (c) had to pay more or endure other difficulties when buying a vehicle and/or driving to their jobs, and (d) had to pay higher costs for locally produced goods. Or consider those who similarly suffered because productive resources were drawn out of the economy to set up the state agencies to write, implement, and enforce these regulations, when these resources might have otherwise been used by the private sector to employ these people or produce more and cheaper goods for consumption.

Since a single trade-off was coercively imposed on everyone, we cannot say that the centralized solution was the most efficient way to organize scarce resources to maximize the satisfaction of millions of individuals given their different trade-off preferences.

In addition, such imposition by force was, of course, immoral.[39]

Fourth, what invariably happens when the state is involved in regulating industries is that the individuals at the regulating agency start to develop a career dependence on the industry's survival, and a bias in favor of the regulated industry (this is known as "regulatory capture"). Leaving aside actual instances of trading favors between the regulated and the regulators, there are three natural, job-related reasons for regulatory capture.

To do his job effectively, the regulator needs detailed information on the regulated firms, and the only way in which he could get that data is from the regulated firms themselves. Thus, as the saying goes, he has to "be careful not to bite the hands that feed him."

In addition, it is highly likely that the public wouldn't pay much at-

[39]The free market might have provided several solutions. Those arguing for these centralized regulations who suffered loss from the poor air quality could have sued the relevant factory, car, or road owners for an injunction or damages, or made claims on their health and/or property insurance policies and let their insurers sue instead. Or, if they weren't able to prove liability to an acceptable standard, then they (or their insurers) could have paid for the pollution controls out of their own pockets, for instance, by purchasing and shutting down the offending factories or paying for their modification, and by paying to fit all cars with pollution-control equipment. In this way we could measure how much these people really valued such pollution control. Instead, they simply took the easier but immoral and less economically efficient route of renting the state's coercive powers to impose their preferences on others.

tention to the nuances of how regulations get written, but the regulated producers, for whom each regulation imposes new costs, would be all over the regulation-writing process and, as another saying goes, "The squeaky wheel gets the oil." When the regulator has to decide between two choices on how a regulation is to be written, he cannot help but be influenced by the lobbying from the regulated producers, for which there is little to no counterbalance.[40]

Further, a regulator who creates too many problems for his industry puts his job at risk, since, without a healthy industry, his role would be less important or viable. Thus the regulator will be careful to impose regulations sufficient to look like he is doing his job, but not so severe as to cause real problems for his industry.[41]

For all these reasons, when the state gets involved, instead of implementation of effective, pro-victim regulation, we get a careful career balancing act by the regulator. In the pollution example cited above, the real interests of those downstream who suffer loss would quickly become of secondary importance relative to the regulator maintaining good relationships with industry participants.

Contrast this with victims pursuing private lawsuits against a polluting producer, which would put the interests of the victims first.

---

[40] As noted earlier, often times the largest producers in an industry seek to have the regulations written to fit with what they are already doing or with what they could afford, with the objective of making it very expensive for new competitors to enter the industry. This restriction of competition is ultimately to the detriment of consumers.

[41] One of the clearest examples of this is the states' lawsuit settlements with the major tobacco companies in the late 1990s. The states struck an agreement with these tobacco companies to settle the lawsuits against them, and to exempt these companies from liability to private citizens, in return for receiving hundreds of billions of dollars from these companies over time, and imposing certain marketing restrictions on their activities. Despite the original intention that these settlement funds be dedicated to discouraging children from smoking, and reimbursing Medicaid for tobacco-related illnesses, only a very small percentage is used for these purposes, with the bulk going to finance general government spending (as do excise taxes on cigarettes). Thus the states now are fully invested in the continued survival and growth of tobacco companies. Some states even sold bonds backed by tobacco-settlement revenues, and so became dependent on tobacco companies to avoid default! As another example, consider the user fees charged by the U.S. Food and Drug Administration (FDA) to the companies that the FDA is regulating, which fund a material portion of the FDA's staff costs.

In fact, the history of environmental regulation in the U.S. is an interesting case study in regulatory capture.

Originally, before state-imposed regulation became the norm, the U.S. operated under a relatively free market in environmental regulation. The private tort lawsuit was the primary way in which producers were regulated; those individuals who suffered damage sued these producers, and won.

Over time, industrial producers found that this regime became too onerous, so these producers sought out the individual U.S. states to help stem the tide of these lawsuits. Producers preferred to become subject to the states' regulations instead of private lawsuits, because they could have significant input into how the regulations were drafted, which they obviously saw as an opportunity to live under a friendlier regime.

However, as time went on, it became difficult for the largest producers to comply with the multitude of different states' regulations, and some states became stricter than others. Thus producers sought out the federal government and, in an odd alliance with environmental activists, supported the creation of the Environmental Protection Authority. Producers decided that a uniform regulatory regime over which they would have significant influence would be preferable to state-by-state regulation.

Of course lost in all of this regulatory evolution are the actual interests of those who suffer damage from pollution but whose lawsuits are prohibited or stymied by the regulations promulgated through this regulatory capture process.

Fifth, and related to the prior point, even if the regulator were not captured by the regulated, the individuals at the state would act against the interests of the victims of an environmental problem if one of the state's key cronies had a conflicting interest.

For instance, after the 2010 deep-water oil spill in the Gulf of Mexico, the U.S. federal government received a number of offers by foreign ship operators to use their advanced technology and highly relevant experience to contain the spill. However, the government rejected these offers because they involved using non-union labor, and labor unions are very important cronies of the state.

As explained earlier, unlike those in the private sector, the state has immunity from suit by private citizens who suffer damage from its decisions, and also the state cannot go out of business for failure to provide a valuable service. Accordingly, in the above situation, there was little risk to the state in keeping cronies such as unions satisfied, even though this conflicted with the state's supposed environmental regulatory role; keeping the unions satisfied was a much more effective way for individuals at the state to advance their own interests than addressing the needs of the mere victims of the pollution.[42]

Sixth, consider under a state regulatory regime who actually benefits from regulatory fines paid by the errant producers. The fines are paid to the state to support the state's operations, and many times it is the actual regulatory agency itself that benefits directly. Perversely, the fines are *not* paid over to the individuals who actually suffer losses caused by the relevant producers' violations (see the example cited earlier relating to the tobacco-company settlements).[43]

Contrast this with private lawsuits, where those who suffer loss receive damages payments directly from the guilty defendants.[44]

The result of the state regulator being able to feed off its ability to levy fines is that this becomes one of its core objectives. Every organization is naturally interested in expanding its revenues because this enables its members to do more. However, this is particularly troubling when the organization is a state regulator, since it could write rules which would enable it to forcibly increase its revenues by conjuring up violations having nothing to do with punishing individuals for infringing the rights of others.

One of the most egregious examples of the state feeding off its regulatory

---

[42]Presumably the unions were a more important crony than the environmental lobby, but this must have presented an interesting "crony conflict" dilemma for the state!

[43]Note that many times fines are levied for actions that cause no actual losses, such as failure to comply with paperwork or certification rules or other victimless, regulatory breaches.

[44]Sometimes, as part of a settlement with an errant producer, a regulator will require the establishment of a fund to compensate private citizens who claim to have suffered loss. However, this is still sub-optimal. It substitutes the regulator's centralized views on the appropriate size of the fund and who is eligible to share in this fund for each individual citizen's right to seek appropriate compensation for his specific loss, and the producer's right to require claimants to prove causation and loss. Often times this leads to intense lobbying by different interest groups to become eligible to share in this type of fund. Not surprisingly then, these funds tend to be distributed politically, rather than in accordance with justice.

activities (although unrelated to pollution) is the "civil-asset-forfeiture" legislation in the U.S. This empowers the police to seize private property as part of the "War on Drugs," without the owner even being arrested, never mind convicted. Based merely on a suspicion that property might have been used in activities relating to illegal narcotics, the police regularly seize cash, vehicles, houses, etc. The owner has to go to court to try to free his seized property and, unlike in any other area of the law, the burden is shifted to the owner to prove a negative, namely, that the property is *not* being used in relation to illegal narcotics (note that the state could prevail even if someone *other than* the owner had used the property for these purposes). This process is very difficult and expensive for the owner, whereas the state could spend taxpayers' money—including the owner's—on court proceedings to contest the owner's arguments.[45]

What happens to the seized property? Federal legislation and some states' legislation allow the police to keep all or a portion of the proceeds they seize or can obtain from selling the seized property. This creates a strong incentive to seize more property, because such proceeds supplement the budget that the police receive from taxes; indeed, this is why such seizure has increased dramatically over time (what police force doesn't want more money to spend on shiny new equipment?).[46]

---

[45] Civil asset-forfeiture should be distinguished from criminal asset-forfeiture. In the latter, once someone is *actually convicted* of a crime, the state can seize the criminal's assets under the statist philosophy of "Taking the profit out of crime." Since the state can use criminal asset-forfeiture to implement that philosophy, there is no reason to also have civil asset-forfeiture. However, the state strongly prefers the civil procedure, as it is much easier to use. Duh!

[46] It's worth noting that, in December 2015, the U.S. Department of Justice announced that it was suspending the federal program which allows local police to share in up to 80 percent of the proceeds from seizing assets under the federal government's purview. Of course this was not a result of the federal government reconsidering the morality of civil asset-forfeiture; rather, due to budget cuts, the Department of Justice wanted to keep these proceeds for itself. The new policy didn't end civil asset-forfeiture, it just temporarily changed which arm of the state got to keep the proceeds. Predictably, local law enforcement groups cried foul, and made the case that cutting off these funds would significantly impact their ability to "protect the public." The irony is that it is the police's use of civil asset-forfeiture from which the public needs protection! In the end, after local police simply stopped seizing assets because they couldn't keep the proceeds, the Department of Justice reversed course and re-

This regime sets up some strange incentives. For instance, if the police seize drugs, then it is hard to legally monetize them, and thus hard to supplement the police budget. Yet if the police first allow drug traffickers to sell their drugs, then the police could seize the cash proceeds, which would be much easier for the police to benefit from. There are actually cases where it has been shown that the police allowed drugs to be sold before moving in to seize the proceeds. So much for civil asset-forfeiture being a tool to combat the drug trade.

In addition, given the financial incentives for the police to focus on civil asset-forfeiture, and therefore on the "War on Drugs," they devote less time and fewer resources to dealing with actual violent crimes, such as murder, theft, rape, etc. Working on those violent crimes just doesn't have the same payoff for the police, and there is no downside to allocating their resources in this manner. If the rates of these violent crimes increase, then the police cannot get fired; in fact, if violent-crime rates increase, then typically statists will then support the police's request for an even larger taxpayer-funded budget.

Note that the "War on Drugs" is clearly an immoral "war." When A puts a drug in his body or sells a drug to someone who wants it, he harms no other person; it is a victimless "crime."[47] Since A has caused no harm, it would be immoral to punish him by imprisoning him or seizing his property, as this would constitute unjustifiable coercion by one man against another. Yet that is exactly what happens with civil asset-forfeiture, making it an immoral action in furtherance of a phony, immoral "war."

And, perversely, the spoils of this "war" enrich the only aggressors in this whole ecosystem, namely, the police. Precisely because there are no victims in these "drug crimes," there is no one else to whom the proceeds could be paid over. That should tell us something.

---

instituted the sharing policy a mere few months later. At least we can all now fully appreciate what motivates local police.

[47] Statists will claim that drug users commit crimes against real victims. However, there are already laws against theft, murder, etc., so the drug legislation adds nothing to those. Second, there is drug-related crime mainly because the product has been pushed underground by its illegality, just as during Prohibition there was illegal activity associated with alcohol, which disappeared once Prohibition was repealed. The reason Wal-Mart doesn't go to war with Target is because they can openly sell their products and compete, and it is always much cheaper to avoid violence.

Enforcement Issues

Statists also argue that, in two respects, state-based regulation regarding negative externalities is a more efficient system of enforcement than private lawsuits.

The first argument statists make is that, in some cases, it might be difficult to show sufficient evidence in a private lawsuit that an entrepreneur accused of, say, pollution damage, is actually guilty of causing a loss to someone, but he should nevertheless be held liable if he violated the state's regulations.

The retort to this is quite obvious: a just system of punishment requires symmetry, namely, if A is to be punished by suffering some physical loss, such as a fine or imprisonment, then this should only occur if he has actually first caused some physical loss to B. Merely violating some arbitrary regulations established by individuals at the state is not sufficient to justify physically sanctioning A. Accordingly, if the evidence of loss and causation cannot be satisfactorily adduced by B in a private lawsuit, then, by definition, A should not be punished. To argue in this instance that the state should be able to penalize A as if he were guilty, merely for breaching the state's regulations, makes decisions about guilt and innocence completely arbitrary. The standard becomes violation of a regulation, rather than causation of loss.

Statists also believe that the state regulator would be more effective than private parties at collecting the required evidence, because the state has independent agencies which specialize in this type of thing. However, this overlooks three points.

First, since the state's "independent" agency is staffed by humans who have their own interests, namely, job security and expansion, the agency's activities are likely to be geared towards whatever would support those objectives. This may mean being sympathetic with industry participants (regulatory capture), or hiding the agency's errors, safe in the knowledge that, unlike in the private sector, no state agency is ever bankrupted for incompetence. Such agencies also tend to purposely increase complexity, by creating many processes and procedures for industry participants to follow—the intricacies of which are known only to the agency's personnel, and the relevance of which to the perceived issues at hand may be quite tenuous—thereby increasing the scope of the agency's activities and the importance of its role, coincidentally providing support for increased budget requests.

Second, state agencies don't offer their personnel the same compensation structure as in the private sector. There is no upside reward for satisfying end-users, and there is no personal financial or career risk in causing delay, complexity, or increased costs for those with whom the personnel interact (nor for preferring on-the-job leisure). Accordingly, such agencies tend to hire lower-quality staff who are less focused and motivated than those in the private sector.[48]

Third, there already *are* independent agencies in the private sector, such as Consumer Reports, UL, and private detective agencies, and there are good reasons to believe that more such agencies would arise and prosper in the free market.

For instance, an entrepreneur's liability insurer would have to indemnify the entrepreneur against successful damages claims by individuals who have suffered loss caused by the entrepreneur's polluting activities. This means that the insurer would have a very strong interest in trying to prevent the entrepreneur from causing such losses in the first place. Accordingly, the insurer may look to hire a private, outside consultant to suggest ways to make the entrepreneur's processes environmentally safer, and to monitor compliance.[49]

This consultant would have its business reputation at stake each time it takes on a client, and thus it would be motivated to do a good job in suggesting effective processes, and monitoring the entrepreneur. If the consultant did a poor job, then it would lose business from insurers in favor of those of its competitors that do a better job. Contrast this with the state's agency, which has no competition or financial incentives to motivate it to be highly effective.

[48]State personnel often receive higher *fixed* total compensation than comparable workers in the private sector, when one considers the combination of cash, benefits, and job security (it's almost impossible to get fired in the public sector). However, the most talented people who want to take more job-security and compensation risk in return for the potential for upside reward, through *variable* compensation, tend to avoid the public sector, because such upside doesn't exist.

[49]In addition to protecting his reputation in the market, the entrepreneur would have another incentive to comply with the insurer's or the consultant's directives, namely, to keep his insurance premiums lower (insurers typically offer premium discounts for insureds who demonstrate that they are lower risks).

The second statist argument in favor of state enforcement is that often times it might be difficult in a private lawsuit for a plaintiff to round up all the relevant defendants. For instance, if someone living next to a highway were suffering damage from exhaust pollution, then he might want to sue all the drivers who have poor exhaust controls, but this is impracticable. However, this example only reinforces why the existence of the state is problematic. The easy way to resolve this problem would be to sue the owner of the road for allowing cars with poor exhaust controls to drive on its property, but the problem is that the owner of the road is normally the state itself, and, as noted earlier, the state has immunity!

If roads were fully private, then the resident could sue the road owner. In addition, faced with this prospect, the road owner (either of his own volition, or as required by his liability insurer) would likely experiment with various processes to prevent cars with poor exhaust controls from using his highway.

The state has no such incentive. Even where it does appear to take action to forestall such problems, it would likely be "captured" by the motor vehicle manufacturers (or any other interest group that is better organized than the residents living next to the highway).

The State Itself Creates Massive Negative Externalities

The final point to make about the alleged necessity of the state to prevent negative externalities from arising is that, in arguing this, the statist doesn't take into account that the operation of the state itself creates many substantial negative externalities. In fact, perhaps it is *only* the state that could actually create negative externalities on a grand scale.

Most directly, and as already noted above, if the state imposes taxes or regulations on private firms to try to deal with alleged, potential negative externalities, then the costs of those taxes or regulations incurred by these firms may cause existing firms to relocate or reduce their operations, thereby creating a negative externality in terms of local employment. In a similar vein, firms not already operating in that area may shelve their plans to establish operations there, thereby creating a negative externality in terms of potential jobs foregone.

For a more general example of the state's impact, consider that the users of state services usually don't pay their full cost directly, because provision of these services is also funded by (i.e., externalized to) taxpayers who don't use such services. This leads to relative under-pricing and thus over-use of these services. This is precisely the logic used by statists to argue against the free market when it comes to negative externalities and the environment, so why is this not an argument against the state when it comes to the services it provides?

For a further example, consider the issuance of state bonds, which is how the state borrows money from investors. The state typically takes these borrowed funds and "invests" them in various state programs.

In the private sector, typically a borrower would only borrow funds if he anticipated that the project or business in which he proposed to invest the funds would yield sufficient proceeds at least to repay the loan and interest (but hopefully more). This is because: (a) the borrower personally has to repay the loan, even if the project or business fails and, if it fails, then he would have to dip into his other assets; and (b) borrowers who develop a reputation for not repaying loans would develop poor credit records, and then would find it difficult to borrow from other lenders in the future.

On the other side, a private-sector lender would undertake a similar type of repayment analysis to try to ensure that his loan is sufficiently "safe," and that the interest rate he is charging is appropriate for the risk.

Yet when the state issues bonds, neither the lender (the buyer of the bonds) nor the borrower (represented by the responsible individual at the state) really expects that, nor particularly cares whether, the proceeds will be used in a productive manner to enable repayment of the loan plus interest. In fact, neither party bothers performing a project evaluation, and the lender charges a very low interest rate, as they both regard the loan as "riskless." This is because both parties know that, regardless of how the proceeds are used, the individuals at the state could always repay the loan through future direct taxes (forcibly seizing taxpayers' income), or through the implicit tax of monetary inflation (by creating new money).[50]

Accordingly, the individuals at the state can borrow money for their pet projects—which brings significant benefits to state personnel in terms of rewarding their cronies and other supporters—and externalize the costs

[50] This is the technical definition of "inflation," namely, an increase in the money supply. This is a tax on those individuals who don't get the new money first, since while the amount of goods available for purchase wouldn't have increased, these individuals' relative share of the money available to purchase those goods would have decreased.

of those loans onto taxpayers. Thus there is a significant, relative over-production of state-bond issuance.[51]

As a final example of the state causing negative externalities, consider that there are unseen negative externalities that arise from the thousands of regulations that already exist, and the new regulations that are implemented by the state each year.

It is impossible for the average citizen to be knowledgeable about the vast majority of these regulations, many of which are vague and thus subject to expansive interpretation, are at odds with local custom, and have nothing to do with protecting private-property rights (in fact, most of them violate private-property rights); indeed, it is likely that each of us is violating some regulation each day of our lives.[52] It is also impossible for the state to realistically enforce all or even most of these regulations against everyone who violates them. In addition, since no one knows in advance which new regulations will be passed each year—although everyone knows that there will be more coming—we live under a highly uncertain legal regime. Thus regulation and enforcement are seen as incomprehensible and arbitrary, instead of understandable and principled.

As a result, there is a complete loss of respect for "the law," which has significant, negative cultural implications for society. This leads to a loss of respect for law-makers and law-enforcers, growth of "grey" and "black" markets, increased conflict in society, as people see themselves racing against their fellow citizens to try to get regulations written and enforced in their favor, and increased opportunities for official corruption.

Yet the statist never considers these negative externalities when arguing for the state. And because these negative externalities from regulations are not factored in, we get a massive, relative over-production of regulations.

[51]The U.S. federal government's explicit outstanding debt currently stands at around $21 trillion, for a negative externality of around $67,000 per citizen. Note that this excludes all the implicit promises to pay that the federal government has made through various welfare programs, such as Social Security and Medicare, which are many times larger than this explicit debt.

[52]The plethora of regulations also leads to many absurdities. For instance, depositing more than $10,000 at a time triggers certain banking regulations based on the suspicion that this is evidence of criminal proceeds, but depositing less than $10,000 at a time triggers related regulations based on the suspicion that the depositor might be trying to avoid the $10,000 threshold. So every deposit is caught!

Myth #12: We Need the State to Deal with Anti-Competitive Behavior

Another twist on the idea of "market failure" is that statists claim that we need the state to curb so-called "anti-competitive" behavior by entrepreneurs. The legislation which has been passed in the U.S. to combat this behavior is known as "anti-trust" legislation. The argument runs that large firms will try to bankrupt their smaller competitors by undercutting these competitors' prices at loss-making levels, so that the large firms could attain monopoly status (so-called "predatory pricing"), and then afterwards these large monopolists would cut production and jack prices up to very high levels, so that they could generate significant profits (so-called "monopoly pricing"). Apparently, only the state can act to thwart this societal menace. Well, this argument is wrong in many respects.[53]

First, this phenomenon has never happened. This whole idea is merely a theory; there is not one single example of this occurring in U.S. history prior to the anti-trust legislation being passed. In fact, prior to passage of the legislation, the industries that have often been cited as the monopolistic villains justifying such legislation were actually *increasing* production and *lowering* prices faster than what was happening in the overall economy.[54]

Second, it makes no economic sense for an entrepreneur to engage in this practice.

Customers would stock up at the unusually low prices and simply shift

[53]One amusing note about the area of anti-trust legislation: some experts have noted that if a company puts its prices up, then it could be investigated for monopoly pricing; if it lowers its prices, then it could be investigated for predatory pricing; and if it keeps its prices constant, then it could be investigated for price-fixing (colluding with competitors to charge the same prices). Moreover, as Austrian economist Don Boudreaux has noted, it's odd that low pricing is singled out for attack by the state, since it is just one of many possible ways to attract customers and thus "harm" competitors. Other ways include more or better advertising, and investing in higher-quality products. It should be up to entrepreneurs, and not the state, to figure out the optimal way to best serve customers and thereby defeat competitors.

[54]See the historical work done in this area by Thomas DiLorenzo, which he wrote about in "The Origins of Antitrust: An Interest-Group Perspective," *International Review of Law and Economics*, Fall 1985, and "The Truth About Sherman," *Austrian Economics Newsletter*, Summer 1991.

their demand from the future to the present, so that when the entrepreneur later jacks up his prices, demand would be lower than it otherwise would have been.

Further, the losses could be potentially enormous for a large firm operating in many markets. Such a firm would have to price at a loss in *each* market to drive out all competitors in those markets.

In addition, once the entrepreneur has bankrupted his competitors and jacks up his prices, he would create the impetus for new competitors to enter the market and offer customers a better value-proposition. In fact, the new competitors would be able to purchase the bankrupt former competitors' assets at bargain prices, and thus be even more effective competition for the incumbent.

Third, the whole notion of anti-trust legislation is actually anti-consumer. The purpose of economic activity is to organize scarce resources to maximally satisfy consumer wants. Consumers benefit significantly from lower prices and, if firms want to engage in pricing wars, then all the better for consumers. No "predatory pricing" complaints ever come from consumers (why would consumers complain about lower prices?!); these complaints always come from the inefficient firms in an industry, which are trying to enlist the state's help to combat the lower prices offered by the more efficient firms.

However, in protecting firms that are inefficient—in that they are doing a relatively poor job of organizing scarce resources to satisfy consumer demand—the state only helps these less effective entrepreneurs tie up resources, when these resources could be better used by the more effective entrepreneurs.

Statists often retort that if inefficient firms go out of business, then jobs would be lost, but this is essentially an argument that it is more important to protect jobs than to satisfy consumer wants. We can see how absurd this idea is through a thought experiment. Imagine a world where all material consumer wants are satisfied by a deity, so that no one needs to work (although people could still choose to do so); in this world, everyone could devote their lives to leisure activities if they wish. Now consider a world where everyone has a job, but the job is to break large rocks into small stones; while everyone has a job, no one's actual wants are satisfied. In which world would you rather live? I repeat, the purpose of all economic activity is to satisfy consumer wants, not to provide jobs.

To the statist's follow-up argument that the state needs to use anti-trust enforcement to strike a balance between (a) allowing firms to satisfy consumer wants, and (b) protecting jobs, one could respond in two ways. First, who at the state is so omniscient to be able to strike this exquisite balance, knowing the wants of all relevant consumers and the economics of all relevant firms? Second, on what moral basis does anyone at the state have the right to forcibly interfere in the peaceful trades between entrepreneurs and consumers?

Anti-trust legislation is just another example of crony capitalism, where the weaker firms engage in political lobbying—making the "jobs" argument—to rent the state's coercive powers to help them compete.

Fourth, enduring monopolies are *only* a feature of a statist system; a monopoly cannot be sustained in the free market.

In the free market, customers only purchase products voluntarily, and entrepreneurs are free to enter an industry as new competitors at any time. Even if at any one point in time there is only one producer in an industry, if he is not supplying the right types of products at the right prices, then customers would abstain from purchasing. This would then create an opportunity for other entrepreneurs to enter the industry to serve the unsatisfied customer demand.

Just because other entrepreneurs have not entered the industry at any particular point in time doesn't mean the incumbent is doing anything wrong. In fact, just the opposite: if his products are in demand, then he should be lauded as the *only* entrepreneur who is currently satisfying customer demand! Think of all the individuals in society who are *not* taking business risk to try to satisfy this demand. They are the problem, not the incumbent.

Statists claim that there are some industries where the upfront financial capital investment required is so large, that long-run average costs would decline significantly as output expands, and thus a single producer would be able to produce at a lower cost than two producers, and hence offer lower prices. As such, this theory states that consumer welfare would be maximized if there were only one producer, the so-called "natural monopoly." Yet history shows that, absent state interference, (a) there has never been an instance of a single producer attaining lower long-run average costs than everyone else, thereby establishing a permanent monopoly, and (b) in every industry where it is claimed that a "natural monopoly" exists (e.g., utilities), there have been multiple producers. What the statist really means by a "natural monopoly" is that he believes that this product should be produced and priced in a particular way, and he cannot conceive of how multiple entrepreneurs and capital-providers, through trial and error, might be able to figure out how to produce it in a competitive environment at prices that customers would be willing to pay. It represents the arrogant substitution of the statist's intellectual limitations for the combined intellects of market entrepreneurs.

Only the state can create a sustainable monopoly, through granting an exclusive license to a firm to operate in a particular territory. This is what happens in those industries in which the state has determined a "natural monopoly" is appropriate. The entrepreneur who obtains this license—usually he is the most effective at lobbying, rather than being the most effective organizer of resources—has the state's power backing his monopoly status, meaning the state makes it illegal for any other entrepreneur to compete. There is nothing "natural" about that at all.[55]

Fifth, the idea of the state enforcing anti-trust legislation against perceived monopolies is really just a cruel joke. It is a perverse self-contradiction that the state—which is itself a coercive monopoly—acts to prevent private-sector monopolies from arising. Yet it exempts itself and its friends (the "natural monopolists") from this regime.

Myth #13: The "Hobbesian Fear"

Probably the most common reason a statist will cite to justify the state is what is known as the "Hobbesian fear." This refers to the concept that, without a state, everyone would be at constant war with everyone else, because this is man's nature.[56]

Under this line of thinking, the only way to prevent this constant state of war is to have a strong state, which is defined as an entity with a legal monopoly on the use of violence in a given geographical territory. The idea

[55] For a very good analysis of so-called "natural monopolies," see Thomas DiLorenzo's article, "The Myth of Natural Monopoly," *The Review of Austrian Economics* 9 (2), 1996.

[56] This is a loose rendition of the principle articulated by the English philosopher Thomas Hobbes in his 17th century book, *Leviathan*. Hobbes is often credited with creating the thought process behind the modern state.

is that this state would use (or threaten to use) force to prevent citizens initiating aggression against each other (as well as to protect them from foreign aggressors). To keep the peace, the state would be the only entity entitled to adjudicate disputes in its territory, including those in which the state itself is a party. In order to fund its operations, the state would be able to levy taxes on its citizens.

At this point, a number of rather obvious objections to this line of thinking should be jumping out of the page.

First, it's important to recall that "the state" is not an entity that can actually act; only individuals can act. Thus "the state" is just a code word for a select group of individuals.

Re-framed that way, what the Hobbesian argument is actually saying is that, in order to prevent person A from initiating or threatening aggression against person B or his property, and vice versa, person S is required to "keep the peace." However, what is it that S is actually doing in this function? Assuming either A or B has not explicitly consented to this arrangement (as to which, see the earlier discussion about true consent), S is forcibly expropriating some of the income of A and/or B (in the form of taxes), and forcibly telling A and/or B how they may live their lives and what they may do with their bodies and property (in the form of regulations). In other words, S is himself initiating or threatening aggression against A and B and their property.

This creates a self-contradiction: the alleged property protector is actually a property expropriator and violator. S might be ensuring peaceful relations between A and B, but the cost of this is S doing to A and B what they can no longer do to each other.[57] Thus we've simply substituted one Hobbesian danger for another. This is best illustrated by how the state acts against its own citizens when it is engaged in hostilities with declared "enemies," ostensibly protecting its citizens against such threats.[58]

For instance, in the U.S., the state has always used war to expand abuses against its own citizens. Examples include: **enslaving citizens** through

[57] Although this assumption about peaceful relations between A and B is dubious given that, as discussed earlier, A and B would lobby S to rent his coercive powers to use against the other.

[58] Never mind that most of these threats, if real, are caused by the state's prior interventions or, if not, are self-serving, falsely portrayed "crises."

military conscription to fight its wars (during the so-called "Civil War",[59] World Wars I and II, the Korean War, and the Vietnam War); **outlawing criticism** of the state and its key personnel, including censoring or closing down the press (through the 18th century Alien and Sedition Acts; by President Lincoln and his supporters during the "Civil War"; and again by the federal government in World Wars I and II); **harassing, incarcerating, plundering, torturing, and executing people** supporting or merely suspected of supporting the enemy (by President Lincoln and his supporters during the "Civil War"; the internment of those with Japanese backgrounds during World War II; the harassment of those suspected to be Communists during the Cold War; and, as part of the "War on Terror," using drones to execute Americans deemed by the president to be appropriate targets); **covertly tapping into private network communications** under the pretext of needing to ferret out the enemy within (most recently with the PATRIOT Act powers, and National Security Agency eavesdropping);[60] and **increasing the forced confiscation of its citizens' income** to pay for these hostilities, through higher taxation.[61]

Note that the alleged "threat" identified by the state as a pretext for its ac-

[59] This is a misnamed conflict. A "civil war" is when rival factions are fighting to seize control of the country's government, which was not the case in this conflict; rather, the U.S. government went to war against the government of the confederation of southern states, which had seceded from the U.S. More factually appropriate names include the "War of Northern Aggression," the "Second War of Secession" (the first being the American Revolutionary War), and the "War to Prevent Southern Independence."

[60] Statists will often respond, "If you're not doing anything wrong, then why do you care if the state monitors your private communications?" Leaving aside the creepy and uncivilized idea that one man is entitled to have access to the private communications of another, the problem is that "wrong" is defined by statists as an action or omission that the state arbitrarily defines as illegal at any point in time, as opposed to an actual act of violence against someone's person or property. Thus the state could use these intercepted communications to take direct action against someone for a victimless, regulatory "crime" (which is not a "wrong" in any natural sense of the word) or, more broadly, to pressure someone to act or refrain from acting, by threatening to disclose legitimate but nevertheless private or personally embarrassing information or activities.

[61] Taxation can be levied in one of three forms: direct, current taxation (the least politically feasible); deferred taxation through present borrowing (requiring future taxes to repay the debt); or implicit taxation through inflating the money supply (the most

tions could sometimes simply be an inanimate object, such as in the "War on Drugs." Some of the state's abuses listed above are now regular state actions in this *faux* war. The state's police are now highly militarized, and engage daily in many violent raids on its citizens' properties in search of the nefarious illegal narcotic, leading to death, injury, and property destruction.[62]

In addition, the state's police track citizens' movements,[63] seize their property, and generally ruin their lives for countless other victimless "crimes." These "crimes" are merely violations of arbitrary, state-created regulations, whereby individuals at the state tell citizens how they may live their lives and use their bodies and property.

The ability to forcibly control the population is a powerful "drug" for individuals at the state, but they need to keep coming up with new pretexts to keep selling this to the population. This is why the state is forever creating hysteria over "crises," where it can roll out "experts" to argue speciously that, without state intervention, the probability of death, destruction, economic impoverishment, and/or misery is substantial. Consider how the state has used the swine flu, Y2K, the occasional mass shooting, 9/11, global warming/climate change, the Global Financial Crisis, inequality, racism, Ebola, ISIS, the "Iran threat," the "Russia threat," trade deficits with China, illegal immigration, etc. to justify significant action by the state to forcibly interfere in citizens' lives.

So, given all of this, I say, thank heavens for S! Where would A and B be without him?

Second, in what other area of life does it make sense for one man to

---

politically feasible since it is the least discernible, which is why states jealously guard their monopoly on money creation).

[62] Even some of the glorified American Founding Fathers were guilty of this type of thing. In 1807, President Jefferson implemented an export embargo on private U.S. citizens in response to British aggression; his successor, President Madison, then implemented some legislation to strengthen enforcement, allowing the military to raid U.S. merchant ships and seize goods on the mere suspicion that they were intended for export.

[63] In early 2015, the U.S. government's program of capturing citizens' license plates to track their movements around the country came to light. Ostensibly this database was first established as part of the "War on Drugs" but, as is often the case, it is now being shared broadly among various law enforcement arms for other reasons.

allow a second to adjudicate disputes between the two of them, and for the second to tell the first how much it will cost him for this alleged benefit? The fact is, no man in his right mind would explicitly agree to this type of arrangement.

Third, the Hobbesian argument claims that the true nature of man is to go to war with his fellow man, instead of first looking for a way to peacefully resolve disputes. However, S is just as human as A and B. Thus if the true nature of A and B is to be at each other's throats, then that must also be true of S. Why then does it make sense for S to rule over A and B?[64]

Fourth, we ought to question the assumption that man's true nature is to go to war with or otherwise aggress against his fellow man. It is clear from everyday life that the vast majority of people do not commit violent crimes against their fellow men or their property, even when there is little to no risk of getting caught.[65] It is rarely the fear of punishment that produces this outcome but, more likely, one or both of the following reasons: (a) it is personally safer and cheaper to avoid violence, and to establish norms to settle disputes peacefully; and (b) man's innate sense of right and wrong.

Moreover, if the Hobbesian assumption were true, then mankind would have died out long ago; the fact that it hasn't, even when there were no strong states for long periods of time, shows that man is capable of devising non-violent means to resolve disputes.

As much as we are troubled by individual violent crime, it still constitutes a very small percentage of human activity. On the other hand, state-caused violence—external war or internal repression—is a much larger source of death in the world. This is because the individuals in charge of the state don't have to get involved in the actual violence, or directly bear its cost.

Fifth, if we need a state to prevent the initiation of aggression among citizens within a state, then shouldn't we also require a state to prevent the initiation of aggression among the individuals running different states? Those at the state are human too, and thus, if there is no world govern-

[64] Unless one believes in one of the Tooth Fairy Theories.

[65] Similarly, most people will perform acts of good, even if they aren't forced to do so, such as leaving tips, giving to charity, helping a neighbor, etc.

ment, then wouldn't they initiate aggression against the individuals running other states?[66] In other words, if the "Hobbesian fear" argument is true, then why should we ever settle for more than one state in the world?

Yet if you ask anyone who is part of running a nation-state if they too should be coercively governed by a higher power, the response is a resolute "no." They point to the concept of state sovereignty: internationally, all states are equal, none can rule over another, and all actions between states are generally worked out by consensual agreement. However, these state entities are just collections of humans. In other words, those at the state believe that they are equal with, and can work things out peacefully with, their fellow statesmen. But, importantly, they don't believe that their own citizens could work things out peacefully among themselves without a coercive ruler.

If these individuals at the state regard themselves as having sovereignty vis-à-vis other statesmen, meaning the full right and power to act without any coercive rule by these other statesmen, then why couldn't all individuals *within* their state claim similar sovereignty? Is there something magical about a geographical area known as a "nation-state," such that within this area there is no respect for individual sovereignty, but as between the rulers of different nation-states there is?

Sixth, if the "Hobbesian fear" is truly the justification for the state's legitimacy, then the state should be strictly limited to two activities, namely, preventing violence against its citizens and resolving disputes; essentially, police, national defense, and courts. Yet the modern state undertakes hundreds of activities costing billions of dollars per year that have nothing to do with "keeping the peace." Perversely, many of these state activities actually involve *outlawing* peaceful activities by citizens (regulatory "crimes").

Thus the state has grown well beyond its alleged Hobbesian rationale, rendering this argument even less credible.

[66]See footnote 64.

V. Busting the Myths about Libertarianism

Statists are very quick to dismiss libertarianism, but few statists, if any, spend much time studying libertarian ideas in depth. It seems odd that, even when presented with the opportunity to take a fresh look at the question of the state versus the individual, a statist wouldn't first explore libertarian ideas before reaching a definitive conclusion. It's almost as if the statist is afraid of what he might discover.

Due to their lack of substantive knowledge about libertarianism, statists subscribe to a number of myths about this political philosophy. There is a very rich body of intellectual work underlying the libertarian philosophy which answers all of the usual questions statists pose but which, sadly, is mostly unexplored by statists (a small subset of this work is listed in the Reading Guide at the end of this book).

This section is not intended to be a treatise on how a libertarian world might operate; that could be the subject of an entire book in and of itself. Instead, this section is merely intended to try to address some of the most common myths about libertarianism, and to whet the appetite of the intellectually curious reader.

What Is Libertarianism?

For the human species to survive and flourish, man must use his body to work the earth's physical resources to transform these resources into products that satisfy humans' needs. However, people and physical resources are scarce relative to needs, and thus conflicts necessarily arise as to the control of these human bodies and physical resources. In fact, it is more basic than that: the *only* reason that conflicts arise in society is due to disputes over who has the right to control physical property (i.e., human bodies and physical objects). This is because one person's control of physical property necessarily excludes another's. For instance, either I can stand in this physical space or someone else can, but we both can't; either I can decide what to put in my body or someone else can decide for me, but we both can't; either I can control this widget or someone else can, but we both can't.[1]

Given that these disputes arise in all societies, political philosophy is essentially the search for a set of principles to determine who in such disputes has the better right to the physical property in question. These principles are known as "property rights," and, if generally adhered to, can minimize conflict by heading off disputes in advance. Different political philosophies claim to have different property-rights regimes.

To the socialist, conceptually "the people" (as one mass) own all physical property. However, when it comes to actually making decisions about what can be done with this property, a much smaller group gets to make these decisions—the ruling elite—and thus in fact the ruling elite exercises all the powers normally attached to ownership. The rest of the people are forcibly prohibited from challenging the ruling elite's decisions.

To the theocrat, conceptually either the deity owns all physical property, or individuals can own property but subject to divine constraints. However, when it comes to actually making decisions about what can be done with this property, a much smaller group gets to interpret the deity's desires—the priesthood—and thus in fact the priesthood exercises all the powers normally attached to ownership. The rest of the people are forcibly prohibited from challenging the priesthood's decisions.

To the democrat, conceptually individuals can own their own bodies

[1]Consistent with this analysis, libertarianism doesn't recognize property rights in intangibles, such as information or ideas, because there cannot be a conflict over their use; my use of an idea doesn't preclude your use. Statists claim that if A uses B's original idea, then A has deprived B of the "value" he has created with that idea. However, B cannot have a right to any particular "value," since this only comes from customers voluntarily paying B for his products, and B cannot have a right to his potential customers' funds! What if B's products were simply shoddy and no one bought them? What if A didn't use B's idea but, nevertheless, competed successfully against B and lured away B's former customers? B has no right to his customers' funds and, therefore, no right to any particular "value" for his ideas, products, or business. Accordingly, if A uses B's idea for A's own benefit, then A has not wrongfully taken any property from B for which B is entitled to restitution.

and other physical property. However, when it comes to actually making decisions about what can be done with bodies and other physical property, a much smaller group gets to make these decisions—the elected class and their appointed agents, through legislation—and thus in fact the elected class exercises all the powers normally attached to ownership. The rest of the people are forcibly prohibited from challenging the elected class's decisions.[2]

If the description of democracy sounds like a duplication of the descriptions of how socialism and theocracy work, then that's because it is! In a democracy, the political class—meaning the combined executive, legislature, judiciary, and bureaucracy—can tell a person (a) what he is entitled to or must do with his body (e.g., to where he can travel, what he can put in his body, what work or leisure activities he can perform with his body, with whom he must work or otherwise associate, what he can say, what he can read, who he must or can kill, etc.), and (b) what he is entitled to do with his property (e.g., what he can keep from what he earns, what he can buy and at what price, how he can use what he is allowed to keep or buy, to whom he can sell it and at what price, etc.). The only material philosophical difference between socialism, theocracy, and democracy is how the rulers are chosen: in socialism and modern theocracies, it has most often been through violent revolution; in the case of democracy, it has been through a subset of the population voting. However, the voting process in a democracy doesn't change the fact that no one who objects to the rulers' decisions about property usage may opt-out, and do with his body and property as he pleases.

The libertarian property-rights regime, however, is quite different from every other political philosophy. It is this: no person may initiate aggression (or threaten the same) against another's body or legitimate property. This is known as the "non-aggression principle" or "NAP."

Consistent with the NAP, legitimate title to non-human property can be acquired only in one of three ways: (a) by a person physically work-

[2]Note that today's democracies are technically fascist in an economic sense. Under economic fascism, private ownership is recognized, but the state uses such a heavy regulatory hand that in essence the state controls the use of all factors of production, even if it does not technically claim ownership over them (this differs from socialism only in that, under socialism, the state actually claims ownership of all factors of production).

ing previously unowned property using peacefully obtained means, so as to objectively evidence the earliest direct control ("homesteading"); (b) through a voluntary transfer agreement entered into by one person with another who legitimately owns the property ("contracting"); or (c) by one person seizing the legitimately owned property of another who has initiated a violent act against the first person ("restitution").[3] In none of these ways does the new owner initiate aggression against another to acquire the property: in the case of homesteading, no one yet owns the property, so there is no one from whom to take it with aggression; in the case of contracting, the current owner is voluntarily agreeing to transfer ownership; and, in the case of restitution, the current owner, through his initial commission of a violent act, is "estopped" (prohibited) from objecting to the seizure of his property, on the grounds that he who initiates aggression cannot then complain about retaliatory force being directed back at him by the victim.

While the contracting and restitution principles probably don't require much more explanation, the homesteading principle might.[4]

The first thing to note about the homesteading principle is that it is based on the idea that everyone has the best claim to his own body.

If a person has the best claim to his own body, then he must surely have the best claim to anything his body physically and peacefully produces (leaving aside any voluntary agreement that he enters into to the contrary). Thus if a person works previously unowned property, then he must have the best claim to the product of that work. It would be very hard to argue that someone else has a better claim to this product, for this would imply that this other person somehow has a superior claim to the first person's body. And if every man has a superior claim to every other man's body, then there is the problem of circularity—A controls B's body and yet B controls A's body—and it would mean that no man could ever act without getting everyone else's consent, which would be impossible to obtain. Mankind would not survive.

[3] I am assuming that it is not necessary to discuss why a person should be the sole decision-maker with respect to his body, but there is significant libertarian work on even this point ("self-ownership").

[4] This is not to suggest that there are no nuances with respect to contracting and restitution. Matters such as what is a valid contract and what evidence can be adduced as proof, and what is reasonable restitution, would all need to be worked out by a libertarian justice system, just as is the case in a statist "justice" system.

The second thing to note about the homesteading principle is that it invalidates the notion that individuals at the state can claim previously unowned property as "public property."

A mere verbal claim of ownership is insufficient; the person claiming to have homesteaded unowned property must have applied material physical effort to the property, and made it obvious to others that he is in control, e.g., by constructing a fence around virgin land, by putting apples picked in the wild into his basket, etc. A mere verbal claim fails to meet the previously mentioned objective of establishing a property-rights regime which minimizes conflict. If all that were necessary is a verbal claim—which only requires a trivial effort by the claimant—then everyone could allege that they made the first verbal claim, and they could allege that their claim related to all unowned property on the face of the earth. That would increase conflict, not minimize it.

In addition, since homesteading is intended to be a peaceful means of property acquisition, the person claiming to have homesteaded property must not have used violently obtained means, for then all the things that he does with such means would be tainted. Thus if the state were to use forced labor (e.g., prisoners, conscripted draftees, etc.) to apply effort to and delineate borders around some unowned property, or to use taxes to purchase the requisite labor services and bordering materials, then this would not qualify as homesteading, because the labor and/or taxes were coercively obtained.

The third thing to understand about homesteading is to consider the consequences of what it would mean to reject this principle. If the first person to work some unowned property is not to be regarded as the permanent owner (assuming he doesn't voluntarily transfer it to someone else, or have it seized in a restitution procedure), then who should be so regarded? There are only three other possibilities.

First, everyone in the world owns such property in common, and thus everyone's consent would be required before anything could be done with it. However, in this case, how could any decisions ever be made about what to do with this property? It would effectively be rendered useless. Mankind would cease to exist if no decisions could be made about how to use property.

Second, the property remains unowned despite the act of homesteading, i.e., no one could ever own property. If this were the case, then the effect would be that either all property would be rendered useless, or there would be perpetual conflict over property which could never be peacefully resolved.

Third, some other person who later acts on the property is to be regarded as the owner (a "latecomer"). However, if this were the case, then ownership would only ever be temporary. A person who owns some property at any point in time would have to live with the perpetual fear that a latecomer might come along and seize the property (and it's not clear *how* a latecomer could legitimately "seize" the property from the current owner). This would reduce the current owner's incentives to apply more resources to the property (i.e., to invest in improving it), as he would be liable to lose control over it at any time, and it would truly be survival of the strongest. Imagine the state of an apartment which has no permanent landlord and is liable to be taken over by a new tenant at any time. Mankind certainly wouldn't flourish anywhere near its maximum potential if everyone viewed property in this way.[5]

There is not much more to libertarianism than the above principles, but the libertarian insists that they be applied consistently to every single human being, on the grounds that all men are metaphysically equal, so there is no cogent justification for some men being entitled to live by a different behavioral code.

Thus, based on the NAP, the libertarian *rejects* the notions that: (a) someone can force another person to do with his body as the first person requires, which is what the individuals at the state do when they regulate people's actions, conscript them for war, and require them to serve on juries; (b) someone can take or control another person's existing property without his voluntary agreement or a proper restitution procedure, which is what the individuals at the state do when they tax, seize, or regulate people's property; and (c) the individuals at the state can legitimately claim ownership of previously unowned land, water, air, and natural resources lying beneath the surface, since these are claims made over unowned property using other resources which were illegitimately acquired.[6]

---

[5]Indeed, this is how the modern state operates! Citizens can only keep and use their property until such time as the more powerful state personnel take away all or some of the benefits of ownership, which they do through taxation, eminent domain seizure, and regulation. Similarly, citizens can only do with their bodies those things which state personnel don't restrict through regulation.

[6]The corollary to these principles is that the state cannot even legitimately own property

To anticipate a statist objection, when the libertarian states that people should be able to use their body and property as they see fit, this does *not* mean that they may use them to initiate murder, rape, kidnap, or assault, or theft or destruction of another's property. Those actions would themselves be a breach of the NAP, and thus would be illegitimate in a libertarian society. However, the corollary to this is that those at the state may also not initiate these actions, which therefore rules out taxation, regulation, conscription, involuntary incarceration for non-violent crimes, etc.

To anticipate another statist objection, the NAP only proscribes the *initiation* of aggressive actions, but does not proscribe *responding* with such actions in appropriate circumstances. Thus A may legitimately use force against B in self-defense, provided B initiated the violence, and C may legitimately seize D's property as restitution or retribution for D having initiated aggression against C or his property.[7] The libertarian objection to the traditional actions of individuals at the state is that, through taxation, regulation, and enforcement, they *initiate* the taking of the property and/or the incarceration of others when these others have not themselves breached the NAP.

Libertarianism, then, is simply a philosophy about when actual or threatened violence is acceptable. However, libertarians recognize actual or threatened violence in *all* areas of society, rather than giving a "pass" to those at the state, i.e., libertarianism is a universal standard, not a selective one. But, beyond this, libertarianism does not prescribe any particular behavioral norms for mankind. Those norms are left to be defined by one's culture, ethnicity, regional customs, family traditions, religion, trade, education, etc. Accordingly, the NAP is only a minimum, and not a comprehensive, behavioral standard.

Put another way, libertarianism is a philosophy which minimizes aggression while maximizing personal freedom. What's not to like about that?

---

which the current owner voluntarily agrees to sell to the state, since the state is using illegitimately acquired resources (tax funds) to purchase this property.

[7]Obviously lots of questions arise as to when someone "initiates" violence, and what punishment and compensation theories are valid (deterrence, rehabilitation, restitution, retribution, etc.). However, these are questions that any system has to work out over time, and are not unique to libertarianism, although there is significant scholarly libertarian work on these issues.

Myth #14: Libertarians Are Utopian!

Statists like to claim that libertarians are utopian, and that libertarianism is unworkable. It's worth exploring these concepts a little further.

The Kids Get It!

Statists reliably teach their young children two basic rules governing interaction with other children, and these rules neatly sum up libertarianism: "Don't hit the other kids, and don't take their stuff."

Yet when the statist's child is old enough to learn about politics, the statist turns his philosophy around 180° and tells his child that, provided you can get enough people to support you (i.e., get elected), you are free to effectively hit or threaten to hit others, and to take their stuff.

Thus, by their own characterization, statists start out as "utopian" teachers to their children! If they only stopped there...

Exactly Who Is Utopian?

A commonly accepted definition of "utopia" is a place of ideal although unattainable perfection, especially in laws, government, and social conditions.

Consider, however, what the statist believes: (a) that individuals at the state, who have an awesome monopoly on coercion in a region, will only act selflessly and will impose limits on themselves;[8] (b) that, as a result, "limited government" is possible, even though, in the history of the nation-state, all that has ever happened is that the state has grown enormously; (c) that there are some individuals who are so omniscient as to be able to discern a "common good" for millions of other people, and to efficiently manage the flow of society's resources to attain that end; (d) accordingly, with respect to any particular economy, that relying on a coercively imposed, central-planning monopoly is more likely to maximize individual consumers' satisfaction than decentralized competition; and (e) that use of centrally directed force as the first tool to resolve societal conflicts is likely to lead to a more peaceful society.

[8]In other words, that the Tooth Fairy Theories are credible explanations of humanity.

On the other hand, libertarians accept human foibles for what they are, and believe that these foibles are inherent in everyone, without exception, and thus look to mitigate the impact of these foibles by objecting to the centralization of coercive power in any individuals. The libertarian recognizes that there is no "common good" among millions of different people (or, if there is, no human could discern it), but that each individual has his own preferences, and that since no man could produce sufficient goods to satisfy all of his preferences, he must trade with others to obtain what he cannot produce for himself. In a truly voluntary society, the norm would be that, to obtain something you want, you first have to produce something someone else wants, and then engage in an exchange, which, by definition, means that there would be mutual gain (this is not a fantasy: although we live in a statist world, millions of these exchanges occur daily). Accordingly, everyone who is compliant would be looking to peacefully "please" others as the route to their own happiness, as opposed to being able to forcefully impose their needs on others (which is what the state allows people to do). Those who are not compliant, and who initiate aggression, could still be restrained or excluded by force.

To think about these differences in another way, consider goals. The statist has very lofty goals for which he wishes to employ the state, such as "equality," "save the planet," "no discrimination," "free or low-cost healthcare, housing, and education for all," "spread democracy," etc. To attain these goals—if any of them are actually attainable—requires complex interactions among millions of humans, in specific sequences, and at specific places and times. No one brain or group of brains is able to comprehend, never mind plan and implement, the actions that need to take place. On the other hand, the libertarian goal is entirely within the control of each individual: don't hit anyone or take their stuff.

Now, exactly *who* is utopian?

The statist never really compares the state as it *actually* works against the few glimpses of the free market that we could find in the real world, presumably because the evidence is so dauntingly adverse to his position; for instance, what serves consumers better, our state-controlled military, healthcare/health insurance, financial, and education systems, or the private-sector iPhone and bread-supply systems? Instead, the statist imagines that the individuals at the state have super-human powers to achieve the statist's ambitious, but wholly unrealistic, central planning objectives, and compares this to the imperfection of the decentralized free market, which is operated by mere humans. This is not utopian thinking?

The libertarian, rather than expecting utopia, simply believes that the NAP is the most just governance principle, because it outlaws (although by no means eradicates) the initiation of force, and thus violent conflict. In contrast, the statist believes that the most just way to run society is to institutionalize violent conflict by empowering those individuals at the state to initiate or threaten force.

Only "Negative" Rights (Duties) Are Workable[9]

Moral philosophy deals principally with the search for just principles of interaction among humans. Three minimum requirements for a just system are that the principles (a) are technically feasible, (b) are universal, and (c) promote human survival. The first requirement hopefully is self-evident; it makes no sense to argue for principles that cannot work in the real world. The second requirement simply recognizes that all men are metaphysically equal, and thus no man has any natural entitlement to special treatment (for better or worse). The third requirement recognizes that the other two are not sufficient if we are trying to sustain humanity and human interaction (if we are not, then it is pointless to try to reason out a moral philosophy!). For instance, a philosophy that advocates all men commit suicide would be workable and universal, but hardly achieves much in the way of sustaining humanity.

So how do libertarianism and statism measure up as moral philosophies?

Libertarianism's central principle is non-aggression, which is a negative right. As such, it is a behavioral standard that, as a technical matter, *can* be universally applied, meaning that it is technically possible for every man to live by this standard concurrently with every other man. This is because

---

[9] In philosophy, a duty is the correlative of a right. Thus if A has the "duty" not to initiate force against B, then B has the "right" not to be aggressed against by A. Accordingly, one could describe the NAP as a "negative right" or a "negative duty." The commonly used terminology which captures the general concept is "negative rights," which I have therefore used here.

the NAP simply outlines what one *cannot* do to his fellow man, namely, initiate interference with his body or property. There cannot be any conflict among men if everyone's negative rights are respected. Everyone could live with and profit from the non-initiation of force at the same time (however, as noted earlier, but it bears repeating, the NAP is a minimum, as opposed to a comprehensive, behavioral code). Thus the libertarian philosophy provides a workable, universal standard and, as noted above, it also inherently discourages (outlaws) violent conflict, and hence promotes human survival.

In contrast with libertarianism, the statist's philosophy has many positive rights embedded in it, meaning that it prescribes what one man can take from another's property or require of another's body (through taxes and regulations, backed up by the threat of force).[10] The reliance on positive rights backed by the initiation of force means that statism *cannot* provide a workable, universal standard that promotes human survival. **First**, one man's positive rights necessarily conflict with another man's negative and positive rights. As to the positive/negative rights conflict, the person who is forced by another to give up something he owns, or do something with his body, has his negative right to be left alone violated, so the statist must necessarily argue that some men don't have these negative rights (but why, and how are these men to be identified?). As to the positive/positive rights conflict, given scarcity, positive rights cannot be universally applied to and enjoyed by every man concurrently, as not everyone could enjoy the right to the same physical object at the same time. In fact, only one man could use any physical object at a time, so who gets to choose who prevails? **Second**, if the statist argues that his philosophy involves a universal princi-

[10] As a technical matter, libertarianism also recognizes positive duties, but *only* if they are voluntarily assumed, as opposed to involuntarily (forcibly) imposed by legislation, which is the hallmark of statism's positive duties. In libertarianism, one could voluntarily assume a positive duty either by entering into a contract, or by actively putting someone in a precarious position. As an example of the latter (per libertarian attorney Stephan Kinsella), if you push someone into a lake, then you assume the positive duty to rescue them, whereas if you merely walk by and see someone in the lake struggling, then you cannot be forced to rescue them (even though it might be the right thing to do as a fellow human). As another example, the parents of a newborn, by bringing the helpless child into the world, assume a positive duty to arrange for the due care of the child, until he is independently capable of looking after himself.

ple, then he would have to argue that every man has the right to use force to take what he wants. Does that really make sense as a behavioral standard to promote human survival?

Accordingly, whereas the NAP is technically feasible, universalizable, and designed to discourage conflict, statism's use-of-force principle is either not universal (if it implies that only some men are entitled to initiate force), or is an "all against all" principle that can only lead to ultimate societal degradation. Hence I would argue that it is statism, as opposed to libertarianism, that is not a workable moral philosophy.

* * * * *

To the extent that the statist is aware of the NAP, he often misunderstands its implication. One major criticism levied by statists is that believing in the NAP is nice, but it's just like saying "Do the right thing," namely, it's apt to regularly fail, since some people would still act aggressively. However, the purpose of the NAP is *not* to eradicate aggression (although the more people who subscribe to the NAP, the less aggression there would be) but, rather, to *allocate liability* based on this principle. Libertarians fully recognize that there will always be aggression and disputes, but suggest that the NAP be the guiding principle in resolving these disputes.

Myth #15: It's Every Man for Himself!

This is a favorite among statists. They envision the libertarian as a rugged individualist, perhaps a survivalist, who wants to "live off the grid," on his own island, barely interacting with others. This only shows how poorly statists understand libertarianism, society, and basic economics.

There's More to Society Than the State

In between the individual and the state, there are many voluntary forms of association. There are families, neighborhoods, businesses, marketplaces, religious groups, common interest associations (e.g., athletic groups, artistic groups, musical groups, etc.), charities, mutual-aid societies, etc. All of these groups allow humans to voluntarily interact with each other to serve their needs. Since they are voluntarily formed groups, interactions only occur because the respective parties believe that they will each benefit.[11]

All of these forms of association and their related human interaction would continue to exist in a libertarian world; *only* the state would cease to exist. Statists wrongly perceive the libertarian as being *for* only one thing, namely, himself. In fact, the libertarian is not for any one thing, rather, he is *against* only one thing, namely, the initiation or threat of force, whether by an individual aggressor or the state.

Only Individuals Have Rights

Statists misinterpret the libertarian focus on "individual rights." This does not mean that libertarians are against groups. Rather, it simply means that, to the libertarian, rights are defined at the individual level; only individuals can have rights and be wronged. While the libertarian advocates for every individual to have the right not to be coerced, he is not arguing in any sense against the existence of, or participation in, broader societal groups (if voluntarily formed).

In contrast, the statist is category-focused. He puts each individual into one or more categories (e.g., "blacks," "women," "workers," "the wealthy," "immigrants," etc.), regards each individual in a category as being identical to every other when it comes to advocating for state policies, and believes that rights are "group rights."[12]

Libertarians regard each individual as unique and irreplaceable. Thus the libertarian is the champion of each individual as his own sovereign being, and not just as some member of a category.

---

[11] This is not to say that these groups don't have rules which "bind" members. They do. However, unlike with the state, each member is free to join the group and to leave the group if he no longer wants to be bound; without his explicit consent, a person cannot be obliged to pay anything to such a group; and a person can be a member of multiple groups at once.

[12] The most abhorrent aspect of the statist's classification of humans into categories relates to national aggression. If state X (either through its military or one of its citizens) attacks state Y, or offends the sensibilities or refuses to comply with the demands of state Y, then when state Y responds, it does not differentiate between the guilty and innocent individuals in state X. All are "fair game" for retribution, threats, sanctions, etc., since all belong in the same category, namely, "the enemy, state X."

Not Isolationist

The libertarian is a staunch advocate for free trade between individuals, which contradicts the notion that libertarians are isolationist.

As discussed earlier, no man could produce for himself all that he needs, and any man would be foolish to try to do so, since every man can profit from specializing in what he does relatively better, and trading with other men who do other things relatively better. This concept—the division of labor—has been one of the greatest boons to global wealth creation over the past few centuries, and is partially responsible for moving man out of a subsistence existence to where he is today.

The libertarian recognizes this, and his "individual rights" principles do not in any way reduce his appetite for specialization and trade. All libertarianism demands is that specialization and trade be voluntary, not coerced.

Only Individuals Can Act

The statist assumes that his preferred form of collectivism is superior to the so-called "individualism" that he sees within libertarianism, without really thinking too hard about what collectivism means.[13]

A group cannot think or act; only individuals can think and act. Thus, even within collectivism, some individual has to make and implement a final decision. That individual, as a human being, would bring to that decision and its implementation his personal biases, incompetence, and ideology.

Under statism, the ruling individual's personal biases, incompetence, and ideology would, through his enactment or enforcement of legislation, or execution of foreign policy, be coercively imposed on everyone under his rule, whether they want to have any interaction with this person or not. In contrast, in a libertarian society, no individual's personal biases, incompetence, or ideology would be imposed on anyone except for those who voluntarily choose to interact with that individual (assuming, of course, that such individual is not violating the NAP).

In other words, statism is really just one person's individualism forcibly imposed on others.

---

[13]Note that the libertarian has no quarrel with "collectivism" if it is voluntary, such as many forms of societal groups. It is *forced* collectivism (the state) that is objectionable.

Myth #16: Libertarianism = Chaos!

Statists assume that the absence of govern*ment* in a libertarian society means an absence of govern*ance*, and thus that libertarianism implies societal chaos. Nothing could be further from the truth.

The Market Could Provide Law and Security

Libertarianism assumes that there would be conflicts that would need to be resolved, requiring adjudication tribunals using developed bodies of law, similar to how today's courts function. Libertarianism also assumes that there would be aggression, both from individuals and, if they exist, states, thus requiring protective services, similar to today's police and military forces.

The principal way in which libertarianism differs from statism in the areas of law and security is that libertarianism implies that policing, courts, and defense would, like all other services, be provided by competitive suppliers who would only earn revenues from customers who have freely entered into contracts with them. Accordingly, these service-providers would have to provide ongoing value and innovation to keep their customers. Contrast this with statism, where these types of services are generally provided by a state monopoly, which means compelled revenues in the form of taxation (likely increasing over time), and ever-lower service levels.

Libertarianism also assumes that bodies of law would be developed locally from the ground up through adjudication of actual disputes, as was the case historically before states forcibly assumed legislative power (as discussed earlier). Contrast this with the arbitrary, top-down, statist legislation of today that applies to all citizens prospectively, even those not involved in any dispute.[14]

The statist's argument in the area of law and security is essentially the

[14] Note that top-down, "one-size-fits-all" legislation requires more heavy-handed enforcement than adjudication principles developed from the bottom up from actual disputes. This is because, in the case of the former, there is no communal "buy in," because citizens have not been involved in arguing for and against the rules, and these rules may not reflect local customs but, rather, the arbitrary whims of distant legislators.

"public goods" argument, namely, that if we don't have a state monopoly providing these services, then these services wouldn't be provided at all, or else only in insufficient amounts. Earlier I detailed the problems with the "public goods" argument from the historical, moral, and economic perspectives, and so will not do so again here.

However, the statist's argument also fails because it does not acknowledge that history shows quite convincingly that, if there is demand for a product, then individuals will rise to the occasion and develop the product without the state's involvement (sometimes as entrepreneurs, other times as end-users). Simply because the statist sitting in his living room can't envision how this would unfold doesn't mean that it wouldn't get done; it just means that the statist is clearly not going to be the person who develops the solution! No one ever sat down and centrally mapped out how money or language might develop. There was a need for these two concepts, and so individuals engaged in trial and error until they found the optimal solutions (at least until money was forcibly taken over and debased by the state for its own ends). The statist cannot explain logically why the default should always be a coercive, monopoly provider simply because he cannot conceive of how something might develop differently.

It is beyond the scope of this book to go into detail about how law and security services might be provided in a libertarian society. No one could say for sure, just as no one could have predicted in advance how things such as today's communications technologies or variety of breakfast cereals would develop. Indeed, if it were possible to specify exactly how things would be configured in the future, then that would be the best argument for statism, as then central planning might work!

There is, however, a very rich body of intellectual work that exists in this area to provide some guiding thoughts, based both on historical and current examples, and compelling logic. Drawing on this material, below I will provide a glimpse of what a libertarian law & order system *might* look like. I will discuss national defense separately, later.

Self-Defense

The first thing to note relates to self-protection. To minimize resistance to the state's edicts, states typically seek to disarm their citizens through gun-control legislation. The alleged "deal" imposed coercively by the state is that citizens give up their right to arm themselves in return for the state's protection from violent crime. Yet when the state's police cannot realistically be at the scene of every (or perhaps any) violent crime while it is actually occurring, of what value is this "deal"?

In a libertarian world, there would be no restrictions on firearm ownership, which would significantly increase each citizen's self-defense options.[15] Of course there would be liability, as there is today, for misusing firearms to initiate aggression against others.

Policing

Beyond enhanced self-protection, in a libertarian world, instead of being forced to pay taxes to the state to fund a "one-size-fits-all" police force, individuals would choose among different "protection services" firms, and voluntarily pay them for their services. These service-providers would compete on price and service, and would offer a menu of different options. Unlike the state's police, those providers that fail to serve actual customer demand would go out of business, and those that meet demand would make profits.[16]

There might be firms that specialize in residential-premises protection, and others that specialize in commercial-premises protection. Some might emphasize "feet-on-the-street," preventive community policing, others might prefer the technology-based approach to surveillance, and still others might provide undercover policing. Some might arm their personnel with firearms, others merely with less lethal means. Some might focus on hiring certain ethnic types to provide ethnic-group-oriented services in the appropriate neighborhoods.

Unlike the state's police, security firms would have no special immunity for their actions. Those firms that act with excessive violence when performing their services would lose customers who do not support this

[15]Note, however, that in a libertarian society, all property in use would be privately owned, and it would be entirely consistent with libertarianism for a private-property owner to prohibit possession of firearms on his property.

[16]This is not fanciful; the industry already exists in the U.S. today. In fact, there are more private security personnel than state police.

type of policing and, as word gets around, they might not be able to attract new customers. They might also face lawsuits from those against whom they act with excessive violence; if they lose these lawsuits, then payment of the judgments would increase their operating costs. Such companies might then try to pass these higher costs on to their customers in the form of higher prices or reduced services. However, this would cause these firms to lose customers to competitors which have lower operating costs because they are less violent, and thus could offer better pricing and/or service options.

Criminal Justice

Crime would no longer be something for which the state takes action; it would exclusively be a matter between the victim and the aggressor, and victims would be able to take action against aggressors without being stymied by state intervention.

The definition of "crime" would be limited to initiating aggression against another person's body or legitimate property, i.e., there would be no victimless "crimes" arbitrarily created by state regulation. Thus the law would once again become comprehensible to everyone, and policing by security firms would be more focused and thus more efficient; these firms would only be concerned with protecting against or investigating actual violent acts against person or property.

Instead of the state's approach to punishment—which tends to be focused on deterrence and rehabilitation (although the state's system is woeful at achieving even these objectives)—different punishment systems would arise in different communities, based on what is acceptable in those communities. It is likely that these systems may all be based on restitution, but some might also provide for retribution.

Victims who, for ethical or practical reasons, don't want to exact the maximum acceptable punishment on their aggressors could agree with the aggressors on lesser punishments on a customized basis. A victim who exacted more than an acceptable punishment on an aggressor would himself be liable to be sued by the aggressor for unjustified violence, which would therefore place limits on how aggressively victims act.

Adjudication of Disputes

Disputes would be adjudicated by private mediation and arbitration firms.[17] Different firms would offer different types of dispute-resolution procedures, with some specializing in different subject matters, and others specializing by geography, religion, culture, or other factors.

Those "judges" who develop a reputation for fairness and subject-matter competence would garner more business, and those who develop a reputation for undue bias and/or incompetence would lose business.

Different groups—such as Catholics, orthodox Jews, Quakers, those against capital punishment, etc.—might prefer to use their own forums to adjudicate intra-group disputes, so that they could ensure that their own customs are taken into account. For inter-group disputes, the parties would have to agree on an independent adjudicator, and when successful, independent adjudicators render judgments acceptable to both groups, this would cause the different groups' legal norms to converge.[18]

Enforcement

If a victim couldn't or didn't want to pursue an aggressor himself, then he might be able to retain an enforcement company to do this for him (or even sell this company his right to punish the aggressor).[19] Perhaps the enforcement company would be entitled to a fee based on the speed of solving the crime, and/or the amount of compensation it recovers for the victim from the aggressor. Therefore, unlike today's police, such a company would be aligned with the victim's interests, and would be highly motivated to solve the crime, pursue the aggressor, and exact the punishment. Yet, unlike today's police, this enforcement company would have no special immunity. Accordingly, if this company employed excessive violence in its activities, then it could face lawsuits from the original aggressors, and thus poten-

[17] This actually happens today; private mediation and arbitration is a large and growing industry due to dissatisfaction with state court systems.

[18] Historically, this is how all legal systems developed: use of local customs, and community acceptance of gradual changes in norms to deal with new situations that arise.

[19] The transfer of enforcement rights is generally a feature of insurance today. Policyholders agree to let their insurance company pursue the other party, in return for quick payment from their insurer.

tially incur higher operating costs, as well as develop a bad reputation, all of which could spell trouble for its business model.

If an aggressor developed a bad reputation by (a) being a repeat offender, (b) not submitting to dispute-resolution procedures, or (c) not complying with judgments against him, then, depending on societal norms, then he would risk being subject to force and/or being ostracized by his personal and/or business community, and he could be excluded from local trade or employment or, since all property would be privately owned, by the owners of local roads, stores, schools, etc.

Companies might arise which specialize in tracking such aggressors, creating easily accessible "reputation reports" like today's credit reports; these reports would be used by the community to deny such aggressors access to all sorts of private property, employment, or trade. Thus, rather than forcibly remove these aggressors to the brutal confines of today's state prisons, the community's punishment might be widespread physical exclusion.

Detention

For those aggressors who are sufficiently ostracized and thus have nowhere else to go, detention companies might arise which offer room, board, and employment, provided these aggressors agree to certain behavior guidelines and supervision. If aggressors owe debts to their victims (or the victims' enforcement companies) which they cannot pay, then these detention companies might purchase these debts, and give the aggressors the opportunity to work off their debts in the employ of the detention companies (or their nominees) while being confined as agreed.

The detention companies might offer to the aggressors to certify to the reputation-tracking companies that, once the aggressors have worked off their debts and/or maintained certain behavior standards, they are deemed "rehabilitated" and could be taken off the list of those to be shunned by society.

Unlike today's state prisons, the detention companies might compete with each other to attract aggressors, since they could make a profit on the aggressors' labor, and thus there would be some efforts to provide acceptable living conditions for the aggressors. If these detention companies breach their agreements with the aggressors, or employ undue aggression against them, then they could in turn be sued by the aggressors. In this type of environment, the aggressors are much more likely to be rehabilitated, and gain/maintain valuable job skills, than they are in today's "rape factories" and "violence training camps" that masquerade as state prisons.

The Role of Insurers

As a final thought, it's likely that individuals and businesses wouldn't necessarily have to contract with all of these different companies separately to obtain these services. Instead, life, health, property, and liability insurers might undertake the effort to choose, contract with, pay, and monitor the various service-providers, and bundle a "law & order package" into their insurance policies.[20] The benefit to the insurer arises because the insurer is the firm which would be liable to compensate a policyholder who is the victim of aggression, so if the protection services could reduce violent crime, and the adjudication and enforcement services could speed resolution of disputes, then the insurer's costs would be lower.

In the case of a dispute between two policyholders with the same insurer, the insurer could easily direct resolution of the dispute, because the two policyholders would have agreed in advance to be bound by the law & order systems the insurer put in place.

With respect to disputes between policyholders with different insurers, insurers would be motivated to establish among themselves, in advance, dispute-resolution procedures to cover these instances. This is because (a) each insurer knows that there will be multiple such situations over time, in which sometimes their policyholders would be the victims and other times the aggressors, so they have to act fairly at all times if they expect reciprocity from other insurers, and (b) it is always less costly to resolve disputes peacefully rather than violently.[21]

---

[20]Other alternatives might include landlords building these packages into their leases with tenants, and property developers building these packages into their maintenance agreements with residents.

[21]This is exactly what happens today among insurers. For instance, when there is an automobile accident, the two insurers don't go to war; they resolve things peacefully, based on procedures established in advance.

Insurers would also be motivated to try to alter the behavior of their policyholders to reduce the incidence of violent disputes and the quantum of losses. This happens today: insurers offer reduced premiums for defensive living (e.g., for installing a burglar alarm, taking a "safe driving" course, etc.), and use deductibles to ensure that policyholders have some "skin in the game" before the insurance kicks in (to reduce moral hazard).

Myth #17: We'd Be Defenseless!

The last thing a statist will ever concede is that defense against external aggression does not have to be provided by the state. The statist just knows that this is *the* "public good" *par excellence.*

To the contrary, earlier I discussed the defects in the so-called "public good" argument in favor of state-provided national defense. There is nothing distinctive about any good or service, even national defense, that could ever justify such good or service being supplied coercively by a monopoly.

So how might this work in a libertarian society?

A Stateless World Would Have Less Conflict

In a stateless world, there would likely be much less need for collective defense capabilities against external aggression.

Much of today's international conflict arises because one state acts aggressively towards another, either attacking that state, or provoking an attack by seeking to interfere in the other state's operations. States do this because the individuals at the state responsible for this aggression (a) do not do any of the fighting themselves, and (b) can coercively seize their citizens' income to pay for this aggression.

In a stateless world, very few men would travel to foreign territories at their own cost to physically fight strangers to try to conquer their territory, or stay there to try to influence their society.[22] Likewise, few men would

[22]This raises the question of the volunteer soldier, who *does* agree to travel overseas to kill others at great personal risk. This is likely a function of the statist political and education systems, which indoctrinate citizens from a very young age to believe that killing foreigners in the name of the state is honorable, even in the absence of a genuine "defense-of-the-homeland" concern (either that, or the volunteer soldier is simply a psychopath). In a stateless society, there would be no state to revere and no state-

be able to afford or want to spend the billions of dollars spent today to hire other men to travel overseas to seize territory or influence another society.

Another source of conflict today is individuals at the state oppressing segments of their own population based on race, religion, ethnicity, etc. And sometimes internal oppression by state A also leads to inter-state war, as another state, state B, attacks state A to try to stop this internal oppression. Again, the individuals leading state A can engage in this oppression at minimal personal cost, because they have others both doing the "dirty work" and coercively funding these activities (so too with the individuals leading state B in attacking state A).

Imagine if these men had to engage in and/or fund the violence themselves; there would be a lot less of it.

Internal oppression is partly facilitated by the state disarming its citizens through gun-control legislation. The most oppressive regimes in history have generally preceded their program of violence by prohibiting the private ownership of firearms, often justified as necessary to reduce violent crime. However, if only the state is armed, then the group targeted for oppression is defenseless.

In a libertarian world where there would be no restrictions on firearm ownership, it would be much harder for one group to oppress another, since the target group could be fully armed too.

Widespread firearm ownership would also be a reason to expect less inter-societal conflict. If a man wanted to hire a group of aggressors to travel overseas and seize territory, then they would face an armed population fighting to defend their own families and property, which history has shown is the most difficult force to defeat, e.g., in ancient times the Greek cities holding off the Persian Empire, the Viet Cong vs. the U.S. invaders in the 1960s, and the Afghanis vs. the Soviet invaders in the late 1970s.

Another factor tending to increase conflict in today's world of highly centralized states is that it is relatively easy to control vast amounts of territory simply by winning a state-versus-state war. In highly centralized states, a relatively small number of people and institutions control all of the internal territory, and thus an aggressor state only has to win control of the

controlled education, so such indoctrination wouldn't exist (psychopaths would still exist, but few citizens would voluntarily pay for them to go on killing sprees overseas, unlike now where we are forced to pay for these gross adventures through taxation).

other state's locus of power in order to gain control over the other state's entire territory, as opposed to physically fight on each square foot of this territory.

In a stateless world, however, there would be no locus of power to seize control of. In a sense, the aggressor would have to defeat every single household, one at a time. That is almost an impossible task that would surely stretch an aggressor's resources intolerably, particularly given that, after seizing each house, the aggressor would also have to *hold* it indefinitely. History has shown that the most difficult part of a prolonged war is seizing and holding more and more ground, because this stretches supply lines to the breaking point.

The final point to make relates to the importance of free trade. States often erect prohibitions or restrictions on individuals in one state trading with individuals in another state, through the imposition of sanctions, tariffs, quotas, exchange controls, regulatory distortions, etc. These trade barriers make war less costly; if individuals in state A already cannot fully and freely trade with individuals in state B, then the cost of state A going to war with state B is lower, since there is no (or less) commercial trade that would suffer.

In a stateless world, however, there would be no artificial trade barriers. Everyone would be free to trade with everyone else. This effectively increases the cost to any society of starting a conflict with another society, since such a conflict would risk damaging or destroying actual or potential customers and/or suppliers. Put another way, the more free trade that exists, the less likely is war, since it makes no sense to degrade key parts of one's own economic ecosystem.

Libertarian Defense in a World with States

That is all well and good if there were no states at all, but what if a libertarian society existed in a world with states?

The first point to note is that a few of the above concepts would still be valid: there would be no aggressive activity by the libertarian society directed towards states, so there would be less provocation sparking conflict; an aggressor state would face an armed population in the libertarian society; and there would be no locus of power to seize to obtain control of the libertarian society's territory. In addition, individuals in the libertarian society would be eager to trade with individuals in the existing states, and, to the extent that such trade existed, as noted above this would increase the cost to those states of attacking the libertarian society.

However, there is also reason to believe that individuals in a libertarian society would still demand *some* protection against potential aggressor states. Where there is demand, production is sure to follow.

Of course the general demand for protective services would be quite different in a libertarian society. Since there would be a range of services to purchase, and each individual would be voluntarily choosing whether to purchase these services and, if so, which ones, he would be a lot more discriminating than are citizens of states (who get no choice, and are compelled to pay). There would likely be little to no demand for offensive capabilities to project force around the world and interfere in other societies; demand would likely exist only for purely defensive and rescue capabilities. Indeed, some individuals might decide that, since their society is no threat to others, the chances of an invasion are low enough to conclude that it would not be worth purchasing any protection at all.

Instead of the coercive, monopolistic provider of protection that is characteristic of today's states, in a libertarian society there would be numerous competitive providers offering different products tailored to customers' actual needs. Such providers would have to offer value to their customers, since they would need to persuade customers to voluntarily part with their money.[23]

Perhaps those in coastal societies would want to pay for some waterborne defense services, but those in the middle of a large land mass might not. Those in difficult-to-reach mountainous regions might decide to forego purchasing much in the way of defense services, figuring that the terrain is sufficient protection against invasion. Those living in high-profile cities which could be likely targets might want to pay up for more protection, and those living in rural areas might want less.[24] Those who

[23]Under statism, if you do not like what you are paying for national defense, or do not agree with the defensive or offensive policies of the state, then your only remedy is to try to move countries (which is not easy). In a libertarian society, you wouldn't have to change location, you could stay and just change provider.

[24]This would properly price consumers' decisions about where to live. In today's regime, residents of rural areas are subsidizing the defensive protection of residents living in high-profile cities, such as New York, since everyone pays for national defense based

live in high-risk target areas might want to purchase missile-defense protection, and, if this is too expensive, then they could either move, or try to persuade others of their fears and have them pay for such protection too. Those who travel overseas a lot might want to purchase highly mobile, skilled bodyguard and/or hostage-rescue services, while those who don't travel much wouldn't have any interest in spending their money on these types of forces.

Just as in any other industry, competition among defense-service firms would tend to bring (or at least hold) down prices, and increase innovation and quality. A provider of defense services that engaged in the type of aggressive activities undertaken around the globe by the U.S. government today, and/or which is constantly involved in violent conflict with states, would find its costs increasing dramatically, and thus it would have to increase its prices or cut its other services to remain profitable. If its customers were not willing to pay higher prices or accept a reduction in service, or they disagreed with the service-provider's actions, then they would look to competing, less-aggressive, and thus lower-cost providers. Likewise, a provider that didn't deliver adequate protection would gain a bad reputation, and would lose customers to competitors.

What if a private protective-services-provider fails in its duties? Lives are at stake. Yet this is no different from today with the state. What if the state fails? In the U.S., see Pearl Harbor, the first attack on the World Trade Center, 9/11, the Boston Marathon, etc. The difference is that, in a libertarian society, such a private provider would go out of business, whereas today the state just continues to be the monopoly provider (and in fact grows its budget with each failure to protect!).

Collective Defense

As noted earlier with respect to law & order services, it is not likely that individual consumers and businesses would have to select, contract with, and monitor each provider for each type of defense service.

For instance, developers of residential communities, and owners of

on the same income-tax scale. If, for instance, New Yorkers had to pay based on risk profile, then fewer people would be able to afford to live there, and/or they might demand that the U.S. reduce its provocative activities around the globe to reduce the city's risk profile.

industrial parks, office buildings, hotels, malls, roads, etc., might purchase defense protection for their properties for the benefit of their residents/tenants/customers. Such owners could build the cost of this protection into the fees that they charge for use of their properties. Indeed, even these owners might not have to purchase defense protection individually; they could form associations or federations across a broader region to purchase such protection as a group.

However, it is more likely that life, health, and property insurers would purchase defense protection for their policyholders. Since these are the insurers that would have to pay out on claims if someone were killed or injured or their property damaged by an external aggressor, these insurers would be motivated to purchase the most efficient form of protective services for their policyholders. Also, since insurers are in the business of assessing and pricing risk, they could charge different premiums for different risk profiles; this would ensure, for instance, that those who choose to live in higher-risk locations would pay for that choice. Further, since insurers aggregate the interests of millions of policyholders, they would have the economies of scale and financial clout to purchase large-scale defense protection.

What about the *Really* Expensive Stuff?

How would a libertarian society pay for certain defense products that today are very expensive, e.g., a nuclear arsenal, a submarine fleet to guard the coastline, an air force, etc.? There are several responses to this.

First, part of the reason that these products are so expensive today is that the buyer is the state and the seller universe is restricted by state licensing rules.

As a buyer, the state doesn't have the same pricing discipline as private citizens do. This is because the individuals at the state are not paying with their own funds, and thus have no financial incentives to bargain for lower prices, and may even be motivated to overpay, if the defense vendors are cronies who could provide other benefits to the relevant state personnel. In a libertarian society, the buyers would all be private, expending their own funds, and thus they would be much more demanding of sellers; sellers would have to compete, including on price, to accommodate buyers' preferences.

On the sell-side, the state only permits certain vendors to operate in the defense industry, using excuses such as "security clearance" to restrict the number of sellers. In a libertarian society, there would be no coercive restriction on the number of sellers, which would tend to put downward pressure on pricing through the impact of greater competition.

Second, it's not clear that the really expensive products would actually be in demand in a stateless society. It's not a valid question to ask how, in a libertarian society, we could afford the national defense the state provides today, because, as discussed above, in a libertarian society the defense protection demanded might be very different.

Third, as also noted above, the likely involvement of insurers would enable the efficient pooling of expenditure on behalf of millions of policyholders, which could be directed towards expensive defense products which are in actual demand.

Fourth, the private sector might develop innovative ways to enable the purchase of the most expensive defense products. Defense-product vendors or the capital markets might provide financing options to buyers, so that payments could be made over time, instead of upfront. Large businesses (or associations of smaller businesses) might figure that it's worth voluntarily contributing to the defense bill, because if potential customers were killed or their property destroyed, then that would be bad for business. People might make voluntary contributions over and above their contractual payments, just because they believe that this is the right thing to do (like tipping a cab driver or waiter, even though you might never see them again). Wealthy philanthropists might feel inclined to establish charitable foundations to contribute.

Myth #18: There Goes the Environment!

Statists assume that the environment would go to hell if we don't have the wise custodians at the state looking out for us (and Mother Earth). Their incorrect assumption is that, in the absence of centralized, coercive regulations, there would be no regulation at all of human activities.

The shortcomings of state regulation of the environment were discussed earlier. I'll provide below some ideas of how environmental regulation might work in a libertarian society.

Rely on Private-Property Rights

What the statist line of thinking misses is that environmental problems are nothing more than property disputes: A's activities cause damage to B's body or property, for which B could take action against A to stop the activities (through an injunction), or to be compensated for his losses (through an award of money damages). This is no different from any other property dispute in society.

Thus, in a libertarian society, these issues would be properly resolved as property disputes. For instance, if A's activities emit pollutants which cause B to lose some enjoyment of his property, or damage to B's body, then, subject to one exception, A would have initiated aggression against B's property, and would be liable.

The exception relates to homesteading. If A were engaging in these activities on his own land which was adjacent to some unowned land, and subsequently B homesteaded the unowned land, then A would be regarded as having homesteaded the right to continue these activities before B homesteaded the unowned land, and thus B would acquire a property right in this land *subject to* A's right to continue with his prior level of activity. In other words, B could not complain about A's activities if he moved in and these activities were already going on. However, if A increases the volume of his polluting activities, or changes their nature, then A *would* be liable to B, as A would not have homesteaded the right to these increased or different activities.

Conversely, if B homesteaded the land before A commenced these activities, then B would be deemed to have homesteaded the right to a pollutant-free enjoyment of his property, and A's subsequent initiation of these polluting activities would render him liable to B.

Any subsequent purchasers of either A's or B's land would purchase these plots of land with whatever homesteaded rights the seller (A or B) had.

In all cases, either party would be free to approach the other to try to negotiate a different set of rights. Unlike what happens under statist regimes—whereby regulations are made without taking into account the preferences of the respective property owners (instead, the preferences of those at the state and their lobbying interests are imposed coercively)—such a private negotiation would enable a true expression by the parties of their relative value preferences for continuing to pollute, or for clean air, as the case may be.

For instance, if B had the right to stop A from polluting, then A could do one of several things: (a) pay for technology and processes to reduce or eliminate the pollution; (b) offer to pay B sufficiently for B to install protective features on his property to reduce or eliminate his losses; or (c) offer to buy B's property outright. Whether A chooses to do any of these things would reflect how valuable he regards his polluting activities, and whether B agrees to (b) or (c), and for what price, would reflect how valuable he regards remaining in place free of pollution.[25]

If an environmental group took a different view from B regarding what is acceptable on his property, and thus, regardless of B's views, wanted to reduce A's polluting emissions further, then that group would be free to do one of several things: (x) offer to buy A out of his land, and then shut down his factory; (y) offer to pay for A to reduce his emissions to the level that the group feels is acceptable; or (z) offer to buy B's property, and then sue A as the new adjacent-property owner. How much the environmental group would be prepared to pay for each of these options would reflect how valuable they regard the reduction of emissions.[26]

Private vs. "Public" Property

One of the main environmental issues with statist regimes is that a lot of land and waterways are publicly owned.[27] This has three ramifications.

[25]Obviously no individual at the state could know what A's and B's value preferences are, and it would be highly coincidental if centralized regulation just happened to accurately reflect these preferences (and it would be impossible for state regulation to keep up with changes in preferences). Also, state regulatory regimes would not recognize the sequencing of homesteading, and thus would generally assume that B has an absolute right to live on his land free of pollution, when in fact A might have been there first, engaging in his polluting activities.

[26]This is very different from how things work in today's statist regime, where the environmental group would, instead, rent the state's coercive powers, at little cost to that group, to forcibly impose its preferences on A and B through regulation. This outcome would not reflect in any way the respective value preferences of the two property-owners.

[27]As noted earlier, to the libertarian, the state cannot legitimately "own" any property, since it uses funds or labor coercively obtained to claim such ownership. I use the word "own" here to mean the *assertion* of control.

First, no one maintains property as well as the actual owner who has his own financial capital invested; look at the state of public housing and public parks, compared with private housing and private parks, respectively.

Second, when the state owns property, at best it tries to balance the interests of different groups, and generally ends up satisfying none or few of them; if one of these groups owned the property itself, then it could protect its interests more vigorously.

Third, what often happens is that the most aggressive lobbying group ends up effectively controlling the property through getting state regulations written in its favor, and thus it coercively "buys" the property at a huge discount (it really only has to pay the lobbying costs), compared with what it would have had to pay in the free market.

Contrast this with the libertarian world in which all property would be privately owned (unless unowned). Consider the case of a privately owned river. The owner would have invested effort and financial capital in homesteading the river, or buying it from a prior, legitimate owner, and therefore would have the best incentive to keep it pollutant-free, either for his own use, or because he wants to supply clean water to his customers (e.g., local residents or businesses). The standard of cleanliness of the river would be much higher when privately owned than when controlled by the state, where no one has any vested interest.

If the river owner contracted with local customers to supply them with clean water and fails to deliver such water, then he would lose customers and could be sued. He would therefore have a strong incentive to take remedial or preventive action against upstream polluting factories (or other bad actors). The downstream users wouldn't have to get involved with the factories to determine who was responsible; their grievance would be directly against the river owner.[28]

[28]When discussing the notion of private ownership of resources like rivers, the statist worries about what would happen if a river owner decided to cease supplying water to his customers. Well, that would be commercial lunacy, and therefore highly unlikely (we don't see private suppliers of other critical items, such as energy, food, or shelter, hoarding their inventories). Of course the owner might insist on different pricing regimes, which would ensure that those who valued the water the most would pay appropriately. However, there would always be an opportunity for competitors to supply water to these end-users. For instance, today in the U.S. there are companies that deliver bottled water to businesses and households which are already connected

Air pollution would be dealt with in a similar manner. For instance, all of the roads would be privately owned, so if someone living adjacent to a road (who has homesteaded a right to clean air) suffers from air pollution, then he wouldn't have to worry about which cars caused this pollution; instead, as noted earlier, his cause of action would be against the road owner. The road owner would thus have the incentive to manage the traffic on his road to ensure that impermissible levels of pollution were not emitted; for instance, he might require inspections of vehicles before granting them permits to drive on his roads.

The Roles of Insurers and Pollution Consultants

Note that it is likely in the above examples that the river owner, the road owner, and the factory owner would all have liability insurance. The relevant insurers would require or financially motivate these owners to take appropriate preventive action to minimize the risk of environmental lawsuits. These insurers would bring current "best practices" from their portfolio of similar clients, so in this way those methods that were most effective would spread among different regions, but be tailored to the specific circumstances in each case, and be updated in real time as circumstances change.

Contrast this with the centralized regulations imposed by the individuals at the state, which are "one size fits all," typically lag market or technological developments, and are written based on input from lobbying interests, as opposed to what is most effective.

The insurers would not necessarily be expert in matters such as measuring pollution, determining causation, assessing pollution-control technology, and compliance and monitoring. In a society in which such services would be in demand from insurers, businesses, and litigants, it is likely that expert firms—call them "pollution consultants"—would arise to provide these services. Unlike today's state regulators, who purport to serve as expert consultants but are really coercive monopolists lacking proper fi-

---

to public water supplies. Other competitors might install rainwater tanks, or come up with other ideas we cannot conceive of from our armchairs. Besides, the feared cessation of supply happens today under statist regimes: if the environmental lobby is particularly successful, then water could be coercively diverted away from end-users in favor of endangered species; if the farming lobby is particularly successful, then water could be coercively diverted away from residential users in favor of farms.

nancial incentives, in a libertarian society the pollution consultants would have to compete to win customers. Those that develop a good reputation would garner more business, and those that provide shoddy services would lose business.

Myth #19: Somalia Disproves the Case for Libertarianism!

Prior to the 1990s, Somalia operated under a repressive statist regime, and then in 1991 this regime was thrown out, and the country operated without a central state at least up until 2006. Somalia has always been desperately poor and dangerous, both when it had and did not have a central state. Statists love to point to Somalia and ask "Is that how a libertarian society would look?!" However, this is an intentionally disingenuous rhetorical question.

Comparisons Should Be Apples-To-Apples[29]

When comparing libertarianism to statism, it is unreasonable to compare this across different cultures. Each culture has a different set of norms, propensities towards violence, respect for others, capital stock, etc. The libertarian is not suggesting that libertarianism would cleanse a rough culture of its inherent characteristics; he is saying that, *for a given culture*, a libertarian society would be more peaceful, just, and prosperous than the statist version. In other words, it is unreasonable to compare Somalia without a state to the U.S. with a state; the latter may still be a better place to live because of its preferable inherent characteristics. The more reasonable way to approach this is to look at Somalia without a state compared with Somalia with a state.

As it happens, there is some research that has been conducted on this point. The paper summarizing that research suggests that living standards improved once the state was eliminated.[30] Per the conclusion in that paper,

---

[29] The key article to read on this topic is "But Wouldn't Warlords Take Over?" by Robert Murphy, *Mises Daily Articles*, available at https://mises.org/library/wouldnt-warlords-take-over.

[30] "Somalia after State Collapse: Chaos or Improvement?" by Benjamin Powell, Ryan

"[T]his paper's main contribution to the literature has been to compare Somalia's living standards to those of 41 other sub-Saharan African countries both before and after the collapse of the national government. We find that Somalia's living standards have generally improved and that they compare relatively favorably with many existing African states. Importantly, we find that Somali living standards have often improved, not just in absolute terms, but also relative to other African countries since the collapse of the Somali central government."

The Danger of Centralization

In a culture where violence is widespread, the worst political configuration is to have one group in central control of the state, visiting its violence on the population as a whole with no limiting factor. This is particularly so where the state has first disarmed the population through gun-control legislation. In these situations, the cost of such violence to those at the state is minimal.

This has been a big part of the problem in some of the most despotic parts of Africa, including Somalia. In these situations, it would be better to have (a) no central authority, but rather a range of competing warlords, each of whom acts as a countervailing force to the others, and/or (b) a fully-armed population. Then the cost of violence to any would-be overlord would be much more significant.

Culture Is Key to Outcomes

Statists irrationally fear that a place like the U.S. would become Somalia if we didn't have a state. However, a culture which is relatively non-violent, and relatively respectful of individuals' rights, is likely to remain so in the absence of a state, simply because those cultural norms are inherent in each individual. In other words, a place such as the U.S. is not likely to devolve into Somalia if we moved to a stateless society, because that is not how people operate in the U.S. today when they have some degrees of freedom to act.

Ford and Alex Nowrasteh, *Journal of Economic Behavior & Organization* 67 (2008). Peter Leeson also has some substantial commentary on Somalia to similar effect, in his book, *Anarchy Unbound*.

To elaborate, in the U.S. today, the vast majority of people peacefully accept temporary rule from the political party which obtains a majority in any election, even if they don't agree with that party's policies and legislation. Statists who voted for the opposition generally don't go around killing people who voted for, or who are part of, the winning political party; they wait until the next election to try to elect their preferred party. If that is the culture we have now, then it doesn't make sense to worry that if the U.S. were to become a stateless society—where each group could voluntarily choose its own policies *all the time*, instead of waiting for the next election—then we would descend into depraved, inter-group violence.

To put it a different way, if Americans are not particularly violent when living under the opposition's ruler, then they're not likely to become more violent when they don't have to live under any ruler.

Myth #20: Libertarians Are Shills for the Powerful!

Statists typically assume that the libertarian's advocacy of the free market means that the libertarian is for the interests of big business, and against the interests of the "little guy." However, it is actually the case that libertarianism is the *only* philosophy that is *for* the "little guy."

Statism is characterized by special-interest groups renting the state's coercive powers to benefit themselves (i.e., crony capitalism). Whether it is big pharmaceutical companies, big agricultural companies, big oil companies, defense companies, alternative energy companies, labor unions, Wall Street, the environmental lobby, etc., the groups that do best under statism are those that lobby most intensively for state support, through subsidies, favorable regulations, patents, tariffs, quotas, eminent domain, money supply expansion, etc. This has happened throughout all of history whenever there has been a state; it is not unique to any time period or region.

However, the one group that does not and cannot lobby as effectively as the above interest groups is the group of individuals often each described as the "little guy," or the "average Joe." As noted earlier, the interests of this group are too diffuse to organize, and the benefits to these individuals from lobbying on any particular issue are outweighed by the costs of doing so, even though the benefits from lobbying on all issues together would be enormous.

As an entrepreneur, the "little guy" has to try to make a living navigating through the horrendous and costly maze of state regulations which special-interest groups (a) help write, to make it harder for the "little guy" to compete, and (b) have much less trouble complying with. The "little guy" takes whatever portion of his income the state allows him to keep after the myriad of taxes levied—which the special-interest groups can avoid through structuring, or minimize by hiring expensive tax advisors—and tries to support his family or reinvest in his business or career.

As a consumer, the needs of the "average Joe" are left to be satisfied by products that (as discussed earlier) are more expensive and less available than they would be absent the state's interference. Unlike special-interest groups which rent the state's coercive powers, his life is simply subjugated to these powers.

Similarly, as a potential employee, the "average Joe" faces higher-cost and lower-quality education, and fewer sustainable employment opportunities, than would be the case if the state did not interfere in the market.

In advocating for the free market, libertarians are simply asking that everyone, big and small, play by the same rules, namely, whomever best pleases the voluntarily purchasing customer will succeed. Libertarians should therefore be understood to be pro-market—which really means pro-consumer—and *not* pro-business. Libertarians believe that the sole purpose of economic activity is to organize scarce resources to best satisfy consumer preferences, and not to safeguard any particular businesses or interest groups, nor to privilege those who want to rely on coercion.

Indeed, as Austrian economist Don Boudreaux has noted, it is the notion of robust private-property rights—the hallmark of libertarianism—which eliminates the distinction between the "powerful" and the "weak." While some may be wealthier than others in a free-market society, no one exercises power over others, in the sense of being able to force them to act against their wills. The wealthiest individual cannot (without legal consequences) take the poorest individual's property unless the latter sells or gives it to him, or tell the poorest individual what he must or cannot do with his body. Only the state does these things, either directly, or through those who rent its coercive powers.

As libertarian historian Tom Woods has noted, statists don't appreciate the irony that often the most vigorous opponents of the free market are so-called "capitalists." In the free market, businesses would face intense competition every single day; however, if they can get the state on their side, then this makes things much easier for them. Thus we have the paradox that businesses—big businesses in particular—may be against the free market, while libertarians are very much for the free market.

That's difficult to reconcile with the notion that libertarians are shills for the powerful.

Myth #21: Libertarians Don't Care about the Poor!

Statists pejoratively ask of libertarians "How would the poor survive in a libertarian society?" The implication is that it is only through the state that the poor can be clothed, fed, employed, etc. There is a lot to unpack here.

Free Markets Rescue the Poor

The statist shows a remarkable lack of appreciation of economic history. Poverty has been the default, the natural state of man, for all of history. It was only the advent of (nearly) free markets, as first embodied in the Industrial Revolution in Great Britain in the 18th and 19th centuries (but which then ultimately took hold in the U.S. and other countries), that lifted the common man out of his dire straits. When the state's influence was at its minimum—meaning there was sound, commodity-based money (generally gold and silver), and the ability to freely exchange private property and freely associate without interference from the state—man was able to dramatically increase his living standards. He did this by specializing in his labor, and by deferring some consumption to provide pools of savings to be invested in developing new technologies and processes, thereby increasing worker productivity.

Importantly, almost every consumer-oriented business that has been successful has achieved this success through constant innovation to bring down the price of goods to make them accessible to the masses; it is much harder to achieve success on a grand scale by selling only to the rich. Thus the poor in the U.S. are able to afford things like wide varieties of food, clothing, and shelter, color televisions, air conditioning, refrigerators, flushing toilets, cars, and air travel, not to mention the ubiquitous mobile device (even in the most poverty-stricken neighborhoods). As noted earlier, the poorest members of free-market-oriented societies live better now than royalty lived a couple of hundred years ago.

We can also see this effect in the U.S., even using government statistics. The so-called "poverty rate" declined dramatically over the course of the 20th century in the midst of a relatively free-market regime, until the massive expansion of the state in the late 1960s and early 1970s as part of the launch of President Johnson's "War on Poverty." At that point, however, the poverty rate flattened out, and has declined much less since, despite trillions of dollars having been spent by the state in this *faux* war.[31]

Looked at another way, where would you prefer to be poor: in freer markets such as the U.S., or in less-free markets such as Cuba, North Korea, and Venezuela? If more freedom is better for the poor, then why is total freedom not the best?

Statism is really just central planning, which surely has been repudiated by the implosion of the Soviet Union and the desperate statuses of Cuba, North Korea, and Venezuela, to name a few examples. The only difference economically between those regimes and the statist U.S. is the *amount* of central planning: in those countries, *every* industry was or is *completely* centrally planned; in the U.S., *every* industry is *partly* centrally planned.[32]

If central planning as a concept does not work, then why tolerate any of it? Statists believe that there is a "correct" amount of central planning, and that only they know this amount, but they will never tell you what this amount is definitively. Generally it is defined as whatever amount they are proposing at any one point in time. This just strains credulity.

[31] Statists really can't explain this phenomenon, not that they even bother to try. As libertarian historian Tom Woods likes to note, had the inverse been true, i.e., had the welfare state been in operation for all of the 20th century and then been terminated in the late 1960s, with the same poverty-rate flattening trend as noted above, statists would be crowing about the obvious benefits from state interference.

[32] And the worst industries in the U.S. are the most centrally planned: education, financial services, healthcare/health insurance, and the military.

There Are Plenty of Non-State Resources to Help the Poor

What about the statist's perennial favorite, namely, that leaving everything "to the market" wouldn't help those who "fall between the cracks"? There are several ways to respond to this.

One way is to note that "the market" is not some impersonal machine but, rather, millions of individuals interacting voluntarily on a daily basis. Likewise, "the state" is not an impersonal machine, but also comprises (unfortunately!) millions of individuals. When the statist claims that the state is superior to the market in preventing some people from "falling between the cracks," he is implying that *only* those at the state have the awareness, compassion, and ability to help these people. On what basis could we conclude that the millions of people not working for the state are not concerned to help their neighbors in need, and that this concern is held exclusively by the millions of people at the state?[33]

Moreover, even if this were true, in a libertarian world these millions of people now working for the state would still be around—just not as part of a state—and thus they could still express and act on their concerns, and the poorest could still benefit from their magnanimity.

Another response is that (as noted earlier) civil society comprises many parts: the individual, families, neighborhoods, religious groups, charities, mutual-aid societies, self-help organizations, businesses, trade groups, and the state. In a libertarian world, the only one of these societal parts that would be missing is the state. Is it not possible that for the few who might "fall between the cracks," there might be some part of what remains of civil society, absent the state, that could help these people? One of the shortcomings that statists suffer from is the "tyranny of the present." What this means, in this context, is that they assume that a libertarian world would look exactly like the present world, minus the state's welfare programs. To the contrary, many aspects of society would be very different. For instance, it is highly likely that, at a minimum, institutions of civil society that once existed, but which have been crowded out over time by the expanding welfare state, would have room to flourish, perhaps growing

[33] Perhaps the Tooth Fairy Theories?

again to the prominence they once had in helping the neediest, before the state's role exploded in the 1960s.[34]

In fact, if the statists in civil society who elect the state into being do so primarily to help the neediest, then presumably they would still care about the neediest in the absence of the state. Are statists claiming that they themselves would become less interested in helping the neediest if there were no state?

Boiling it all down, both a libertarian society and a statist society would comprise all the same individuals, and all the same social institutions bar one: the state. Thus the only difference between a libertarian society and a statist society is the ability to coerce others. The statist is effectively saying that he cannot envision marshalling sufficient resources to help the neediest through his own actions and persuasion, and thus must rely on force.

The statist must hold a very dim view of his fellow citizens; one wonders why he would even want to live among them. Nevertheless, this does not justify the immorality of one man coercing another.

There Would Be Fewer Poor

Another example of "tyranny-of-the-present" thinking is the statist's implicit assumption that, if the state ceased to exist, then we'd have (at least) the same number of poor as we do now (however one counts them). Yet in a libertarian world with the free market, we would expect that there would be fewer destitute people.

As discussed earlier regarding the free market, without a state there would be: (a) more and better-paying jobs, since, absent taxes and regulations, the cost of employing workers would be lower, there would be more capital equipment available per worker to increase each worker's productivity, and workers would be free to make their own risk/reward trade-offs when accepting employment; (b) more opportunities for entrepreneurs to pursue, freed from the costs and restrictions placed on them by taxes and regulations; and (c) more goods in the market, at lower prices, as the costs of production and the range of permissible products are freed from the impediments imposed by taxes and regulations.

[34] See, for example, the history of mutual-aid societies in the U.S., as detailed in the book by David Beito, *From Mutual Aid to the Welfare State*.

In addition, one of the key insights of Austrian economics is that the state's central planning of the money supply and interest rates, and control of the banking system—primarily through the actions of the state's central bank—have major, adverse consequences for the economy. The key state action in this respect is causing and/or facilitating the artificial expansion of the money supply, which causes both the artificial suppression of interest rates, and effective (even if not always visible) economy-wide price inflation over time. There are three main consequences of such state action, all of which hit the least well-off particularly hard, and none of which would occur in the free market.

First, economy-wide "boom-bust" business cycles are caused by the artificial manipulation of interest rates, and the downturn portion of these cycles has a more significant, adverse impact on the least well-off than it does on others.

Second, when new money is created and injected into the economy, the resulting price inflation impoverishes the least well-off relative to those who are the closest cronies of the state. This is because the new money is not injected uniformly, but typically first goes to the "connected few," who therefore get to spend it before prices rise, and it is the least well-off who get the new money last, well after prices have risen.

Third, due to the artificial suppression of interest rates and effective price inflation, everyone is pushed to take on much more risk in saving for retirement than they would otherwise, and the least well-off can least afford to take these risks. In the free market, one could build up a reasonable retirement fund through the low-risk methods of simply accumulating money in a checking account (or holding it as physical cash), and/or lending money to a bank through the use of a savings account bearing a decent interest rate. The value of such money would actually grow over time, due to the general price deflation we would see in the free market (as more goods are produced with very little increase in the money supply), and, in the case of savings accounts, the interest income earned. However, in today's low-interest-rate, positive-price-inflation world, those methods would lead to a real decline in wealth (i.e., after adjusting for price inflation), and so individuals now feel compelled to speculate in the securities markets, real estate, or other high-risk endeavors.

More broadly, societal prosperity is directly linked to the amount of "stuff" produced to satisfy consumers' wants. The amount of "stuff" produced is, in turn, directly linked to the number of man-hours devoted to appropriate, productive activities. When there is a state, a significant number of man-hours are devoted to activities that have nothing to do with satisfying consumers' wants. These man-hours include: the time spent by individuals who work for the state in either creating or enforcing regulations; the time spent by individuals in lobbying the state to rent its coercive powers; the time spent by individuals who have successfully rented the state's coercive powers in producing "stuff" otherwise than in accordance with what would be produced in the free market; and the time spent by individuals in complying with the state's regulatory whims. Then there are the man-hours devoted by individuals trying to avoid the state's whims.

Imagine all of the additional prosperity we would have if all of the aforementioned people, time, effort, and resources were instead engaged in appropriate, productive activities.

Finally, the state incarcerates in cages thousands of potentially productive individuals for victimless "crimes," which substantially and probably permanently impairs the earning power of these individuals—never mind the destructive effect this has on their lives and families—likely condemning many of them to impoverishment. Without a state, these individuals would be free not only to better their own lives, but the lives of those with whom they enter into voluntary exchanges.

Freedom of Movement

Another aspect of the state that adversely impacts poverty is the state's regulation of immigration.

Many of the world's poor would have much better lives—better job prospects, more goods and services available to purchase, and at lower prices—if they were free to move to places with more liberty than where they live today. States create and enforce artificial national borders, and establish category-based immigration restrictions (based on geography, ethnicity, family ties, etc.). All of these restrictions prevent the poorest individuals from moving to places where they could better flourish.

In a libertarian world, these centrally imposed restrictions would not exist. All property in use would be privately owned, so whether someone from another region could move here would be based on the individual decisions of transport-providers and local private-property owners. Businesses would be free to invite, host, and employ immigrants from other regions, as would relatives, ethnic associations, charities, etc. These decisions would be made on an individual basis using privately established criteria, and it is likely that more of the world's poor would be able to more easily move to where the opportunities lie.

The statist who advocates both for the poor and for state-based immigration barriers is essentially saying that his concern for the poor only extends to those located inside an artificially created geographic area. However, why should the plight of someone inside this area be more important than that of someone outside this area? It certainly makes sense that people feel more compassion for those in their immediate neighborhood, as they live with and see these people all the time. But by what logic should a statist in New York feel more strongly about a poor person in Seattle than a poor person in Toronto? He knows neither personally, and the poor person in Toronto is actually geographically closer to New York than is the poor person in Seattle. It is as if the U.S./Canadian border possesses some magical, anti-compassion feature.

Why should anyone allow the individuals at the state to define which poor people in the world they are allowed to be concerned about?

The Morality of It All

The argument that the state is necessary to help the neediest is a utilitarian argument. Such an argument is, in effect, saying that the statist believes that if he perceives some people as being in need, then he is justified in coercively taking resources away from others he perceives as not being in need, because the ends are worthy. The statist does not, or at least cannot, deny that his means involve coercion (nor that the definition of "in need" is entirely subjective).

On the other hand, the moral perspective looks at the means used. As noted earlier, it is immoral for one man to initiate force against another. Thus, in the case of state-managed welfare, the fact that the objective is to help the needy doesn't alter the fact that the proposed use of coercion is immoral. In a libertarian world, all welfare would be voluntary, and thus the means would be moral as well as the ends being worthy. And, as discussed earlier, there are many non-coercive alternatives for aiding the poor.

One final point. If the utilitarian argument is to prevail over the moral argument, then why not just cease treating robbery as a crime and allow the neediest to freely rob the well-off directly? Why bother using the state as a middle-man to engage in this robbery, with all of its overhead costs and the complicating personal incentives of those who work at the state?

Myth #22: Libertarians Are Pro-Prostitution and Pro-Narcotics!

The statist believes that if he regards an activity as undesirable, then the state should prohibit it. Accordingly, statists also believe that if libertarians are against the state prohibiting an activity, then libertarians must be *for* the activity itself, either personally, or as a statement of values that "society" ought to hold.

To pick on prostitution as an example, the myth runs as follows: since the libertarian does not believe that the state should forcibly throw people into cages for voluntarily purchasing and selling sex, the libertarian therefore likes to use prostitutes, wants to be a prostitute, or believes that society should endorse prostitution.

This myth suffers from two fallacies.

First, as discussed at length previously, libertarianism is simply about the appropriateness of the initiation of force in personal dealings. Being against the use of force says nothing about how one evaluates the merit of the personal dealings in question. Staying with the prostitution example, it is not inconsistent for the libertarian to believe that if two people want to engage in consensual sex involving payment, then they should be free to do so, while at the same time not wanting to personally engage in this type of activity nor wanting his loved ones to do so.

The libertarian believes that the question of whether a voluntary activity which doesn't breach the NAP is a virtue or a vice should be answered for each person through privately developed standards, and not through centralized legislation backed up by force. However, the statist's first thought whenever he wants to "suggest" a set of values for society is to use the coercive powers of the state. But the state is the bluntest possible instrument to use, not only because it relies on force, but also because whatever solution it resolves on would be a "one-size-fits-all" solution.

Second, in suggesting that we need the state to enforce (purported) societal values, the statist is conflating society with the state.[35]

[35] I've discussed earlier how it is logically impossible to talk about the values of "society,"

However, society is *not* the same as the state; society is much more extensive. As noted earlier, society comprises many different voluntary institutions, as well as the state (e.g., families, neighborhoods, religious groups, charities, mutual-aid societies, businesses, etc.). To the libertarian, one of the key roles of these non-state institutions, as has always been the case historically, is to create and promote local norms, values, and ethics to help people lead "better" lives (however defined).

Thus for the statist to claim that, without the state's use of force, things like prostitution and narcotics would run rampant in a stateless society is to shortchange the role and impact of these non-state institutions. Both history and logic suggest that, compared with the brutality of imprisonment, these institutions could be very effective in developing norms to discourage self-destructive activities, promote healthier practices, and allow for a more open, humane, and effective way of dealing with those who engage in these activities.

Again, it's critical to be clear about what libertarianism is and is not. It is *not* a statement of personal values. It is simply a philosophy about when the use of force is justified.

Myth #23: If It's so Good, Then Why Hasn't It Ever Been Tried?

Statists believe that there are no historical or current examples of libertarianism in practice. However, there are plenty of examples of societies or segments of societies which have interacted, or are currently interacting, on a truly or mostly voluntary basis. Statists read but they do not comprehend; they see but they do not observe.

History

There are a number of historical examples of stateless societies, as well as "low-state" societies, i.e., those without the coercive control of a large, centralized, all-pervasive, professionally administered state.

At the outset, the most basic point to note is that the concept of the civilized world comprising only large, formal nation-states really only began

since only individuals can hold values, and it strains credulity to suggest that we could discern a common set of values on most topics among millions of unique individuals.

in the 17th century with the Treaties of Westphalia. Before then, societies were organized in numerous different forms. Some societies were stateless (e.g., clans, tribes, and feudal societies), others had a "low-state" form, such as monarchies existing in parallel with private society (with well-defined boundaries between the two) and the ancient Greek and Renaissance Italian "city-states," and of course there were also the large, ancient empires (e.g., Egyptian, Persian, and Roman). In many of these societal forms, unlike with today's nation-states, there was no abstract "state" which was regarded as separate from the persona of its ruler(s).[36]

There is significant scholarly work noting that a substantial portion of medieval Europe was anarchistic, in the sense not only of being stateless or "low-state," but being anti-state, meaning that societies (supported by bodies such as the Catholic Church, guilds, universities, and towns) were fiercely opposed to the centralization of political power in, and legislative edicts issued by, large sovereign states.

The development of the "law merchant" in the Middle Ages and the Renaissance is a very good example of individuals voluntarily developing their own legal system and customs. The law merchant was based on what was generally perceived to be fair, and to work effectively, to facilitate peaceful trade among a highly mobile population across different regions. Within this merchant community, the threat of being ostracized by one's trading partners was the most important reason to accept adverse judgments rendered by the private courts.

In terms of other stateless legal systems, medieval Iceland and Ireland operated with purely voluntary conflict-resolution regimes, and in the U.S., the development of the West initially operated quite efficiently and peacefully before the federal and state governments got involved (it turns out that the "wild, wild West" was not so wild after all).[37]

---

[36]Once nation-states arose, this redirected loyalty away from an individual ruler to the state itself, from which the concept of nationalism arose.

[37]See Terry Anderson and Peter Hill's book, *The Not So Wild, Wild West*. In addition, Peter Leeson's book, *Anarchy Unbound*, and Edward Stringham's book, *Private Governance*, detail a number of very interesting and sometimes counterintuitive historical examples of self-governance without a state. And Elinor Ostrom's book, *Governing the Commons*, provides some examples of how, contrary to mainstream thought, "public" natural resources have been effectively managed by small, private user-groups which create their own rules, apply them consistently to everyone in the group, self-monitor, and internally enforce.

In addition, in Europe in the 19th and early 20th centuries, the small region known as Moresnet operated peacefully and prosperously as a "low-state", neutral zone for about one hundred years. And, as noted earlier, contemporary Somalia, while no stateless paradise, saw a measurable improvement in living standards when it was stateless in the 1990s and 2000s relative to when it had a central state.

More generally, as noted previously, every single function that is carried out by the modern nation-state—including defense, policing, courts and law, roads, education, etc.—was at one time carried out by private parties on a non-coercive basis until the state took it over for its own purpose. Most importantly, many of these functions are still carried out privately today in different parts of the world.

The International Community

The most obvious and significant current example of libertarianism is the international community: vis-à-vis one another, the various nation-states exist in a condition of political anarchy. There is no "world state" coercively governing all nation-states. Accordingly, many aspects of what a libertarian society would look like domestically are in operation today internationally.[38]

For instance, taking the collection of nation-states as a single society, there are competing protection forces, courts, bodies of law, currencies, approaches to regulation, etc. There is no group of central planners taxing and/or subsidizing nation-states, handing out special privileges to crony nation-states, or dictating which nation-states may produce what, at what price goods must be sold, etc.

The NAP is generally respected among nation-states, in the sense that no nation-state asserts the right to coerce another.[39] The individuals working at each nation-state interact with individuals working at other nation-states on a completely voluntary basis.

In some sense, the homesteading principle is also respected. Nation-states have delineated boundaries of property that they control, which they claim as their own, and these boundaries are, for the most part, accepted by

[38]To be clear, this is not an endorsement of existing nation-states, which of course would not be part of a libertarian society!

[39]With the exception of the U.S. government.

other nation-states. Similarly, when a nation-state peacefully declares borders around ocean-based "economic zones," and portions of outer space for their satellites, this homesteading is generally respected too.

If one nation-state trespasses onto the claimed property of another, then the right of self-defense is well recognized.

The most acceptable form of interaction within the international community is not through coercion but, rather, via voluntary agreements (treaties) and voluntary associations (such as the United Nations, World Trade Organization, NATO, etc.). Each such association freely decides on which nation-states may join and which may not; if some nation-states are not invited to join a particular association, then they are free to set up a competing association. If invited, a nation-state is free to join and financially support an association, but is also free to leave. Yes, there are wars and other conflicts (just as there is within a nation-state), but these constitute the minority of the millions of interactions that happen daily among nation-states.

As discussed earlier, it's noteworthy that the individuals at a nation-state are content to live in a libertarian existence relative to their contemporaries at other nation-states, but they are not prepared to live this way among their own citizens, whom they prefer to rule by force.

Local Communities

At the smaller-unit level, today we have cruise ships (which are essentially floating, stateless societies), private residential communities, the private cities of Columbia in Maryland, Co-Op City in New York, and Reston in Virginia, Walt Disney World, shopping malls, corporate campuses, hotels, kibbutzes, etc. They each have their own civic goods (i.e., roads, parks, waste disposal, security, etc.) and regulations and customs (or "law"), and they operate efficiently and fairly without state-style coercion.[40]

In fact, every voluntary association is a case study of libertarianism: people come together (and may leave) voluntarily, make their own rules of interaction, financially support the objectives on a voluntary basis (and may

[40] For an excellent theoretical discussion of these concepts, as well as some in-depth case studies, see Fred Foldvary's book, *Public Goods and Private Communities*.

similarly withdraw such support), and for the most part interact peacefully. There are no implied or actual threats of incarceration at gunpoint for failure to carry out or finance these groups' stated objectives.

One objection that statists might raise to the applicability of these examples is that these voluntary groups only operate on a relatively small scale, and thus voluntarism may not be an appropriate form of interaction for a nation-size population. That might be true, but this objection would be another example of "tyranny-of-the-present" thinking, and would miss the point. In a libertarian world there wouldn't be any nation-states, so there would be no need to find forms of interaction that work at the national level.

Even in a world with nation-states, as we have today, a small-scale group with shared interests, where the governors and governed are very close, is the most natural, accepted, and therefore effective method of ordered association. Thus, even within large regional populations, voluntarism could work well to provide order if the governance model were a mosaic of many small, voluntary, shared-interest groups (and any individual might belong to a multitude of such groups).

On the other hand, nation-states—where the rulers are distant, the populations large, and interests diverse—necessarily try to create unnatural, less accepted, and thus less effective large-group interactions, which therefore require force to implement. Thus, by its very nature, the nation-state governance model is doomed to ultimately fail.

But Even If These Examples Didn't Exist...

As relevant and illuminating as these examples are, even if these examples did not exist, it would not weaken the case for libertarianism. Just because a particular form of governance hasn't existed yet doesn't mean that it couldn't arise in the future, and that it couldn't be superior to what came before it.

Notwithstanding this logic, statists often argue that if there hasn't been an enduring stateless society, then that must prove that such a governance form is not technically feasible, and/or is inferior.[41] But by this logic, the

[41] It's worth noting that Ireland existed in a stateless model in medieval times for longer than the U.S. has existed as a constitutional, federative republic.

present form of any idea is always the evolutionary end point. Framed that way, I'm sure not even the most ardent statist would agree; in fact, most statists are always arguing for changes to the state's form (mostly to increase its powers). Imagine if, before the first modern democracy arose, a monarchist had pointed out that the idea of democracy died in the ancient world, and thus it must not be technically feasible, and/or is inferior to monarchy. Should that have been conclusive as to the feasibility of democracy, or the desirability or probability of democracy arising again? In addition, since statists believe that modern democracies are an improvement over the pre-existing monarchies, how can they honestly argue that it is impossible for societal governance to evolve again in a positive direction (and into a very different form)? Is it possible to reach the end of history?

In that respect, a quick survey of history would show that societal governance has never been static, but continually changes, and, from the perspective of individual liberty, zigs and zags, sometimes changing for the better, and sometimes for the worse. For instance, the European continent has had clan-based societies, democracies, republics, empires, feudal societies, stateless societies, highly fragmented, anarchistic-tending societies, city-states, monarchies, communist dictatorships, fascist dictatorships, and modern nation-states, just to name a subset.

Finally, consider the abolitionists in the U.S. in the 19th century trying to make their case against slavery; at that time, slavery was and always had been ubiquitous. Are we to believe that the abolitionists had no valid case to make, because there had never been a world without slavery?

Myth #24: Libertarianism Is a Futile Endeavor!

Statists often criticize libertarianism on the basis that it is unrealistic, and that libertarians are too idealistic. We are told that a stateless society has never existed and never will exist, so why bother believing in it and pursuing it as an organizing principle?

There are a number of ways to respond to this, both in terms of principle and in practice.

Principles

First, by the above metrics, statists are idealistic too. For instance, they would desire a world without murder, yet none has ever existed or will exist, but statists still try to educate others as to why murder is wrong and try to reduce it where possible.[42]

If "idealistic" means advocating for something different from the current state of affairs, then who *isn't* idealistic?

Second, as noted earlier, political philosophy and the organization of society have been evolving for thousands of years. Who is to say that such evolution is over?

When the Roman Empire was at its zenith, ruling much of the known world, it might have been difficult to conceive that an alternative would one day emerge; likewise when monarchy was the prevailing system in western Europe. In the 18th and 19th centuries, when slavery was a global institution in the so-called "civilized" countries, it might have been very difficult to conceive that one day most of the world would recognize its abhorrence. For those living under eastern European communism in the 20th century, it might have been very difficult to conceive that one day they would be living free of that yoke.

Political organizational forms change over time, and it seems that, as time goes on, the changes happen more rapidly, perhaps because new technologies allow new ideas to spread more rapidly. So who is to say that it is impossible that growing numbers of people could reject the idea of the state, and form stateless mini-societies?

Third, if you believe that a particular principle for organizing society is just—in this case, the NAP—then even if you cannot hope to immediately attain 100 percent of your ultimate goal—in this case, a stateless society—how could you work to move society towards that goal until you first set that goal? In other words, you first need to know your destination before you can set out on your journey. You don't need to magically appear instantly at your end destination to achieve success (although that would be nice!); you could set your destination, and then continually take incremental steps towards it.

[42] Here I mean "murder" as statists define it, which excludes killings by or on behalf of the state.

Libertarians believe in the moral superiority of a stateless society and, by setting this as the destination, it becomes very clear which policies in today's society to oppose and which to support. It means having a guiding principle, as opposed to just going by "gut," or blindly following a political party or personality.

Practical Steps

Even in today's overwhelmingly statist world, it is not true that libertarians have no means to advance our cause. There are a number of meaningful things that libertarians can do and are doing to promote libertarianism.

Pursue and Promote Alternative Education. As discussed earlier, the state can only exist with the acquiescence of the majority of the population, because the individuals in the private sector vastly outnumber the individuals at the state (as large as that number is). Thus, educating people about the true nature of and problems with the state, and the fact that there is a real alternative to the state, must surely be a first step in turning that acquiescence into skepticism, if not outright opposition.

Historically, the state has had a huge advantage in influencing the content taught in schools and at college, given the all-pervasive, purposeful control of education by the state and the intellectuals who support it. However, with the advent of the Internet and powerful mobile devices, alternative content is now easily within the reach of those who want to learn about different political philosophies, whether at home or on-the-go. And there is a growing array of homeschooling and self-study resources available at one's fingertips. Thus there is good reason to be optimistic in this regard.[43]

As the societal conflicts caused by statism grow more extensive and more intense, and as more national crises cause people to question whether the

[43]Because this means the Internet represents a real threat to the state, watch for increasing momentum within the state to control the flow of content on the Internet, perhaps disguised by seemingly innocuous phrases such as "net neutrality," "common-carrier regulation," "hate-speech laws," or "campaign-finance reform," or as part of the "War on Terror" or the "War on Drugs." This already happens in totalitarian states for the same reason, but it is coming to a democracy near you!

current system is the best we can hope for, many people—particularly the young—are looking for new ideas. The libertarian should not only keep improving his own understanding of libertarian principles but, even more importantly, should provide those who are looking for an alternative with guidance on how to find the rich body of libertarian educational resources that exist.

Refrain from Participating in Elections. Of all the arguments for the state, the statist's favorite is that elections indicate the consent of the population to the state and its policies. The state gleefully uses voter-turnout figures to claim that there is a post-election mandate for this or that, and that "The people have spoken."

Thus, to do his part to reduce voter turnout, the libertarian should refrain from voting, and try to convince others to do the same. To the statist, the fewer the votes cast, the weaker the mandate coming out of an election. If a weaker mandate means less state activity, then that is generally a good thing for the cause of liberty.

Note also that, based on probability, voting is a waste of a citizen's time. Statistically, the chance of a single vote determining the outcome of an election, and then of that outcome leading to implementation of the voter's desired legislative or executive policy, is infinitesimal.

Another way to think about elections is that, in the grand scheme of things, they don't change anything material; all that happens is that a different team is put at the helm of the destructive vessel that is the state.[44] What really changes society is public opinion: the abolition, women's-suffrage, civil-rights, and gay-rights movements all *preceded* state legislative or judicial action. Thus, instead of investing the time to work on a candidate's

[44] A relevant comment often attributed to Mark Twain is that "If voting made a difference, they wouldn't let us do it." For instance, in a typical national election season, Party A argues for a 40-percent tax rate, and Party B for a 35-percent tax rate, but there is no chance that anyone would conclude that taxes per se are illegitimate; Party A argues that the state should bomb or invade state X, and Party B argues for aggression against state Y, but there is no chance that anyone would conclude that all state aggression is illegitimate; Party A blames group J for society's woes, and Party B blames group K, but there is no chance that anyone would conclude that the state itself is the cause.

campaign, or to research candidates or vote, the libertarian might consider a better use of his time to be working to change public opinion through whatever means he prefers.[45,46]

Ridicule "Public Service." Statist's laud "public service"—meaning working for the state in either a civilian or military role—as a very honorable activity.

The libertarian should do what he can to persuade family, friends, and colleagues to avoid joining the state's apparatus, by illustrating how working at the state is actually something to disdain as immoral, rather than something to revere. In this way, the libertarian can not only do his part to reduce the size of the state, but also to keep more people in the productive and moral private sector, which is ultimately better for societal prosperity.

Promote Nullification. Nullification simply means rejecting the legitimacy of a piece of legislation, and therefore refusing to comply with it. Peaceful nullification can be pursued in two main ways in the U.S.: by state governments, and by jurors. I'll deal with each of these in turn.

First, state governments can nullify federal legislation which they believe is unconstitutional, based both on historical precedent and the structure of the Constitution.[47] In general, this is implemented by passing state-level legislation to the effect that no state-government personnel, or resources, will be permitted to assist the federal government in enforcing the relevant federal legislation within the state. This can be a very effective means of constraining the power of the federal government, since it often relies to a large extent on the cooperation of state governments.

---

[45] These comments only apply to broad elections in which there is not a specific question on the ballot subject to a binding "Yes/No" referendum. However, were there to be a specific question up for vote in a binding referendum, such as "Should we eliminate the property tax?", or "Should we approve the public school budget?", leaving aside the statistical argument, it could make sense for the libertarian to vote, since there would be a definitive opportunity to reduce state coercion.

[46] As libertarian investor Doug Casey has noted, one other benefit of not participating in elections is that it reduces the amount of contact you have with state personnel, which by definition improves the quality of your life.

[47] For a detailed analysis and history of the use of nullification in the U.S., see Tom Wood's book, *Nullification*.

This has gained currency in recent times, as evidenced by various initiatives at the state level to restrict or negate such federal-government programs as deporting illegal immigrants, spying on citizens by the National Security Agency, gun control, Obamacare, the "War on Drugs," and the Common Core education curriculum. While the libertarian has no greater affinity for state governments than for the federal government, the libertarian should support and encourage one arm of the state (broadly defined) taking on another arm if the net effect is to reduce the overall state activities.[48]

While state nullification is an effective way to oppose the federal government, it doesn't have any impact on the unjust activities of state governments. As a practical matter, it is of course entirely open for local governments to try to use the same strategy against state governments. However, as a matter of constitutional structure, local governments do not really have this option.[49]

Second, with respect to jurors, they can vote to acquit a defendant whom they believe is guilty of a "crime" where they believe that the "crime" itself is based on unjust legislation, in the sense that the legislation is not legitimate pursuant to the NAP.

For instance, even if the facts supported the case that the defendant had not paid his taxes, if a juror believes that taxes are an immoral act of robbery by the state, then he could vote to acquit that defendant, and no court could question the juror's decision. The juror would not only be judging the facts, but also the legislation.[50]

---

[48] Thus it would not make sense to support an initiative at the state level which simply substitutes state-government activities for the federal government's activities, or which adds more intervention than it reduces.

[49] By "constitutional structure," I mean that the relationship of a local government to its state government is very different from the relationship of a state government to the federal government. There is a solid basis for state nullification because the several states, as principals, established the federal government as their agent, and granted to it limited powers through the Constitution. By definition, those same states could therefore refuse to recognize the federal government's exercise of power if they believe it falls outside what they granted to it in the Constitution. However, with respect to local governments, they too are creatures established by state governments, and thus cannot nullify state-government action; a principal can nullify his agent's actions, but the converse is not true.

[50] However, it would not be a libertarian act to acquit a defendant of murder if the evi-

This can be a powerful act of defiance against not just federal-government legislation, but also state- and local-government legislation. It is one of the few times in which private citizens can have a meaningful, peaceful, oppositional impact. It could even impact the prospective decisions of law-enforcement personnel, who might decide, in the face of continual jury nullification of certain victimless "crimes," to cease trying to enforce or prosecute them (which might lead legislators to repeal such legislation).

There is actually a history of impactful jury nullification in the U.S.: in the mid-19th century, juries in northern states refused to convict under the federal Fugitive Slave Act, as an act of opposition to slavery; and in the early 20th century, juries refused to convict under the federal Prohibition legislation.

Today there is a growing libertarian movement to make jurors more aware of the concept of jury nullification, despite the state's attempts to obfuscate this principle.

More generally, nullification can be pursued more effectively as a societal strategy once enough people are educated in libertarian principles. At that time, each act of nullification would reinforce each other act, and the groundswell of active opposition would become quite obvious to statists. It would then become harder to argue that there is acquiescence to the state.

Support Non-State, Alternative Products. There are situations in which the state has not yet fully prohibited citizens from using non-state alternatives to products that are provided, privileged, and/or regulated by the state. Libertarians should try to use these alternative products where possible, and encourage others to do the same.

Examples of this include using: private mediation and arbitration services, instead of the state's courts; private schools, home-schooling, and online courses, instead of state-provided schools; private residential communities, instead of public towns and villages; private mail services such as FedEx, instead of the state's mail service; new transportation services such

dence supported his guilt, since murder *is* a breach of the NAP, and thus legislation outlawing murder is arguably not contrary to the NAP (although punishment by the state, instead of by the victim, *would* be contrary to libertarian philosophy).

as Uber, and new accommodation services such as AirBnB, instead of state-regulated taxi services and hotels, respectively; and alternative currencies such as Bitcoin, gold, or silver, instead of state-mandated money. In addition, as there is increased traction around the world for "special economic zones" and seasteading—which are stateless or "low-state" communities carved out from existing states—individuals and businesses could choose to relocate to these physical areas.

Some of these are more expensive options, since (a) the state can price its products without worrying about making a loss, and (b), through taxes, one is forced to pay for the state alternative, even if one chooses additionally to pay for the non-state alternative. However, to the extent that the libertarian can afford to choose these options, it would enhance the private-sector's ability to compete with the state, and withdraw some legitimacy from the state's claims that it must be a provider or regulator of these products.

Using these options could be regarded as a "partial secession" from the authority of the state.

Advocate for Secession. Full-blown secession on the political level is the act of one political entity declaring its independence from another political entity. When one entity formerly governed by another secedes, politically it moves from being a subservient entity to a peer entity. In this way, the power of coercion is removed from that relationship, and the two entities must now deal with each other in a state of political anarchy, i.e., on a purely voluntary basis. This can be one of the most dramatic yet peaceful ways for people in a given region to escape the power of larger state.[51]

Indeed, there is an elegance to secession as a solution to escaping an overlord entity. While land is fixed, jurisdictional boundaries are not. Secession doesn't involve moving the land, the citizen, or the overlord, but rather simply the boundaries of the prior overlord's rule.

Secession also initiates a logic train that can lead to the dismemberment of political authority. If one region secedes from a larger entity, then that larger entity could not reasonably object when a second region seeks to secede, and a third region, etc. Similarly, if a region B secedes from a larger

[51]The violent form would be armed revolution.

entity A, then region B could not reasonably object when a smaller region, C, seeks to secede from region B; if that happened, then nor could region C reasonably object when a still smaller region, D, seeks to secede from region C; and if that also happened, then nor could region D reasonably object when a still smaller unit, perhaps a household, seeks to secede.

Accordingly, states have always vigorously fought secession attempts at any level, because they understand where the logic train may lead.[52]

Within the U.S., state-level secession has excellent historical and constitutional underpinnings.[53]

As a matter of history, in 1776, the original 13 American colonies seceded from Great Britain, and in 1781, these independent states formed a union under the Articles of Confederation. However, in 1788, a subset of these states seceded from this union, and established a new union under the United States Constitution (subsequently, all existing states joined this new union). Then, in 1861, a subset of these states seceded from the United States of America, and formed the Confederate States of America under a separate constitution.[54]

There were also secession events within individual states: Kentucky seceded from Virginia, Tennessee from North Carolina, and Maine from Massachusetts.[55]

Turning to the constitutional perspective, it was the colonies—organized as states—that set up the federal government under the Constitution

[52]A rare exception to this point is the Principality of Liechtenstein which, although an absolute monarchy, has provisions in its constitution whereby every village is entitled to secede, and, through a referendum, the population can abolish the monarchy.

[53]A very good source on this topic is a book edited by David Gordon, *Secession, State & Liberty*.

[54]In addition to these actual acts of secession, at various times in the 19th century some of the northern states in the U.S., principally the New England states, seriously contemplated seceding over various matters, such as the federal government's assumption of the debts of the states, slavery, the Louisiana Purchase, and the War of 1812 against the British.

[55]It is also worth noting that secession has not just been a feature of U.S. history, but has occurred numerous times in European history too: Norway seceded from Sweden; Belgium seceded from The Netherlands; the Soviet Union broke apart into 15 separate states; Yugoslavia broke apart into seven separate states; and Czechoslovakia broke apart into two separate states.

as their agent, to carry out specific tasks. Just as with any principal/agent relationship, the principal (the states) can always fire the agent (the federal government) and withdraw from the relationship. Statists often claim that the American "Civil War" settled once and for all the question of whether there is a right to secede, but that is a specious argument, because the outcome was based solely on violence. As libertarian historian Tom Woods likes to note, if a bully on the playground mugs another child and takes his lunch, then would anyone seriously conclude that the bully's right to that lunch is settled once and for all? Sure, he has the lunch now, but he got it illegitimately.[56]

However, the right to secede doesn't rest just on historical precedent and constitutional principles. There are strong moral and logical grounds too.

In terms of the moral grounds, if all men are metaphysically equal, so that no man can rule another without his consent, then every man must be able to secede from any political authority once he withdraws his consent, since that political authority is nothing more than a group of other men.

In addition, since a state always "acquires" its property through coercion—such as through war, seizing private property owned by citizens, or physically claiming unowned property using income confiscated from citizens to fund its operations—none of this property is legitimately held by the state. Likewise, a state's control over citizens within its declared borders is based on coercion. Accordingly, the individuals at the state have no moral grounds to object if citizens want to break away from the state's control, and assert their right to reclaim or homestead "state property."

In terms of logic, to reject secession means to assert that a particular political entity, such as a nation-state, is the precise, God-given size that it needs to be, and it absolutely cannot be one inch smaller! Of course this makes no logical sense.[57]

---

[56] There is another odd aspect about statists' support for the "Civil War." Statists rightly condemn states like the former East Germany and North Korea for killing those who try to flee being ruled by these states. Yet statists see no contradiction in supporting the Union declaring war on the Confederacy when the latter had the temerity to (metaphorically) flee being ruled by the U.S. federal government.

[57] Amusingly, those who reject secession—which makes a state smaller—don't ever seem troubled by *expansion* of a state, through war, land purchases, treaties, colonization, etc.

Secession is also a concept much favored by libertarians because it reduces the size of states (note that *both* the new state and the remaining "rump" state will individually be smaller than the previous combined state). For the libertarian, "small is beautiful" when it comes to states (or, rather, small is the least ugly form).

The smaller the state, the less militarily powerful it is likely to be—in the sense that there are fewer human and other resources within its territory to commandeer—and thus the less able it would be to wage war on other states or act provocatively around the globe. This means that it is less likely that its citizens would suffer all the terrible consequences of war. We can see this principle in operation today, whereby there are many small, relatively prosperous states which don't seek to exert any global power, and which are left alone by the larger states, even though it would be relatively easy for the larger states to conquer them. Examples include Andorra, Costa Rica (which has no armed forces at all), Liechtenstein (ditto), Luxembourg, Monaco, and Singapore.[58]

Moreover, the smaller the state, the more intimate are the personal relationships between citizens and those at the state, and thus there is less that the individuals at the state can get away with, e.g., you can see your mayor at the local diner and complain to him that the garbage is not getting picked up on time, but it's a lot harder to have this conversation with your state governor, or the president. In addition, each individual is more significant in a smaller state than in a larger state, and thus there is less likely to be an emphasis by elected officials on mass-marketing or sloganeering, and more attention paid to individuals' concerns.

Further, to the extent that there could be any commonality of interest among a group of people—whether in terms of culture, language, religion, or economics—it is much more likely to occur within a small village than within a county, state, or country, e.g., the views on immigration in a small, Texan village on the Mexican border are likely to be more homogeneous than the views of everyone in the U.S. Thus, it is more likely that a smaller state's actions would better reflect any shared interests of its citizens than would be the case with a larger state, where the interests are much more diverse.

---

[58]One exception would be Israel, but that small state receives an enormous amount of military-focused aid from the U.S.

In addition, smaller states are at greater risk than larger states of losing their citizens to competing, neighboring states. The smaller the state, the less costly it is for a citizen to move to a neighboring state, in terms of distance from his family, employment, preferred culture, preferred climate, etc.[59] Smaller states are also more sensitive than larger states to losing their citizens. With fewer resources to begin with, smaller states would feel the loss of any citizens and their financial capital more acutely than would larger states. Thus, smaller states must be much more careful than larger states about overreaching in their coercive actions against citizens. In addition to curtailing their coercive activities domestically, smaller states are also likely to prefer open, free trade across borders (both in terms of financial capital and goods), since the smaller the state, the less self-sufficient it can be, and hence the more important imported financial capital and goods would be to the well-being of its population.

Accordingly, to the libertarian, a world with an increasing number of smaller and smaller states is a very positive trend. Thus, libertarians should be in favor of every secession movement, of which there is an increasing number these days.[60] As the idea of secession gains currency, it is entirely possible that small, libertarian communities would be able to break away and live on a purely voluntary basis.

Engage in Low-Level, Civil Resistance. As large as the modern state is, it has simply passed too many regulations for it to effectively enforce them all against everyone. Much to their chagrin—but proving that scarcity is a fact, even for the state—the individuals at the state run up against the constraint that they have limited time and resources, and have to allocate how they use them to selectively enforce regulations. This creates the opportunity for libertarians to simply ignore (and ridicule) the

[59]Obviously this is less of a concern for a state if other states erect immigration barriers. However, a state that is looking to persuade individuals to move from a neighboring state is likely to reduce or eliminate such barriers. A number of states today offer relatively easy citizenship programs for certain attractive types of individuals (particularly those looking to invest, or with needed skills).

[60]Libertarians should even favor secession if the seceding state is initially likely to be more statist than the state from which it is seceding. The decentralization of power, and weakening of both states, are likely to have more important, long-run impacts than any temporary increase in statist intensity at the seceding state.

state's regulations when they are not aligned with the NAP. If this type of civil resistance grows over time, then it is possible that, in certain areas, the state might have to rethink whether its regulations make sense, given the obvious erosion of the public's acquiescence which is necessary to sustain the state.

Obviously the degree of risk one is comfortable taking is up to the individual, but there are many lower-risk ways to ignore the state's unjust rules: when practicable, transact using physical cash, gold, or anonymous cryptocurrencies, to ensure transactions remain untrackable by the state; when turning 18 years-of-age, refuse to register with the Selective Service System, to avoid providing information helpful to the state if it decides to use military conscription to fight its wars; employ and/or provide sanctuary for illegal immigrants; if desired, consume alcohol and narcotics even if prohibited by legislation; ignore occupational-licensing regulations when running a small business; refuse to recycle as commanded by the state; when appropriate, ignore speed-limit legislation; refuse to obtain the state's zoning approval when making small improvements to one's property; and support businesses which are obviously ignoring the most ridiculous state regulations.

It's worth noting that a casual survey of society would show that many statists routinely act in these ways and, what is most amusing and revealing, this includes many individuals who work for the state itself. Often times the retort from statists who are caught in the act is "But I wasn't hurting anyone!"

Exactly.

Perhaps it is innate in all humans to judge rules by the standard of the NAP, even if not everyone can articulate this as clearly as libertarians can.

VI. Why Does It Matter?

Why is it even worth discussing libertarianism vs. statism? What is the point of debating political philosophies?

Minimizing Conflict within Society

Ultimately, political philosophy is about searching for the most just way to govern society. That seems to be a worthy end. As noted earlier, all conflicts in society are conflicts over scarce resources, whether human bodies or physical objects. We should all be interested in defining some acceptable, peaceful standard to govern human behavior with respect to such conflicts.

If we want to live in a society that rejects force, minimizes conflict, and has a principled way to try to non-violently resolve conflicts that do arise, then we ought to advocate a political philosophy that is consistent with those ends.

Statism relies on the initiation or threat of force by the individuals at the state, and is characterized by a vigorous competition among citizens to rent the state's coercive powers, to forcibly take things from fellow citizens. It is therefore a political philosophy based on force, and conflict is a feature of statism, not a bug.

Only libertarianism, with its sole focus on the non-initiation of force, can meet the above philosophical test. Libertarians define this peaceful principle—the NAP—and then demand that it be the standard to which every single person be held to account in everything he does.

In addition, as noted earlier, because libertarianism is based on a "negative rights" principle, it can, as a technical matter, be enjoyed by everyone in society concurrently. This makes it a highly scalable political philosophy.

In other words, not only is libertarianism the only peaceful political philosophy, it is the only political philosophy that can be universally applied.

Opposing War

Libertarians are not just in favor of the NAP domestically. Libertarians also believe that no one should initiate aggression against people who live in different geographies, just because they are engaging in activities we don't like or because we want some physical resources they have.

Yet this is what the state does, habitually.[1]

Why do libertarians oppose initiating or provoking war?

Initiating or provoking war means: (a) sending citizens to their death overseas and/or to kill others who pose no imminent threat, and provoking retaliation in the homeland against citizens (blowback); (b) through taxation and "defense" spending, forcibly diverting scarce resources—which could otherwise be used to produce goods to satisfy consumers' actual wants—to produce things the only purpose of which is death and destruction, and then using these things to destroy other scarce resources; and (c) reducing citizens' liberties to speak, travel, earn income, move assets, etc., based on the fiction that this reduction in liberties is necessary to safeguard the population from blowback.

It's worth emphasizing two critical points about war.

First, when an individual in society wrongfully kills multiple victims, statists are rightly shocked, and correctly label this as "mass murder." Yet when individuals at the state initiate lethal combat operations against people overseas who are not imminently threatening the state's citizens, this is mass murder on a much larger scale, but statists are not troubled by this activity, so long as it is labeled "war." Yet, logically, changing the label applied to an action cannot change its moral status.

Second, with every state-manufactured, alleged danger, the state argues that it needs more powers for defense. Yet the vast majority of the time this is a disingenuous argument, because either it was the state's prior activities which initiated or provoked the danger, or no defense is called for because there is no actual danger. As Randolph Bourne once wrote, "War is the

[1]Recall that the main reason that the state arose historically was to facilitate the financing of the monarch's wars against other monarchs.

health of the state." It is very easy for the state and its beneficiaries to expand their power dramatically amid alleged conflict, since at these times the state can whip up fervor through appeals to patriotism and "defending the homeland." When the alleged conflict is over—if the state ever admits this, which is exceedingly rare—the state never yields, never reduces its powers back to pre-conflict levels. This "ratchet" effect is defended by the argument that the state needs to remain "vigilant" against the alleged enemies, or new potential enemies.[2]

Governing by Principle, Not Arbitrarily

Why should we accept an overarching principle by which to govern society? The answer is that, if we don't govern by principle, then by definition we are governing arbitrarily.[3]

Statism has no universal principle that defines when coercion is justified and how to resolve conflicts. Under statism, the rules which govern society are based solely on who is in power at any one point in time, and the whims of that ruling elite. Under a modern democracy, statists pledge

[2]Americans have been told by the state that they have effectively been in a perpetual state of war over the 20th and 21st centuries, during which time there has been an increasing erosion of liberties. This has resulted cumulatively from the unnecessary entry by the U.S. government into World Wars I and II, the U.S. government's unnecessary provocation of and participation in the "Cold War," and its resulting conflicts (in Korea and Vietnam), the "War on Drugs" (really a war on the state's own citizens voluntarily ingesting substances, so it can never actually be over), and the "War on Terror" (really a war on a strategy, so likewise it can never actually be over). The liberty-destroying PATRIOT Act was passed urgently following the September 11, 2001 terrorist attacks—which were themselves likely blowback from aggressive U.S. military activities in the Middle East—allegedly to prevent the next such attack, but the legislation has never been repealed, even 16+ years later, apparently because of the permanent need for "vigilance" (no doubt due to the permanent U.S. military activities in the Middle East). Unsurprisingly, as part of the "War on Drugs," the domestic police now aggressively use against U.S. citizens (a) the powers grabbed under the PATRIOT Act, and (b) the surplus military equipment made available from the "War on Terror." And so on it goes.

[3]Note that the libertarian has no objection to any individual living his own life using arbitrary, rather than consistently principled, guidelines (assuming that this individual is not violating the NAP). It is only when such an individual tries to forcibly impose his arbitrary guidelines on others that the libertarian's objection arises.

fealty either to process (electoral and legislative) or a personality, or both, but not to a principle. How is this different from a monarchy or a dictatorship? Because arbitrary rulings are sometimes issued by a group, instead of by a single person?

Since state-imposed legislation is such a central part of statism, one should put to a statist the following question: By what standard should legislation be judged as good law, in the sense of being just? The statist is likely to give a blank stare in response, or may respond that, provided it is duly passed by a duly elected legislature, and not overturned by a court, the legislation is good law. However, regarding the latter response, statists' own actions demonstrate that they don't really believe this. Many statists have historically protested certain pieces of legislation as unjust, or ignored such legislation, such as: the Fugitive Slave Act; "Jim Crow" legislation; legislation explicitly or implicitly prohibiting universal suffrage, or homosexual relations or marriage; military-conscription legislation; legislation prohibiting the consumption of alcohol or narcotics; legislation setting vehicular speed limits; and legislation prohibiting or restricting home businesses. In cases like these, statists are actually judging legislation by a higher standard than mere legislative process. Yet if you press statists to articulate that standard, then they would likely be unable to do so, thereby confirming the arbitrary nature of statism. Not so libertarians; to them, the only just law is one that proscribes the initiation or the threat of force against peaceful individuals.

To make this point differently, "partial" statism is internally inconsistent. Most statists believe in the state for some tasks and not for others. Yet they can point to no consistent, cogent, logical principle which allows one to distinguish between the two sets of tasks. If coercive central planning is superior in one area, then it should be superior in all areas; if coercive central planning is unacceptable in one area, then it should be unacceptable in all areas.

Accordingly, to be consistently principled, one either needs to be a libertarian, or a philosophical communist. Anything else in between is unprincipled.[4]

---

[4]The inconsistency of statists manifests itself most obviously in the area of U.S. foreign policy. Anti-war statists on the political left believe that the U.S. government should

The worst implication of the arbitrariness of statism is that it can *only* lead to *more* conflict. If the rules of society are defined only by who is in power, then society disintegrates into what libertarian historian Tom Woods has called a "low-intensity civil war." Every interest group competes aggressively to exercise or rent the state's coercive powers, since on any issue there can only be one winner (to use the example given previously, we all either have to drink Coke or Pepsi). This is what causes, and has always caused, political conflict between different groups: blacks and whites, urban and rural residents, women and men, political left and right, domestic and foreign parties, unions and corporations, environmentalists and industry, the wealthy and the less well-off, police and civilians, etc.

Why should we live like this? We're only harming ourselves.

* * * * *

To return to the original question—Why does it matter?—it matters because we should all want the most peaceful society we can attain. To attain a more peaceful society, you need to start with a peaceful governing principle.

---

not dictate to foreign nations how they should organize themselves, yet these same statists believe that the U.S. government *should* dictate to its own citizens how they must live their lives. Pro-war statists on the political right believe that the U.S. government is not competent to organize domestic society, but that it *is* highly competent to organize regime change in, and the restructuring of, foreign nations.

VII. Conclusion

The very nature of the state means that it is morally and efficaciously untenable, and it is only a matter of time before the state collapses on itself as it confronts reality. The libertarian views the process of moving to a stateless society like riding on a train from where we are now to where we want to be. Sometimes the train will be traveling faster, and sometimes slower; sometimes in a more circuitous route, and sometimes more directly. The libertarian's key tasks are to try to accelerate the velocity and increase the directness of this train.

Along the way, the libertarian is happy for the train to stop to pick up those who might want to ride with us, such as statists of both the political left and right who agree with the libertarian on particular issues. However, the libertarian recognizes that such riders would likely get off well before we reach our final destination. That's fine too.

The libertarian is guided by a very compelling, universally applicable principle of non-aggression, and should never be reticent to articulate this principle when people question why he is riding on this train.

Nor should the libertarian be reluctant to press the statist about which fundamental principle underlying statism can be more compelling than being against the initiation of force. In fact, if you were to ask a statist if he is against the initiation of force, and if he believes that all men should live by the same standard, then you'd likely get a resounding "Yes!" It's only when you point out that this leaves no room for the state that the statist starts to backtrack.

If no man has any natural entitlement to rule another—a euphemism for "initiate force against another"—then the burden of proof must logically be on *the statist* to justify coercion by individuals at the state against others, and *not* on the libertarian to justify freedom from such coercion. Yet, in arguments about political philosophy, statists typically invert the burden of proof, as if coercion by individuals at the state is the natural order of things. Libertarians ought to vigorously reject this framing of the argument.

In this respect, as libertarian historian Tom Woods has noted, the most effective way for a libertarian to frame the argument is as follows: since libertarianism rejects the legitimacy of the initiation of force, to be against libertarianism is to believe *in* the legitimacy of the initiation of force. Therefore, the libertarian ought to challenge the statist to articulate his compelling arguments in favor of the initiation of force.[1]

In this book, I have sought to explain that (a) there is no technical reason that a stateless society could not function, (b) such a society would be economically more prosperous for all, especially the least well-off, and (c) above all, the NAP would be a moral basis by which to govern society. Hence libertarianism is only "unrealistic" presently because the majority of individuals do not understand or support it, but, given the huge cultural changes that have occurred in society over time (e.g., attitudes about slavery, women, and homosexuality), this too could change.

In medieval times, there were many practices carried out which we now regard as absurd, such as trial by ordeal, but which back then were regarded as quite proper, because most people in society believed that a deity would continually and justly interfere in the world upon the invocation of the priesthood. Libertarians see an analogy here with statists' fealty to the state and its rituals, namely, that most people in society believe that the state will continually and justly interfere in the world upon the invocation of the ruling elite. This absurdity, which is on par with medieval practices, will ultimately be unmasked over time. When, we cannot be sure.

To be a libertarian means to open your eyes to all that is wrong with the state, and to open your mind to the fact that there is a much better alternative. Hopefully this book has helped.

[1]Libertarian philosopher Hans-Hermann Hoppe has developed the concept of "argumentation ethics," which shows the illogicality of a statist using argumentation to try to persuade another of the merits of coercion. It is too complex to explain in a mere footnote but, for a taste, Hoppe shows that if a statist takes the position in a non-violent argument that one man can forcibly dictate what another man does with his body (and, by extension, his property), then the statist is engaging in a self-contradiction, which is a fatal flaw in any logical argument. This is because, in resorting to persuasion through non-violent argument to make his point, rather than using force, the statist is necessarily implying that his opponent has free use of his body to stand there and engage in the debate. Put more simply, it is self-contradictory for the statist to argue that disputes should be resolved by force, since he is not resolving the current dispute by force but, rather, by argument!

Afterword: A Personal Perspective

My conversion to libertarianism took place over the last few years. I began as a constitutional conservative, but my quest for intellectual consistency and a universal principle of justice wouldn't let me rest there.

I liken my awakening to what happened to the character Neo in the movie, *The Matrix*. Neo ingests the "red pill," which chemically severs his neural connections to the system run by intelligent machines, and enables him to begin to appreciate reality. He discovers that humans are connected neurally to a simulated world run by the machines—although humans are not aware of this—and that humanity is actually being used by the machines as a physical power source. There is probably no better analogy than this for how we were all educated, how we live under statism, and how a full appreciation of libertarianism can open one's eyes.

My adoption of the libertarian philosophy has provided me with a number of intellectual and psychological benefits:

1. I am politically agnostic. I no longer care about distinguishing between, arguing about, or supporting political parties or candidates. To me, they're all part of the problem, namely, the state. The differences among the various parties and candidates are trivial compared with the differences between statism and a voluntary society.

2. I have a crisper, more consistent view about morality, and what I am for and against. Once you absorb the NAP, it brings a great moral clarity to your life.

3. I am less preachy about the lifestyles of strangers. As long as someone is not interfering with my body or property, I don't have any interest in interfering with theirs (the "live-and-let-live" principle).

4. I try to treat people as unique individuals, and not merely as replaceable members of categories.
5. I am completely against war and offensive projections of force around the world.
6. Most importantly, I have much greater faith in the ability of private individuals to solve complex problems facing humanity when left free to do so. When you better understand the role of entrepreneurial ingenuity in economic history, it gives you cause for great optimism (if we could just rid ourselves of the yoke of the state).

While I would dearly like to see our society evolve into a stateless society, I know that this is unlikely in my lifetime. However, being a libertarian does not mean that I will never be satisfied unless we have a stateless society; rather, it means that I object to every single instance of state action due to its immorality (as well as its economic indefensibility), and I will derive great satisfaction from the elimination or thwarting of each such instance. In other words, it's not all or nothing that counts, it's every single thing.

What ultimately drives me to be a libertarian? Murray Rothbard, the modern father of libertarianism, put it best when he once wrote that a genuine dedication to liberty "can only be grounded on a passion for justice. ...And, to have a passion for justice, one must have a *theory* of what justice and injustice are." As I've tried to detail in this book, I regard the state as the largest and most frequent and dangerous purveyor of injustice, and therefore playing some role in reducing this injustice is what drives me. As Rothbard went on to note, other lofty goals, such as the abolition of poverty, cannot be attained by man simply willing them, but rather they require a complex set of economic factors to operate in a certain way over long periods of time; on the other hand, injustices are deeds inflicted by one man on another and, since they are the actions of men, their elimination is subject to man's instantaneous will. Per Rothbard again, "For instant justice *could* be achieved if enough people so willed." Changing wills, then, is the libertarian mission.

If any of this seems interesting to you, then I invite you to get onboard!

Reading Guide

I have set out below (in publication date order) a list of the books that I have read on philosophy, economics, history, and other subjects which provided me with the intellectual foundation to write this book.[1]

However, these books were not my only resources. I have also learned much from listening to podcasts recorded by, and reading articles written by, a number of intellectuals whom I highly respect. They include (in alphabetical order) Walter Block, Don Boudreaux, Jeff Deist, Tom DiLorenzo, Peter Van Doren, David Friedman, Roger Garrison, Jeff Herbener, Bob Higgs, Hans-Hermann Hoppe, Jacob Hornberger, Jörg Guido Hülsmann, Stephan Kinsella, Peter Klein, Brion McClanahan, Ryan McMaken, Bob Murphy, James Otteson, Lew Rockwell, Murray Rothbard, Joe Salerno, George Smith, Thomas Sowell, John Stossel, Mark Thornton, Walter Williams, and Tom Woods.

* * * * *

- *The Law* by Frederic Bastiat (1850)
- *No Treason: The Constitution of No Authority* by Lysander Spooner (1870)
- *War is a Racket* by General Smedley Butler (1936)
- *The Road to Serfdom* by Friedrich Hayek (1944)
- *Human Action* by Ludwig von Mises (1949)
- *America's Great Depression* by Murray Rothbard (1963)
- *Education and the State* by E.G. West (1965)
- *Education Free & Compulsory* by Murray Rothbard (1971)
- *For a New Liberty* by Murray Rothbard (1973)

[1] Note that, subsequent to publication of this book, I have continued to read many more books on these and other topics, and I keep a dynamic, subject-sorted Reading Guide, which is available at any time on request.

- *Defending the Undefendable* by Walter Block (1976)
- *The Ethics of Liberty* by Murray Rothbard (1982)
- *Civil Rights: Rhetoric or Reality?* by Thomas Sowell (1984)
- *A Theory of Socialism & Capitalism* by Hans-Hermann Hoppe (1988)
- *Governing the Commons* by Elinor Ostrom (1990)
- *Public Goods and Private Communities* by Fred Foldvary (1994)
- *Separating School & State* by Sheldon Richman (1995)
- *The Economic Laws of Scientific Research* by Terence Kealey (1996)
- *Secession, State & Liberty* edited by David Gordon (1998)
- *The Rise and Decline of the State* by Martin van Creveld (1999)
- *The Costs of War* edited by John Denson (1999)
- *From Mutual Aid to the Welfare State* by David Beito (2000)
- *Democracy—The God That Failed* by Hans-Hermann Hoppe (2001)
- *The Real Lincoln* by Thomas DiLorenzo (2002)
- *Chaos Theory* by Robert Murphy (2002)
- *The Myth of National Defense* edited by Hans-Hermann Hoppe (2003)
- *The Not So Wild, Wild West* by Terry Anderson and Peter Hill (2004)
- *The Politically Incorrect Guide to American History* by Thomas Woods (2004)
- *The Economics and Ethics of Private Property* by Hans-Hermann Hoppe (2006)
- *33 Questions About American History You're Not Supposed to Ask* by Thomas Woods (2007)
- *Anarchy and the Law* edited by Edward Stringham (2007)
- *Inclined to Liberty* by Louis Carabini (2008)
- *Hamilton's Curse* by Thomas DiLorenzo (2008)
- *The Ethics of Money Production* by Jorg Guido Hülsmann (2008)
- *The Case for Discrimination* by Walter Block (2010)
- *More Guns, Less Crime* by John Lott (2010)
- *Great Wars & Great Leaders* by Ralph Raico (2010)
- *Nullification* by Thomas Woods (2010)
- *The Enterprise of Law* by Bruce Benson (2011)
- *The Conscience of an Anarchist* by Gary Chartier (2011)
- *Basic Economics* by Thomas Sowell (2011)
- *Intellectuals and Society* by Thomas Sowell (2011)
- *Race & Economics* by Walter Williams (2011)

- *Rollback* by Thomas Woods (2011)
- *Libertarian Anarchy* by Gerard Casey (2012)
- *Organizing Entrepreneurial Judgment* by Nicolai Foss and Peter Klein (2012)
- *The Great Fiction* by Hans-Hermann Hoppe (2012)
- *South Carolina Civilians in Sherman's Path* by Karen Stokes (2012)
- *No, They Can't* by John Stossel (2012)
- *Defending the Undefendable II* by Walter Block (2013)
- *War and Delusion* by Laurie Calhoun (2013)
- *The Problem of Political Authority* by Michael Huemer (2013)
- *Intellectuals and Race* by Thomas Sowell (2013)
- *Environmental Markets* by Terry Anderson and Gary Libecap (2014)
- *Toward a Libertarian Society* by Walter Block (2014)
- *Playing by the Rules* by Tracey Brown and Michael Hanlon (2014)
- *The Moral Case for Fossil Fuels* by Alex Epstein (2014)
- *The Machinery of Freedom* by David Friedman (2014)
- *Anarchy Unbound* by Peter Leeson (2014)
- *Peace, Love, & Liberty* edited by Tom Palmer (2014)
- *Out of Poverty* by Benjamin Powell (2014)
- *Northern Opposition to Mr. Lincoln's War* edited by D. Jonathan White (2014)
- *Real Dissent* by Thomas Woods (2014)
- *Water Capitalism* by Walter Block and Peter Nelson (2015)
- *We Kill Because We Can* by Laurie Calhoun (2015)
- *Chasing the Scream* by Johann Hari (2015)
- *The Primal Prescription* by Doug McGuff and Robert Murphy (2015)
- *Choice* by Robert Murphy (2015)
- *Wealth, Poverty and Politics* by Thomas Sowell (2015)
- *Private Governance* by Edward Stringham (2015)
- *The Problem with Socialism* by Thomas DiLorenzo (2016)
- *Nature Unbound* by Randy Simmons, Ryan Yonk and Kenneth Sim (2016)
- *An Austro-Libertarian Critique of Public Choice* by Thomas DiLorenzo and Walter Block (2017)

Made in the USA
Coppell, TX
09 December 2020